Praise for A New History of Shinto

"Written by two scholars at the forefront of the study of Japanese religions, this book offers much more than a brief history. It is in fact a very bold and lucid attempt to redraw the parameters that govern our understanding of that elusive body of thought and practice we call Shinto. After an excellent overview of the development of Shinto through time, the authors present a series of case studies, of a shrine, a myth, and a rite, that reveal neither a precious fossil, nor the remnant of a pristine, primitive past, but a constellation of institutions and practices that was for ever evolving in response to changing demands. This book will surprise and on occasion shock; it will surely be required reading for all those interested in Japan and the Japanese."

Richard Bowring
University of Cambridge

"*A New History of Shinto* contains fresh material presented in an entirely original format. Co-written by two of the world's leading academic authorities on Japanese religions, this book is a substantial and highly readable introduction to Shinto, informed by the best of recent scholarship. The volume offers a host of surprises for any reader who thinks that Shinto is Japan's ancient indigenous faith, and at the same time provides much new information and fresh insights for those more familiar with the research findings which have radically transformed our understanding of Shinto in recent years. Overall, the book sets a new standard for a concise introduction to Shinto. It should be required reading for anyone interested in Japan and religion."

Brian Bocking
University College Cork

This series offers brief, accessible, and lively accounts of key topics within theology and religion. Each volume presents both academic and general readers with a selected history of topics which have had a profound effect on religious and cultural life. The word "history" is, therefore, understood in its broadest cultural and social sense. The volumes are based on serious scholarship but they are written engagingly and in terms readily understood by general readers.

Other topics in the series:

Published

Heaven	Alister E. McGrath
Heresy	G. R. Evans
Islam	Tamara Sonn
Death	Douglas J. Davies
Saints	Lawrence S. Cunningham
Christianity	Carter Lindberg
Dante	Peter S. Hawkins
Spirituality	Philip Sheldrake
Cults and New Religions	Douglas E. Cowan and David G. Bromley
Love	Carter Lindberg
Christian Mission	Dana L. Robert
Christian Ethics	Michael Banner
Jesus	W. Barnes Tatum
Shinto	John Breen and Mark Teeuwen

Forthcoming

Paul	Robert Paul Seesengood
Apocalypse	Martha Himmelfarb
Islam 2nd Edition	Tamara Sonn
The Reformation	Kenneth Appold
Monasticism	Dennis D. Martin
Sufism	Nile Green

A New History of Shinto

John Breen and Mark Teeuwen

A John Wiley & Sons, Ltd., Publication

This edition first published 2010
© 2010 John Breen and Mark Teeuwen

Blackwell Publishing was acquired by John Wiley & Sons in February 2007. Blackwell's publishing program has been merged with Wiley's global Scientific, Technical, and Medical business to form Wiley-Blackwell.

Registered Office
John Wiley & Sons Ltd, The Atrium, Southern Gate, Chichester, West Sussex, PO19 8SQ, United Kingdom

Editorial Offices
350 Main Street, Malden, MA 02148-5020, USA
9600 Garsington Road, Oxford, OX4 2DQ, UK
The Atrium, Southern Gate, Chichester, West Sussex, PO19 8SQ, UK

For details of our global editorial offices, for customer services, and for information about how to apply for permission to reuse the copyright material in this book please see our website at www.wiley.com/wiley-blackwell.

The right of John Breen and Mark Teeuwen to be identified as the authors of this work has been asserted in accordance with the UK Copyright, Designs and Patents Act 1988.

Library of Congress Cataloging-in-Publication Data

Breen, John, 1956–
   A new history of Shinto / John Breen and Mark Teeuwen.
     p. cm. – (Blackwell brief histories of religion series)
   Includes bibliographical references and index.
   ISBN 978-1-4051-5515-1 (hardcover : alk. paper) – ISBN 978-1-4051-5516-8 (pbk. : alk. paper) 1. Shinto–History. I. Teeuwen, Mark. II. Title.
   BL2218.B74 2010
   299.5'61–dc22
                                  2009029982

A catalogue record for this book is available from the British Library.

Set in 10/12.5pt Meridien by SPi Publisher Services, Pondicherry, India
Printed and bound in Malaysia by Vivar Printing Sdn Bhd

1   2010

Contents

List of Illustrations

Maps

Figures

Tables

Conventions and Abbreviations Used in the Text

In this book we follow the standard convention of giving Japanese names in Japanese order, with the family name followed by the given name. Less conventionally, we refer wherever possible to Shinto kami, often inadequately translated "god" or "gods," as "kami," without italics.

Finally, a note on periodization is called for. A number of conventional period names are used in the text, sometimes without dates. For easy reference, these dates are listed here:

Nara	710–794
Heian	794–1185
Kamakura	1185–1333
Muromachi	1336–1573
Edo	1600–1867
Meiji	1868–1912
Taishō	1912–1926
Shōwa	1926–1989

Perhaps unwisely, we often refer to the Nara and Heian periods collectively as "ancient" or "classical," Kamakura and Muromachi as "medieval," Edo as "early modern." Meiji and after are the "modern" period, and "premodern" thus refers to pre-Meiji. Whenever these terms are encountered in this book, they are used in these particular senses. Note also that the lunar calendar prevailed in Japan until 1873, when the Japanese government adopted the solar calendar.

Abbreviations

NKBT	*Nihon Koten Bungaku Taikei*
SBS	*Meiji Ishin Shinbutsu Bunri Shiryō*
SNKBT	*Shin Nihon Koten Bungaku Taikei*
ST	*Shintō Taikei*

Prologue

The premise for *A New History of Shinto* is the more or less obvious point that Shinto is a construct, that Shinto is not in other words coeval with heaven and earth. At some time in the past, it came into being. It follows from this observation that there must have been a "pre-Shinto," a time, that is, when Shinto did not exist, and there must also have been historical processes of "Shintoization" that led to its construction in particular ways at particular times. In this book we are every bit as interested in exploring this "pre-Shinto" and pursuing these "Shintoization" processes as we are in the Shinto construct itself. The method we adopt is to devote three core chapters to in-depth, historical case studies of three central Shinto motifs: shrines, myth, and ritual. Specifically, and for reasons which will become apparent, we focus on the Hie Shrines, east of Kyoto in Shiga Prefecture, the myth of the sun-goddess and the rock-cave, and the Great Rite of Feasting, known as the *daijōsai*. The other chapters range more broadly and less deeply, but always critically, across different Shinto themes in premodern and modern Japanese history.

A New History of Shinto is a co-authored book, and we shared the research and writing load equally. Mark Teeuwen was responsible for Chapters 1 and 4; John Breen wrote Chapters 5 and 6. Chapters 2 and 3, as well as the Conclusion, were co-written, with Mark Teeuwen being responsible for the early and medieval sections, and John Breen for the early modern and modern. Both of us incurred numerous debts in the researching and writing of our different chapters and sections, which we want to record here. Both authors want to thank Kirsten Berrum of Oslo University for drawing and redrawing the Hie maps. Mark Teeuwen would like to thank Michael Como and Herman Ooms for generously sharing their work on the ancient period with him, Kadoya Atsushi for good company and for directing him to some wonderful sources on the medieval period, and Mori Mizue for giving him free tickets to the Noh play that is discussed in Chapter 4. He is also grateful to Arne Kalland for the photograph of *iwato kagura* at Shingū and to Yajima Arata from Shibuya Kuritsu Shōtō Bijutsukan for the reproduction of *Shichifukujin iwato no kurabiraki*.

John Breen wants to thank Takagi Hiroshi of Kyoto University for lots of advice and friendship, the shrine priests Sagai Tatsuru and Suhara Norihiko, and the local historian Yamaguchi Yukitsugu both for sharing their deep knowledge of Hiyoshi Taisha, and for introducing him to some invaluable written and visual sources. He wants to record his gratitude, too, to the archivists at Shiga Prefectural Library and Shiga Prefectural Office, as well as to Iwahashi Katsuji of the National Association of Shrines and Kase Naoya of Kokugakuin University. It goes without saying that any shortcomings in the arguments presented are solely the responsibility of the authors.

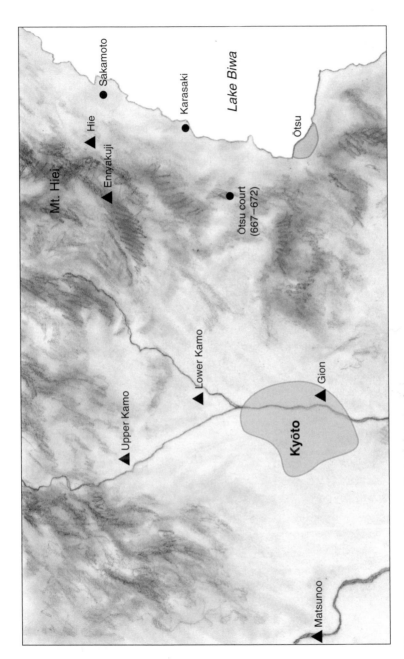

Map 1 The geographical location of the Hie Shrines

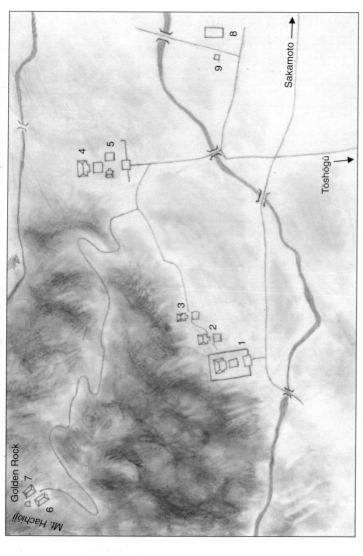

Golden Rock

Mt. Hachiōji

7

6

4

5

3

2

1

8

9

Sakamoto →

Tōshōgū →

Western compound
1 Ōmiya → Ōmiwa (1873) → Nishi Hongū (1928)
2 Shōshinshi → Usa (1869)
3 Marōdo → Shirayama-hime (1873)

Eastern compound
4 Ninomiya → Hongū (1873) → Higashi Hongū (1928)
5 Jūzenji → Juge (1869)
6 Sannomiya
7 Hachiōji → Ushio (1869)

Other
8 Ōmandokoro
9 Ōji → Ubuya (1869)

Map 2   The position of the seven shrines in the Hie precinct

Chapter 1

An Alternative Approach
to the History of Shinto

In today's Japan, Shinto has a distinct identity. Shinto is the religion of shrines (*jinja, jingū*), large and small sanctuaries that are distinguished from Buddhist temples by their characteristic architecture. These shrines, some 100,000 in all, are managed by about 20,000 Shinto priests, who are immediately recognizable from their traditional attire. The shrines accommodate a multitude of deities. While these deities differ from one shrine to another, they clearly belong to the same category (called kami), and they are obviously different from the buddhas and bodhisattvas of Buddhist temples. Similarly, shrines stage a dazzling variety of ceremonies, but it is evident even at first glance that they share a common ritual language.

Still, however clear the contours of modern Shinto may be, in some ways it is also very difficult to pin down. According to official statistics, Shinto is Japan's largest religion, with more than a hundred million "adherents," a number that amounts to well over 80 percent of all Japanese. Yet only a small percentage of the populace identify themselves as "Shintoists" in questionnaires conducted by the media or by Shinto organizations. This reflects the fact that while many Japanese participate in shrine events and make use of the ritual services offered by shrines, only very few regard Shinto as their religious identity. Seen through the eyes of the average patron of shrines, Shinto remains a very vague concept. Shrines may be categorized as Shinto and temples as Buddhist, but this distinction is of little consequence to those who make use of their services. It makes sense to distinguish shrines from temples, but with few exceptions it is impossible to differentiate between "Shintoists" and "Buddhists."

Of course, the fact that Shinto hardly functions as a religious identity does not mean that shrines are taken lightly. As "religious juridical persons" (*shūkyō hōjin*) in law, shrines cannot be supported by public funds under Japan's postwar constitution.[1] They depend for their upkeep on the largess of the inhabitants of their "parish" and the general public. Without a steady stream of income, no shrine can survive; a shrine priest much less so. When a shrine ceases to make itself relevant to the community on which it depends, it will disappear almost instantly. In this perspective, the fact that so many shrines have survived good times and bad over centuries bespeaks a truly astonishing staying power. Ultimately, this remarkable resilience is down to the never-ending efforts of generations of shrine priests, who time and again have succeeded in finding new roles and new sources of income for their shrines, and to the willingness of shrine parishioners and other patrons to make their resources available to them.

Shrines may have a permanent priest, but most do not; such smaller shrines are maintained and run by people in the neighborhood, or share a priest with a number of other shrines. Statistics show that, overall, there is about one priest to every five shrines. There are also a few hundred large and very large shrines: the Ise Shrine, for example, has some 600 personnel, ranging from priests and musicians to office workers. But of course, shrine priests cannot keep a shrine afloat on their own. Equally important is the role played by worshipers' organizations (*sūkeikai, hōsankai*) and neighborhood associations (*chōnaikai*), which organize the community's participation in and funding of shrine events.

How does a shrine work? Shrines are places where kami are believed to reside. The focus of most shrines is the main sanctuary, or kami hall (*shinden*), usually a simple wooden or concrete building in traditional style. The shrine's main deities are said to dwell in this building, often in mirrors or other "kami objects" that are permanently hidden from view. In front of the kami hall is a worship hall (*haiden*), from which the visitor looks up to the sanctuary. Prayers are said in this worship hall. Only priests may approach the sanctuary, and even they seldom enter its inner recesses where the kami is hidden. The area around the two halls is often parklike, and even in an urban environment it tends to look like a small natural forest, or at least it will feature a few trees. Access to the shrine precincts is through a characteristic torii gate. Visitors enter by way of this torii and rinse their hands and mouth at a basin with running water before proceeding to the worship hall. At larger shrines, they will pass by a shrine office (shamusho), where they can ask a priest to perform a ritual or buy kami tablets, amulets, postcards, and a variety of souvenirs. Most will pass the office without a glance, throw a coin into the money box (saisenbako) at the worship hall, clap their hands, and bow their head briefly in prayer before hurrying off once more into the secular world beyond the torii. The most popular opportunity for such a shrine visit is New Year. Some 70 percent of all Japanese visit a shrine in the first days of the New Year (a practice called hatsumōde);[2] outside this rush-hour period shrines tend to be very quiet places.

Shrines perform three categories of rituals. One is personal prayers for individuals or families. After hatsumōde, which also belongs to this category, the most popular practices are hatsu miyamairi, the first shrine visit of a newborn baby, and shichi go san, a shrine visit to celebrate a child's third, fifth, or seventh birthday. These rites are observed by some 50 percent of Japanese. On these occasions, a priest will intone a solemn prayer (norito) and dancing maidens called miko will perform in front of the altar. The participants make a symbolic offering (a branch of the evergreen sakaki tree called a tamagushi) and are offered a sip of sacred rice wine (miki), signaling a mutual promise between the kami and the worshiper. Other popular rituals are purification rites for building sites and cars, weddings, prayers for avoiding misfortune in "dangerous years" (yakudoshi), and prayers for success in examinations.

The second category of shrine rituals is of an imperial nature. These rituals are standardized across the land and occur simultaneously at most manned shrines. The most important ones are kinensai (February 17) and niiname-sai (November 23). Both are classical court ceremonies in which the emperor prays for (kinensai) and gives thanks for (*niiname-sai*) the year's harvest. As we shall soon see, these rituals only entered the ritual calendars of shrines in the late nineteenth century. Other national rituals have a similar imperial theme: *kigensetsu* (February 11) celebrates the founding of the nation by the mythical emperor Jinmu, which tradition dates to 660 BC; *Meijisetsu* (November 3) the birthday of the Meiji emperor; and *tenchōsetsu* (December 23) the birthday of the present emperor. These rituals, which do not draw large crowds, symbolize Shinto's connections with the imperial house.

The third and last category consists of shrine festivals (*matsuri*). Apart from New Year, festivals are the main occasions on which shrines really come to life. Shrine festivals reflect local traditions and are spread across the year. Large festivals last for many days and give a cultural identity to whole cities, as well as attracting thousands of visitors and tourists. Small festivals are intimate affairs, not unlike neighborhood parties. The most common pattern of a festival is a parade, for which the kami is transferred from the kami hall into a palanquin called a *mikoshi*. The *mikoshi* is carried or wheeled through the neighborhood and temporarily installed at various sites where the kami is entertained with dancing, theater performances, wrestling matches, archery contests, and the like. Festivals tend to be run by the local community rather than the shrine priests, who take center-stage only as ritual specialists performing liturgical tasks such as the transfer of the kami to the *mikoshi* or the recitation of prayers. Most of the festivities take place outside of the shrine and are managed by selected community members. Typical of shrine festivals is that they engage large parts of the community in their proceedings, and that they envelop the community in a carnivalesque atmosphere in which much is allowed and all is forgiven. All in all, some 25 percent of Japanese participate in a local festival of this kind.

Where in all this is "Shinto"? For shrine priests, these three types of rituals are all part of a single tradition. For most participants, however, the coherence in their own ritual behavior does not derive from such categories as Shinto and Buddhism. From their point of view, the New Year shrine visit belongs together with the Buddhist *obon* festival in August and the eating of

Christmas cake in December. All events of this kind form part of a single calendrical cycle of seasonal festivities (*nenjū gyōji*) that brightens up the routine of a busy life. For most, "religion" and "faith" have little to do with it.

Conceptualizing Shrine Practice as Shinto

"Shinto" as an overarching construct may have little appeal to the average shrine patron, but it has had a profound influence on the design and operation of shrines. Also, individual shrines are aware of the fact that, without a broader conceptual context, each shrine would be even more vulnerable to social change. Shrines explain their function in society in terms of "Shinto" and market themselves under that flag. Developing Shinto as a concept, then, is of utmost importance to the shrine world as a whole.

In the postwar period, this has been one of the main functions of the National Association of Shrines (Jinja Honchō; hereafter NAS), an umbrella organization working on behalf of some 80,000 member shrines. NAS was founded in 1946, at a time of deep crisis when it was far from obvious that Shinto would survive the demise of the old imperial Japan. All agreed that if Shinto was to be rescued from rapid disintegration, it needed to be reinvented. Yet the direction that Shinto would take after Japan's catastrophic defeat in the war was far from clear. The choices made by leaders of the shrine world at this crucial juncture reveal much about the position of shrines in society, and about the ambiguities of "Shinto" as a conceptualization of shrine practices.

In the turmoil immediately after Japan's capitulation, the shrine world had good reason to fear for its future. Since 1868 shrine ritual had been a matter of political importance to the Japanese state, and especially from around 1900 onwards Shinto had occupied a secure place at the center of Japan's national identity. The allied powers that occupied Japan in September 1945 saw Shinto as the ideological foundation of Japanese "emperor worship" and aggressive expansionism. They moved quickly to remove its influence from the public sphere by drastic measures.

In the face of this threat, shrines fought an uphill battle on all fronts. Budgets were nonexistent, and many of the leaders of the old Shinto establishment were being purged from public life. Nor was it easy to find sympathy among the general public. In the face of Japan's disastrous collapse, most Japanese felt a profound aversion to the propaganda that they had been bombarded with for over a decade, and shrines suffered for their long-standing association with that propaganda. Shinto was utterly out of synch with the times and many could not envision its survival in the new, democratic Japan of the future. The Occupation authorities were in fact convinced that if they left it alone, Shinto would disappear by itself. They abstained from the use of force against even the most militarized shrines in the sure knowledge that, over time, these shrines would fold without their help.

However, as things turned out, Shinto proved more robust than most had imagined. The large majority of shrines not only survived but found renewed prosperity as soon as the worst period of economic hardship was over. In 1946 such an outcome must have appeared less than likely, even to the Shinto leaders who formed NAS's early policies. The possibility that Shinto would fall into the abyss of modernization and democratization was felt to be very real, and those who worked to save the shrine world had strong views on what Shinto was to represent in this new age.

Among the debaters, we can discern three main camps. The first, led by Ashizu Uzuhiko (1909–92), stressed Shinto's role in uniting the Japanese people under the spiritual guidance of the emperor. The second, drawing on the work of the ethnologist Yanagita Kunio (1875–1962), rejected the idea that centralist imperial ideology was at the core of Shinto. Instead, this group stressed the spiritual value of local traditions of worshiping local kami, in all their centrifugal variety. The third, fronted by Orikuchi Shinobu (1887–1953), argued that if Shinto was to survive, it should be developed from an ethnic religion into a universal one.[3]

These three positions reflected radically different approaches to Shinto. Ashizu was an imperial loyalist and activist who saw Shinto in a political context. Yanagita and Orikuchi, on the other hand, were academics with a nativist bent, both specializing in Japanese folklore and dedicating their careers to a search for the deepest roots of Japan's religious culture. Within NAS, Ashizu fought a hard battle to exclude the influence of Yanagita and Orikuchi from the new shrine organization.[4] He feared that their emphasis on regional diversity would tear apart Japan's sense of national unity, and even suspected that their views were being used in a leftist conspiracy to destroy the nation. Initially, Ashizu prevailed, but over time the alternatives offered by Yanagita and (to a lesser degree) Orikuchi have bounced back.

We will return to NAS and the shifting positions of its spokesmen in Chapter 6 of this volume. For now, our main point is that all of the three "camps" that struggled over the authority to give new direction to Shinto in 1946 drew on different aspects of the tradition as it existed at that time. Shinto was a political construct designed to instill a "national spirit" in the people; but it was also a bottom-up complex of local rituals and festivals with little internal coherence; and finally, it included a number of religious groups that adhered to universalistic teachings. Let us take a brief look at each of these strains of Shinto, all of them still alive and well in present-day Japan.

Meiji and the Formation of Shinto as a State Cult

To understand the three faces of Shinto, we need to turn our attention to the prewar period. The formative years of modern Shinto are concentrated in the half-century between 1868, the year of the so-called Meiji Restoration, and 1915, when Tokyo's Meiji Shrine was inaugurated. Many have argued that Shinto was "invented" in this period, and it is indeed beyond doubt that pre-Meiji Shinto was a very different animal from its post-Meiji heir.

In the twelfth month of 1867 a small band of insurgents arranged for the emperor to issue an imperial rescript announcing the abolishment of the shogunate. The rescript called for a restoration of direct imperial rule, as in the days of the first (mythical) emperor Jinmu. Soon it became clear what this meant for shrines. The new regime was to be based on the principle that "rites and government are one" (*saisei itchi*), and in the third month of 1868, all shrine priests were placed under the authority of a newly resurrected ancient institution, the Jingikan, or Council of Kami Affairs. This Council was put in nominal charge of all shrines. In the ensuing weeks shrines were methodically separated from Buddhism. Buddhist priests, deities, buildings, and rituals were banned from all shrines. In the words of Allan Grapard (1984: 245), the Meiji government "forced thousands of monks and nuns to return to lay life and watched without moving when innumerable statues, paintings, scriptures, ritual implements and buildings were destroyed, sold, stolen, burnt, or covered with excrement." It was at this time that Shinto became physically and institutionally distinct from Buddhism.[5]

Why this sudden obsession with shrines? The radical reforms of 1868 drew on a wave of nostalgic nativism that idealized Japan's age of antiquity as a divine era of natural harmony and innocence. Japan needed to make a fresh start; to do this, it had to rid itself of the accretions of history. Many branded Buddhism, which had enjoyed a privileged status under the Tokugawa shogunate, as one of the corrupting influences that had undermined Japan's ancient vigor. In a sense, this was a simple result of the changing times. In spite of the shogunate's continued support, Buddhism had already lost its former position of intellectual dominance to Confucianism by the eighteenth century. By the nineteenth century it had become a popular target of Confucian condemnation. The Meiji revolution itself was fueled by a heady mix of Confucian ethics and imperial patriotism, in which Buddhism was either marginalized or refuted.

Another factor behind the Meiji institutionalization of Shinto was an acute sense of crisis in the face of Western expansionism. It was feared that Christianity would gain a foothold in Japan, with devastating effects on the nation's cohesion and, ultimately, its chance of survival. The new Shinto was also a means to enhance the visibility of the emperor, who was now the sole focus of national unity. The Meiji government looked to shrines as a means to educate the people and make them aware of their new status as imperial subjects.

In effect, the new Meiji cult of shrines functioned as a form of Confucian-inspired ancestor worship. By honoring the ancestors of the nation, a community was created that celebrated a shared past. To this end, shrines were redefined as places that commemorated heroes of the state. The centerpiece of the new shrine system was Ise, the shrine of the imperial ancestor and sun-goddess Amaterasu. It is no coincidence, then, that in the third month of 1869 Emperor Meiji (who was only 16 years old at the time) became the first emperor ever to worship at the Ise Shrine.[6] In 1871 all other shrines were arranged on a hierarchical scale, from imperial and national shrines at the top to prefectural shrines, district shrines, and finally non-ranked shrines at the bottom. At the same time, hereditary lineages of priests were abolished and a state-sanctioned system of appointed priests was put in its place. In this way shrines were appropriated by the state and designated as sites for the performance of state rituals (*kokka-no-sōshi*). From this time onwards, state-appointed priests were to perform an increasingly standardized set of state rituals as local representatives of the emperor. Their performance of these rituals aimed to unite the people with their emperor in a shared act of ancestor worship, in the manner of a family that gathers in front of the family altar to create and renew a sense of shared purpose and solidarity.

The effect of these measures was that, for the first time, "Shinto" took on very clear contours. Shinto was about shrines, the emperor, and Japan, and it had a clear boundary vis-à-vis Buddhism. Yet in many other senses Shinto still remained a disconcertingly vague concept. As the government would soon find out, there was no consistent teaching that was readily available for the Shinto missionaries whom the Council of Kami Affairs began to send out into the country in 1870. Shinto thinkers disagreed on even the most fundamental questions. Which kami should be incorporated in the imperial cult? What is their relation to each other? What do the classical texts teach about life and death, good and evil, reward and punishment? No consensus could be reached on any of these central questions, and under these circumstances an effective missionary campaign was impossible.

Moreover, it was clear almost from the start that the goal of enhancing national cohesion would not be served by alienating

Buddhists. Already in 1872 the Council of Kami Affairs was closed down and replaced by a new institution called the Ministry of Edification (Kyōbushō).[7] This Ministry coordinated a new grand campaign, run by official "national evangelists" (kyōdōshoku), to spread Japan's "Great Teaching" to the populace. The campaign also coopted Buddhist priests, and its Great Teaching was deliberately kept as neutral as possible. It merely stressed three general points: (1) respect for the gods and love for the country; (2) observance of the "Principles of Heaven and the Way of Man"; and (3) reverence for the emperor and obedience to his government. Again, the message consisted of a combination of universal Confucian ideas with Japanese symbolism. The role of shrines in this scheme was to give substance to that Japanese focus, pointing ultimately to the emperor as the father and chief celebrant of the nation.

As the political situation began to settle in the 1870s, the question arose what status this national Great Teaching should have. Buddhist groups, most notably the Jōdo Shinshū (True Pure Land) sect, soon felt ill at ease within the shrine-dominated campaign and objected to having to worship deities that were never part of their own tradition. Adopting the Western concept of "religion," they argued strongly that "Shinto" was not and never should be a member of that category. Buddhist representatives maintained that, in contrast to temples, shrines were not sites of *religion* but of *ritual*. Participation in shrine rites, then, should not be premised on faith or belief. It could not be anything more than a simple expression of respect for the Great Men who had built the nation. This line of reasoning not only served to give Buddhism a monopoly over the "religious" realm; it also allowed the government to combine freedom of religion (eventually guaranteed in the Constitution of 1889) with a continued official shrine cult. As renewed bickering among Shinto ideologues and protests from Buddhist groups reduced the campaign to a shambles, the government took drastic measures. In 1882 shrine priests were forbidden from engaging in any "religious" activities (such as preaching, conducting funerals, or selling amulets); two years later, the Great Teaching campaign was discontinued.

After this debacle the state's interest in shrines waned rapidly. The urgency of the early Meiji years had faded, and Christianity had by now proved less threatening than first feared. Significantly, the government planned to phase out state funding for shrines, which caused all the more hardship because all temple and shrine lands had been confiscated in 1871.

It was only after the Sino-Japanese war of 1894–5 and the Russo-Japanese war of 1904–5 that new opportunities arose for shrines to make themselves relevant to the government. A wave of renewed self-confidence inspired much patriotic enthusiasm, expressed in a ritual format that put shrines center stage. The fallen from these wars were enshrined in newly founded military shrines, including Yasukuni Shrine in Tokyo and a range of "nation-protecting shrines" (gokoku jinja) elsewhere, and shrine visits by the military, as well as school classes, became a new social ritual. At the same time, a growing socialist and communist movement swept over Japan, preaching class struggle and revolution and inspiring fear that national unity was threatened. Under these circumstances Shinto once more became a focus of attention. In 1906 thousands of village shrines were merged with the aim of retaining only one shrine in each community, which could then serve as a stage for national, imperial ceremonies (Fridell 1973). The earlier plan to end state support for shrines was abandoned and a new financing system was introduced; also, the Shinto liturgy was standardized by law. When Emperor Meiji died in 1912, a large plot in central Tokyo was reserved for a shrine in honor of his spirit and that of the empress. This widely advertised project, which was finished in 1915 with the inauguration of Meiji Shrine, finally set Shinto squarely on the map by triggering a national media campaign and engaging large numbers of people in an explicitly "Shinto" undertaking (Imaizumi 2007). Until 1945 Shinto was to serve as Japan's "non-religious" state cult, propagated with increasing zeal especially after 1931 as the country headed into war.

All these changes had a profound effect on shrines. The erasure of earlier ties with Buddhism proved to be only the beginning of an intense period of transformation. Many shrines simply disappeared, while new ones dedicated to national heroes (ranging from the Meiji emperor to fallen soldiers and paragons of virtue from earlier ages) were erected across the country, and even in

Japan's colonies. Pre-Meiji shrines that survived all reforms were often redesigned and given a new identity: a new name, or even a new set of kami taken from the imperial classics. As ancient priestly lineages disappeared, local traditions were lost and exchanged for standardized procedures drawn up in Tokyo. On top of all this, shrines lost their traditional sources of income (notably, shrine lands) and had to adapt to a new social context, marked by increased mobility and modernization in all its different guises.

The first and second categories of rituals performed at shrines today that were mentioned above, namely the personal and the imperial, were products of this short period of intense modernization that began in 1868. We have already noted the introduction of imperial rites; some of the "private" rites that now constitute the mainstay of shrine ritual are even newer. The New Year ritual of *hatsumōde* developed from a variety of earlier customs in the early twentieth century. In Edo (as Tokyo was called before 1868), people had visited shrines dedicated to the Seven Gods of Fortune to pray for luck in the coming year; in many other places, worshipers selected a shrine or temple that was located in a lucky direction from one's house (*ehō-mōde*), as determined by a Yin-Yang specialist of divination (*onmyōji*). Also rites of purification for, say, building plots had before Meiji been a speciality of Yin-Yang diviners; the performance of such rites by shrine priests was a twentieth-century innovation. Shinto marriages only gained popularity after the wedding ceremony of Crown Prince Yoshihito (the future Emperor Taishō) in 1900. *Shichi go san* has older roots in earlier rites of passage for children, but these did not typically involve shrines. This ritual gained its modern form only in the Taishō period (1912–26). Before that time, customs varied from one region to the next; in the Kansai area, for example, there was no tradition for taking young children to shrines, and instead 13-year-olds were taken to Buddhist temples. The custom of drawing lots to foretell one's personal fortune (*omikuji*) at shrines and tying them to branches in the shrine grounds, as depicted on the cover of this book, spread in the same Taishō period. The origins of today's *omikuji* can be traced back to early Edo *Kannon kuji* (Avalokiteśvara lots), popularized first at Tendai temples and later by, again, Yin-Yang diviners (Ōno Izuru 2002). All these rites were actively promoted in the modern era in response to shrines' loss of economic independence. After all, shrines had lost both their landholdings and the right to engage in "religious" activities, including even the sale of amulets. These new practices were designed as "nonreligious" opportunities to draw people to shrines; they were new ritual services that shrine priests could offer without breaking the law.

In December 1945, only months after Japan's surrender, the American-led Occupation issued the so-called Shinto Directive (Shintō shirei). The stated aim of this Directive, made explicit in its first article, was to put an end to "the perversion of Shinto theory and beliefs into militaristic and ultranationalistic propaganda, designed to delude the Japanese people and lead them into wars of aggression." The Directive prohibited all financial contributions to Shinto shrines from public funds, as well as all forms of official support for Shinto rites or ideas. At the same time, shrines were offered a new lease of life as private religious organizations: "Shrine Shinto, after having been divorced from the state and divested of its militaristic and ultranationalistic elements, will be recognized as a religion if its adherents so desire." In February 1946 shrines were registered under a new law as religious juridical persons (*shūkyō hōjin*), and NAS was founded as a new umbrella organization.

Rather than making a radical break with the past, NAS opted to hold on to many elements of the Meiji state cult. It retained the leadership of the Ise Shrine, and to this day the organization makes a great effort to distribute Ise deity amulets (*jingū taima*) to households throughout Japan, for both ideological and financial reasons. The imperial rituals instituted in the Meiji period have a prominent place on the ritual calendar of member shrines, just as they did before the war. Perhaps most importantly, NAS inherited the Meiji view of Shinto as a non-religion. This partly explains Shinto's weakness as a religious identity. NAS sees Shinto as a "public" ritual system open to all members of the community irrespective of their "private" beliefs, not as an exclusivist religion. Thus, if Shinto does not function as a religion, this is primarily due to a choice made by the shrine organization itself.

Shinto as Folklore

The state cult of shrines and its legacy in NAS's policies stand out as a major factor in the crystallization of Shinto, both before the war and after. However, we should not be tempted to believe that before 1945 shrines were simply stages for patriotic ceremonial. If that had been the case, Shinto would indeed have imploded in the aftermath of Japan's capitulation. The fact that the number of shrines hardly decreased at all after the discontinuation of the state shrine cult must cause us to pause, because it proves that the imperial cult was never more than an ephemeral superstructure. Even when nation building was at its most intense, state ritual was not all there was to Shinto. In fact, the evidence suggests it was not even the most important part of Shinto.

In spite of the centralizing policies of the government, shrines continued to function first and foremost as stages for local community festivals. Within the confines of this category, the variety is endless: spring festivals in prayer for a good growing season, autumn festivals in thanks for the year's crops, New Year festivals to pray for good business in the coming year, summer festivals to ward off illnesses, hunting rituals, fishing rituals, purification rituals, and celebrations of local foundational events.[8] In spite of the fact that most of these ceremonial occasions do not primarily address imperial themes, even prewar shrine administrators recognized their importance. Local festivals were far more effective in inspiring the general public to be actively engaged in shrine affairs than the ideological rites of imperial Shinto. Festivals were profoundly affected by the separation of shrines from Buddhism in 1868, but they nevertheless displayed a measure of continuity with the period before Meiji. Their nature was such that they were not easily assimilated into a standardized, secularized imperial cult. A rite in which court emissaries presented imperial offerings was added to the festival proceedings at shrines of high rank, but otherwise local festivals remained peripheral to the interests of Shinto ideologues.

To others, however, it was the mystery of this endlessly variegated body of local practices that constituted Shinto's true appeal. The most influential thinker and writer to call attention to local shrine cults was the above-mentioned Yanagita Kunio.[9] Yanagita was an outspoken critic of officialdom's way of running shrines. As early as 1918 he wrote:

> During the Russo-Japanese war, when nobody could foresee whether we would win or lose, people in villages that had sent many of their youngsters to the battlefield had no other way to deal with their anxiety than to turn to the kami of their village shrines [*ujigami*]. Many shrines performed so-called enemy-quelling rites attended by local politicians and officials, and those rites attracted much attention. But at the same time, mothers and wives fasted, performed ablutions and carried out such practices as *o-hyakudo* [making a hundred successive shrine visits]. Such acts of faith were in fact counted among the virtuous acts of the wartime. It is utterly groundless to ignore all this [religious activity] and claim that shrines are merely places for expressing respect for ancestors and Great Men.[10]

In this passage Yanagita displays an attitude towards the people and their customs that is very different from that of the authorities. Yanagita was much more impressed by private acts of sincere faith performed by the "folk" (*jōmin*) than by official ceremonies such as enemy-quelling rites. In his view, this grass-roots faith was profoundly religious, and he considered the policy to separate shrines from religion as a gross act of cynical opportunism. Yanagita saw the bureaucratic policy to cleanse shrines of all "religious" stains in the name of imperial Shinto as a threat to the authentic faith of the people. For him, shrine worship and other local practices (though not those rooted in Buddhism) bore testimony to the oldest and deepest layers of Japan's culture. In his search for the authentic roots of Japan, Yanagita looked to the periphery where he assumed that ancient practices and mentalities had remained untouched by modernity. In Yanagita's eyes, the official policy towards shrines threatened to wipe out these last remaining islands of uncontaminated folk culture, and thus destroy Japan's unique heritage.

Yanagita had good reasons to be concerned. The separation of Shinto first from Buddhism, and then from "religion," excluded many traditional practices from shrines. Healing, divination, rites of possession as a means of communicating with ancestors or protector spirits, and many other kinds of rituals were banned from shrines, as were the practitioners who engaged in them. Of course, demand for such rituals persisted, and they never disappeared; their practice simply moved to another location or went underground (Bouchy 2003; Liscutin 2000). Even in their new hideaways, though, practitioners of what the authorities regarded as "primitive superstitions" had to live with a constant fear of police harassment, and many felt pressured either to give up their calling or find a government-sanctioned way to carry on.

Yanagita was not above condemning many of the activities of popular religious figures as superstition; but in a carefully selected range of folk practices, he perceived a cultural heritage of great value. In his vision, Shinto appeared as a complex of ancient beliefs and practices that had been handed down, from one generation to the next, by nameless "folk" in the remotest parts of the land. He used rich data from countless fieldwork trips to theorize about a pure and original Japanese essence in which kami worship played a central role. This does not mean that Yanagita was opposed to the central idea of the prewar *kokutai* ideology, namely that the people and the emperor are one.[11] While criticizing top-down imperial Shinto, he stressed the original unity of folk ritual and imperial ritual. In his view, both expressed the same concerns with fertility, life, and growth that can ultimately be traced back to the ancient Yayoi age (c. 300 BC–AD 250) when the arrival of rice cultivation laid the foundation for Japan's culture. Like the official line on Shinto, then, Yanagita's studies were premised on the notion of a single, indivisible Japanese "spirit." The difference was that, in Yanagita's eyes, the local customs of the people constituted the very core of that Japanese cultural essence, while officialdom tended to look down on local practices and beliefs as superstitions that stood in the way of a truly modern Shinto.

Yanagita's vision was to a large degree shared by Orikuchi Shinobu, whom we met earlier as an advocate for a more "religious" Shinto. Orikuchi used textual sources rather than fieldwork, but his findings pointed in much the same direction as Yanagita's. As will be discussed in more detail in Chapter 5,

Orikuchi looked for the roots of imperial rituals in folk practices that had survived in the periphery of modern Japan. Both Yanagita and Orikuchi, then, sketched the contours of a very different conception of Shinto: not as a nonreligious practice of emperor worship, but as the essence of Japan's cultural identity as a *Volk* – which was also reflected in imperial ritual. This "romantic" vision of Shinto has survived into the postwar period as an alternative to the more political model that originated in Meiji.

Religious Shinto Sects

The Meiji period also saw the emergence of a number of "Shinto sects" that were officially recognized and administered as religious groups. These groups were labeled *kyōha Shintō*, literally "Shinto groups with [specific] teachings." By 1908, there were 13 in all. This category arose as a result of the separation of shrines from religion, institutionalized in 1882 (Hardacre 1986; Inoue Nobutaka 2002). The idea was that, while shrines would limit themselves to ritual, the propagation of Shinto teachings would be delegated to private groups approved by the government. Some of these groups were founded by shrine priests as a way to continue their religious activities after 1882. In these cases the Shinto sects were a new way to coordinate the activities of already existing lay "confraternities" (*kō*) connected to famous shrines or sacred mountains. At Ise, for example, an "Ise Teaching Institute" was already set up by 1872; in 1882 it was reorganized as a Shinto sect called Jingūkyō, "the teaching of the Ise Shrine," which served as an umbrella organization for all Ise confraternities scattered throughout the country. At Izumo Shrine in Shimane Prefecture there was a similar development. Other Shinto sects originated as grass-roots popular movements, led by popular healers and other religious figures. These groups found in the new category of *kyōha Shintō* a shortcut to official recognition that seemed to promise an end to police harassment. Often this could only be achieved by adapting the group's teachings and practices to the official line on Shinto.

At least some of these Shinto sects focused on a single site or deity to which they gave universal meaning, as a creator deity seeking a personal relationship with devoted believers. In this sense, these sects were religious in a manner that closely resembled the example of monotheistic Christianity. They built "churches" (*kyōkai*), often performing regular services attended by dedicated congregations, and engaged in active proselytization. As the direct predecessors of the later "new religions" (*shinkō shūkyō*), they brought a new form of religious organization to Japan. Some achieved a remarkable degree of success. In the 1930s the nationalist Shinto scholar and educationalist Tanaka Yoshitō (1872–1946) lost faith in the feasibility of spreading Shinto among the populace by "secular" means, while at the same time discovering in the preachers of the Shinto sects a group of educators who could compete "even with Christians" (Isomae 2000a). It must have been a similar assessment that persuaded Orikuchi Shinobu to argue that Shinto's only chance of survival after the surrender lay in its becoming a universal "religion" in the full Western sense of the word.

Many Shintos; Many Histories

We can sum up the above by observing that Shinto, as it emerged after Meiji, had three faces:

1 A "nonreligious" body of state ritual focusing on the emperor.
2 A broad swathe of local rituals that addressed a range of other concerns, from community prosperity to individual good luck and health.
3 A number of religious groups, defined by the state as "Shinto sects."

All three came with their own definitions of Shinto, ranging from imperial *kokutai* ideology, via Yanagita's folklore-based notion of an authentic national culture with roots in ancient times, to the various teachings of the founders of Shinto sects. If we include the viewpoint of the actual users of shrines, many of whom did not and do not see their shrine practices in terms of "Shinto" at all, the picture becomes even more confusing. With the possible exception of this fourth view, all these attempts at defining Shinto are clearly products of modern Japan. Moreover, it is clear that the theories and doctrines of the ideologues of state ritual, folklorists like Yanagita, and sect leaders do not necessarily have a lot to do with the ways in which shrines have functioned, even in the modern period itself. This places us in a difficult predicament as writers of a Shinto history, however "brief."

In fact, one notion that is shared by all these conceptions of Shinto is that it is the "indigenous" religion of Japan, with roots in the nation's ancient past. Whatever line one takes, Shinto is invariably staged as the "original" essence of Japanese culture. This emphasis on ancient indigenous origins has led both modern and premodern Shinto thinkers to history, and it has determined the basic premise on which Shinto's views on its own history may be constructed. Almost invariably, current historical narratives follow a classical three-part plot: from ancient purity, by way of a "medieval" age in which Shinto was mixed with Buddhism and Confucianism, to final restoration and a return to authentic purity in modern times. Even the best introductory history of Shinto, Inoue Nobutaka's *Shinto: A short history* (2003), follows this overall plot, even though it is careful to avoid depicting ancient Shinto as "pure" and to stress the role of Buddhism as forming rather than distorting Shinto.

These historical accounts are based on the fundamental assumption that there has been such a thing as Shinto throughout Japan's history. The importance of this belief to the self-understanding of Shinto professionals (priests, educators, administrators) explains the enormous impact of the work of Kuroda Toshio (1926–93). This historian of medieval Japan launched a frontal attack on Shinto dogma by arguing that the understanding of Shinto "as the indigenous religion of Japan, continuing in an unbroken line from prehistoric times down to the present" is nothing more than a myth (Kuroda 1981). Instead, he posited that "before modern times Shinto did not exist as an independent religion," and he maintained that premodern Shinto should be understood as a "component" or an "extension" of Buddhism in its Japanese guise (Kuroda 1981: 3). This insight has since served as the starting point of a fundamental reconsideration of Shinto and its role in Japanese history. There is little doubt that a disinterested review of the sources confirms Kuroda's point: an analysis of the historical usage of the term "Shinto" (*jindō, shintō*) reveals that this word took on its present meaning much later than traditional histories would suggest (Teeuwen 2002). Certainly, there was no Japanese religion called Shinto in ancient Japan. By implication, this means that the "pure Shinto" of modern times was not the product of a restoration, but a modern invention.

Yet Kuroda's analysis creates as many questions as it solves. Surely there was a distinct Japanese "tradition" (if we want to avoid the term religion) with some degree of coherence before Buddhism arrived on the islands in the sixth century, even if it was not at the time conceptualized as Shinto? Kami shrines, myths, and rituals appear as obvious elements of such an ancient tradition. Many shrines have existed in the same location where they are today since classical, or even prehistoric, times. Most shrines are much younger, but even these can be regarded as specimens of a genus that has its roots in ancient Japan: kami shrines. Texts of court mytho-history from the early eighth century, most notably *Kojiki* (Record of ancient matters; 712) and *Nihon shoki* (Chronicles of Japan; 720), contain tales about kami that are obviously non-Buddhist in nature. Even though these texts are not free from continental influences, they are in fact less "Chinese" in outlook than one might expect, considering the nature of the court at that time. Finally, many elements of modern Shinto ritual display a clear continuity with documented ancient forms. Much of this is due to later reconstructions of classical ritual forms, but at least there was always a common ground between existing and reconstructed ritual that allowed such reconstructions to be implemented in the first place.

At first sight these observations may appear to lead us back to the traditional view of Shinto as a continuation of Japan's "original" religion. However, such a representation of history would only be justified if kami shrines, myths, and rites had developed as a coherent complex of phenomena, reasonably distinct from other traditions. If a closer look at the sources reveals that shrines through much of their history were affected more profoundly by their connections with Buddhist temples, or by Yin-Yang lore from the Asian continent, it makes little sense to frame their development as a history of Shinto. Vice versa, in mapping the historical development of, for example, a kami myth, it would be a gross distortion of history if we were to focus only on those contexts that fit in with the modern concept of Shinto, especially if it turns out that the myth in question was most "alive" in quite different contexts.

The crux of the matter is that kami shrines, myths, and rituals are a great deal older than their conceptualization as components of Shinto. Therefore, the only way to delve into the history of these shrines, myths, and rituals is by laying the concept of Shinto to one side, at least as a start. Only in this way will it be possible to study these aspects of kami worship in their proper historical contexts. It is only after this that we will be able to look back and try to identify the significance of Shinto in the histories that we have just explored.

For these reasons this book will take a different approach to that of more conventional histories of Shinto. Such histories have typically assumed that Shinto has been an abiding force in Japanese history, and they present a selection of data that confirms this. Of course, as already noted, there were indeed significant linkages between the histories of kami cults long before Meiji, and Chapter 2 will give a brief survey of historical developments that served to bring kami shrines, myths, and rituals together. In the main body of the book, however, we will take the reverse approach of tracing the history of some of the main components from which Shinto was construed at a later stage: shrines, myths, and rituals. The difference is that while Shinto historians naturally stress the "Shinto-like" aspects of shrines, myths, and rituals, we make a conscious effort to put that Shinto angle aside, and thereby gain a less preconceived understanding of shrines, myths, and rituals in their contemporary setting, when there is no evidence that they were understood as ingredients of Shinto.

This fragmenting approach is necessary not only to understand pre-Shinto kami cults in their proper context, but also to bring out the process of "Shintoization" that culminated in the Meiji shrine reforms. To appreciate the impact of the Shinto ideology of modern times, we need to know what kami shrines, myths, and rituals entailed before they were assimilated to that ideology. Moreover, we need to bring out the elements of coherence that were already there before Shintoization set in and that made the conceptualization of kami cults as Shinto credible and feasible.

A Shrine, a Myth, and a Ritual

To root this history solidly in the soil of the real Japan, rather than in some abstraction, this book focuses on one particular shrine (Chapter 3), one myth (Chapter 4), and one ritual (Chapter 5). Of course, this forces us to make a selection that by definition will not be representative; but at least it will slice through history in a different and, we believe, more informative way than a book that begins by imposing the modern category of Shinto on premodern times.

Given the central position of the Ise Shrine in modern Shinto, it would have been both logical and useful to focus on this site. On the other hand, Ise is in many senses a very exceptional shrine, and perhaps the least representative of them all.[12] Other shrines and their rituals were "Shintoized" by way of assimilation to Ise, as the shrine of the imperial ancestors. Therefore, we have chosen to focus on another important shrine that can give us a better idea of what was there prior to Shintoization. Excellent studies of the shrine sites of Kasuga (Grapard 1992a), Konpira (Thal 2005), Kumano (Moerman 2006) and Ōyama (Ambros 2008) already exist; partly for that reason, this book will focus on another shrine complex that is today known as Hiyoshi (in its earlier guises, as Hie), located at the foot of Mount Hiei near Kyoto. This shrine was a pioneer in many different ways: in its symbiosis with the Buddhist establishment on Hiei's slopes; in its economic and political role as a holder of lands and a center of kami-assisted warfare; in its contribution to early formulations of Shinto; in the tragedy of its late medieval destruction and early modern rebuilding, and in its lengthy and, at times, violent struggle to break away from the Buddhist control exerted by Hiei's monks. The site shares many of these developments with other larger shrines, and it may serve as a lens through which to survey some of the major watersheds in the history of shrines.

The myth that we will follow through history is the tale of the sun-goddess Amaterasu who hid in a rock-cave and thus threw the world into darkness. This is one of the most famous episodes of kami mythology, and it has had an exceedingly rich afterlife in many different contexts. The main protagonists of this myth are the kami of central court lineages, including the imperial ancestor Amaterasu herself; still, in many of its later incarnations, the myth was not primarily interpreted as a political one, but rather as a metaphor for enlightenment practices, or as the origination myth of performative traditions such as *waka* composition, Noh, and kami dancing (*kagura*). Only after Meiji were such interpretations purged from the historical record, in what we may understand as a determined attempt to re-establish the court's monopoly on imperial symbolism.

Finally, the ritual that will be examined in detail in this book is the imperial enthronement ceremony called the *daijōsai*, or the "great rite of [rice] consumption." The *daijōsai* was in many ways the defining ritual of modern state Shinto. After all, it was the greatest of the imperial state rites, dramatizing the emperor's exclusive relationship with Amaterasu, and so narrating in the most powerful and persuasive fashion the transcendental nature of the imperial line. A historical exploration reveals that the *daijōsai* had the most interesting of pre-Shinto histories. The ritual is not as old as the modern state maintained; its original meanings were quite different from those now established; and, moreover, it was by no means consistently regarded as a necessary element of imperial enthronements. Once again, it was only with Meiji that the contemporary meanings of this rite and its Shinto identity were determined.

Chapter 2

Kami Shrines, Myths, and Rituals in Premodern Times

In the most general sense, shrines are sites where priests and worshipers interact with kami. Excavations of sites where offerings have been left over many generations reveal that the history of "shrines" in this basic meaning of the word goes back to prehistoric times. However, if we understand shrines to refer to permanent institutions, featuring buildings and dedicated priests, their emergence is much less ancient. Even more fundamentally, it is questionable whether ritual sites in different parts of Japan were perceived as specimens of a single category ("shrines") before the classical period. Shrines came to form such a distinct category only when shrine cults were treated as members of a single species by the imperial court. Therefore, the emergence of centralized court worship of shrines in the seventh and eighth centuries was a landmark in shrine history.

Early Shrine Cults

Perhaps the most common ancient prototype of today's shrines was an open-air site of seasonal worship, located at the boundary between the human realm where crops were grown and the chaos beyond it. A very suggestive description of such a site can be found in an eighth-century account of the shrine of a minor lineage of chieftains, the Yahazu, who were based in the northeastern province of Hitachi:

> During the reign of Emperor Keitai [early sixth century], Matachi of the Yahazu lineage cleared the reed plain in the valley to the west of the [present] district [office] and opened up new rice fields there. Then, *yato-no-kami*[1] flocked together and appeared in great numbers, stopping people from entering and cultivating the fields. According to local people, *yato-no-kami* have the bodies of snakes, carrying horns on their heads. If one looks back at them while fleeing, one's house and kin will be wiped out and one will have no descendants. Matachi was greatly angered by this. Wearing armor and carrying a spear in his hand, he slew them and chased them away. At the mountain entrance he planted a stick in a ditch as a mark, and he announced to the *yato-no-kami*: "We shall give the land above this stick to you, as the domain of the kami, but the land below it will be turned into rice fields for the people. I shall become a priest [*hafuri*] of the kami, and I shall revere and worship you in all eternity. I pray, do not strike us; do not bear a grudge against us!" He set up a *yashiro* and did worship there for the first time. He cleared ten *tokoro* of rice fields, and Matachi's descendants have performed worship here until this day. (*Hitachi-no-kuni fudoki*, NKBT 2: 54–5)

This tale is recorded in a gazetteer (*fudoki*) compiled on court orders under the supervision of Hitachi's provincial governor (c. 720?), and sheds some light on the local worship of deities called kami as it manifested itself in this particular outlying region. It depicts the kami as the original owners of the land. They are dangerous and violent and allow the people to live on the land only if soothed with offerings and prayers. The community exists due to a pact with these deities, renewed periodically through worship. By a combination of force and negotiation, Matachi conquered agricultural land from the kami. He emerges both as the founder of his community and as the ancestor of a lineage of priest-chieftains. His worship of the kami at a sacred place, called a *yashiro*, makes it possible to grow the rice on which the people depend. This *yashiro* (a word that means "temporary shelter") was not a permanent "shrine" inhabited by kami; rather, it was a demarcated site where seasonal ceremonies took place. The kami dwelt in the natural world beyond the human realm, and were invited to this site on the border between these two worlds only for the duration of the offering ritual. As descendants of Matachi, the Yahazu chieftains derived their authority from their status as the hereditary priests of the kami of the land. The act of making offerings to the kami on behalf of "the people" was intimately linked with political leadership, and it served to validate "taxation" – control over the agricultural surplus by chieftains who acted as mediators between the community and the greater forces that threatened it from the outside.

The northeast, where this tale is set, was an area that was little affected by the great changes that transformed central Japan into a "state" fashioned after continental models between the fifth and seventh centuries. In the course of these centuries Japan slowly evolved into a centered political unit governed by the so-called Yamato dynasty; the seventh century saw the expansion of that early state into the north of the main island Honshū. No doubt this was first and foremost a military process, but in the court's account of the subjugation of the Yahazu lands, it is presented in terms of a confrontation between the primitive deities of the land and a much more powerful type of kami:

> Later, during the reign of Emperor Kōtoku [r. 645–54], Maro of the Mibu-no-*muraji* took control over this valley and ordered for an irrigation pond and a dam to be built.[2] Then, the *yato-no-kami* climbed into a pasania tree by the pond and gathered there. Time passed, but they would not leave. Maro raised his voice and demanded: "The purpose of this pond is to give life to the people. Are you heavenly deities or earthly deities, you who resist the imperial will?" To the people who had been called in for corvée duty, he said: "Kill those swimming and creeping creatures, every single one that catches your eye! Do not fear them." Instantly, the ghostly snakes disappeared. (*NKBT* 2: 56–7)

Maro's conquest of Hitachi revealed that the Yahazu were only as powerful as the deities they worshiped. As "earthly" deities, these "ghostly snakes" stood no chance when confronted with the heavenly might of the imperial court. When the court's representatives in Hitachi recorded the Yahazu legend, they made sure that it conveyed a new message: the court does better at "giving life to the people" than the Yahazu because imperial power is heavenly power. As a result of Maro's action, the right to levy taxes was transferred to the imperial court. The notion of "heavenly and earthly deities" (Ch. *shenqi*, Jap. *jingi*) reflected an ancient Chinese categorization, attested in Confucius's *Analects* and other great classics. In Japan this foreign notion became the central concept around which the court organized its priestly power. The court absorbed local authority by incorporating local cults in the emperor's universal worship of the "deities of heaven and earth." In practice, this meant that the most important kami were integrated in a new court narrative, a "mytho-history" that established the origins of the Japanese state, and it implied that the court assumed the authority to make "heavenly" offerings to deities across the land. Together, this narrative and ritual practice constituted a new cultic system that we shall call the *jingi* cult.

Almost all information that we have about shrines in ancient Japan derives from records composed by the court in the context of this *jingi* cult. This presents us with a range of difficult problems. Classical sources mention a great number of shrines; in some places, at least, there appear to have been more shrines than settlements. Yet they reveal almost nothing about the ways in which these shrines functioned. The *jingi* cult subjected a number of these shrines to nominal court control, while at the same time priestly lineages from these shrines used the *jingi* cult to enhance their influence at court. Most shrine sites, however, were not included in this court cult, and about these we know next to nothing. The closest the Hitachi gazetteer comes to a description of actual shrine practice is a short passage about a shrine called Tsunomiya:

> Every year, on the tenth day of the fourth month, a festival [*matsuri*] is held and sake is served. Men and women of the Urabe lineage gather to drink and to enjoy themselves with song and dance for many days and nights. They sing: "They tell me to drink the fresh sake of the kami – that must be why I am so drunk." (*NKBT* 2: 68–9)

Similar incidental glimpses at shrine practice in other sources likewise confirm this image of communal festivities, mostly concentrated in the months of planting in spring and harvesting in autumn.

Jingi *Myth*

Mytho-history was one of the pillars on which the *jingi* cult rested. It is the function of myth to represent the present as rooted in a divine past, and thereby legitimate it and render it unchangeable. The art of writing allowed the court to give its own narrative of origins a new form of permanency and canonized authority, and with the help of Korean scribes, the legends of the royal lineage and its closest allies were codified in a number of works that are among the oldest surviving texts written in Japan. It was on this corpus that Shintoists would later draw in their search for ancient Shinto teachings.

We do not know when exactly the process of codification began, but the earliest surviving texts in this corpus, *Kojiki* (712) and *Nihon shoki* (720), clearly draw on earlier written materials.[3] In outline, both works offer a similar story, although the details are at times strikingly different. The plot of *Kojiki* may be summarized as follows:

1 We learn the names of the first deities who "became" when heaven and earth first originated: Ame-no-Minakanushi, Takami-musubi, and Kamu-musubi.
2 Izanagi and his sister Izanami descend from heaven and have sexual intercourse. Izanami gives birth to the Japanese islands as well as many other deities. She dies while giving birth to the fire deity and disappears to the "Land of Gloom" (Yomi). Izanagi tries to win her back but fails. When Izanagi washes away the dirt of death, he produces the sun-goddess Amaterasu, the moon god Tsukuyomi, and the storm god (?) Susanowo.
3 After a violent confrontation with Susanowo, Amaterasu retires into a cave and the world is thrust into darkness. The heavenly deities gather to lure Amaterasu from the cave in

a grand ritual. On earth, Susanowo and his descendant Ōkuninushi acquire treasures of great power, which are used by Ōkuninushi to build the land.

4 Takami-musubi and Amaterasu decide to establish heavenly rule over the "Central Land of Reed Plains." The earthly deities, led by Ōkuninushi, are persuaded or forced to cede the land to the gods of heaven.

5 Takami-musubi and Amaterasu send their grandson Ninigi down to the Japanese islands to take possession of the land. Ninigi is given heavenly treasures (jewels, a mirror, and a sword), and he descends to a mountain in Kyushu accompanied by an entourage of heavenly deities.

6 Ninigi's great-grandson, later known as Jinmu, is the first human emperor. Jinmu sails from Kyushu and conquers Yamato, defeating the descendants of earthly deities with the help of the gods of heaven and the magical powers of heavenly treasures.

7 Jinmu's descendants conquer the Japanese islands and establish Yamato rule even in Korea. Myths about the Age of the Gods shade into human history, organized by imperial reign.

Kojiki is a treasure trove of mythological motifs, names, unexplained references, and dead ends. Numerous deities make brief appearances in the tale, never to be mentioned again. Clearly, the work presents a small portion from a much larger body of material, which has been compressed into a narrative with a single overarching plot: the establishment of a heavenly dynasty in Japan.

Nihon shoki conveys the same message, but differs radically from the *Kojiki* in three aspects. First, *Nihon shoki* follows the model of Chinese dynastic histories much more faithfully than *Kojiki*, both in its language and its format – for example, by giving precise dates for all entries. Secondly, *Nihon shoki* lists many different versions of the various episodes of the story, presenting first one main version, and then quoting "other texts" with slightly different accounts. Thus, *Nihon shoki* gives us some idea of the breadth in the production of mytho-history in the decades around 700. Thirdly, there are significant differences in the mythological plot.[4] The most conspicuous difference is that *Nihon shoki* omits nearly the entire tale of Ōkuninushi. *Nihon shoki* appears less interested in giving credit to the earthly deities than *Kojiki*, and focuses even more narrowly on the heavenly dynasty of the Yamato emperors. Equally striking is the fact that *Nihon shoki* tones down the solar imagery of *Kojiki*. In *Nihon shoki*, it is Takamimusubi alone who orders the pacification of the land and grants rule over the Japanese islands to Ninigi. This text never refers to Amaterasu as the ancestor of the imperial lineage; it even appears to avoid the character for "sun."[5] We know very little about the actual history of the compilation of *Kojiki* and *Nihon shoki*. Strangely, *Kojiki* is never quoted in *Nihon shoki*, nor in any other text from the Nara period (710–94). There is no good answer to the question why *Nihon shoki* was compiled so soon after *Kojiki*, or to why *Nihon shoki* was given such a different format. We have no reliable contemporary sources that can help us to understand what the differences between these texts mean.

Imperial edicts (*senmyō*) issued between 697 and 749 refer to the emperor as a descendant of the gods of heaven, and more specifically, of the sun, while at the same time stressing that the dynasty is also rooted in Yamato's soil.[6] These same ideas are reflected again in the posthumous names given to emperors in this period, which all contain the phrase *Yamato-neko*, "son of Yamato's roots," in some cases combined with references to heaven or the sun. The combination of allusions to the sun and the "roots" of the land has been characterized as typical of *Kojiki* myth, in contrast to that of the *Nihon shoki* (Mizubayashi 2002: 18). That leaves us with the question why so much effort was invested in the compilation of that latter work. The late seventh century saw the creation of a Chinese-style imperial state in Japan, and it is understandable that it was seen as desirable to adapt the imperial legends to Chinese standards. However, that does not explain why the *Nihon shoki* should include numerous parallel versions, nor why it de-emphasizes both the dynasty's solar symbolism and its "earthly" aspects as a dynasty that, while being of heavenly origin, had allied itself with the powerful deities of the earth through marriage, agreement, and conquest. These are very serious problems, which question the traditional account of Yamato's self-authentication by mythological means.

The long tradition of interpreting *Kojiki* and *Nihon shoki* as canonical expressions of a fixed, coherent mythology of great antiquity has not made it any easier to discern the dynamics of mythmaking in classical Japan. Perhaps the most important finding of recent research is the very fact that there *was* such a dynamic, and that the realm of myth was never static. *Jingi* myth was a product of the decades around 700, when the Yamato kings transformed themselves into heavenly emperors. While drawing on earlier sources and tales, the mythological texts did not simply codify an archaic oral tradition; rather, their authors and editors created a new discourse, which was constantly contested, revised, and rewritten, so that no "final version" ever emerged.

The creation of new versions continued also after the *Nihon shoki* in 720, often with the more limited aim of raising the status of particular lineage. In 807, an account of the Inbe lineage and its roots in the Age of the Gods was submitted to the court, with the explicit aim of rectifying current evils and restoring the Inbe to their old position as leading court priests (*Kogo shūi* [Gleanings from ancient tales]). A much more ambitious attempt at rewriting myth is found in a text called *Sendai kuji hongi* (Original record of old matters from previous generations), which mixes passages from *Kojiki, Nihon shoki,* and *Kogo shūi* with a small portion of otherwise unknown material, some of which clearly favors another hard-pressed lineage, the Mononobe. This text is generally thought to have been compiled at some time in the ninth century by an unidentified Mononobe author.[7] It signals the continued attraction of myth as a source of prestige even at this late date. At the same time, it also demonstrates the lapsing power of *Kojiki* and *Nihon shoki: Sendai kuji hongi* challenges these sacrosanct records by mixing them with material from the private *Kogo shūi* and by introducing new elaborations. Such a bold act would hardly have been attempted in the heyday of court myth a century or so earlier.

Jingi *Ritual*

The mytho-histories were, of course, not widely read, and their message was conveyed much more effectively by ritual means.

The court invested heavily in ritual performances that gave visual expression to the heavenly, solar nature of imperial rule. In the palace, court priests performed a range of kami rituals that combined older rites with new procedures imported from Korea and Tang China. These rituals, too, stressed the hierarchy between heavenly and earthly shrines and kami. From 689 onwards the office that coordinated this court cult was called the Jingikan, the "Council of [affairs of] the heavenly and earthly kami" (the Council of Kami Affairs) and its activities were stipulated in a body of law known as *jingiryō*, "regulations on the heavenly and earthly kami." An imperial sun cult was established at Ise, some 100 kilometers east of the Yamato heartland. As the shrine of Amaterasu, Ise served as a center of kami ritual second only to the palace itself.

The shrines that entered the court cult were divided into "heavenly" and "earthly" shrines during the reign of Emperor Tenmu (r. 672–86) or that of his widow, Empress Jitō (r. 686–90). The Council of Kami Affairs, as we will henceforth refer to the Jingikan, kept lists of these shrines and their deities and determined their rank within the court hierarchy. The priests of these shrines were officially registered as such (implying that they were exempt from the taxes imposed on the agricultural population), and public lands and taxes were set aside for their upkeep. To begin with, "public shrines" of this kind were concentrated in the larger Yamato region; later, their number and geographical spread was gradually increased. A final list, recorded in *Engi shiki* (Procedures of the Engi period; 927), included 2,861 shrines scattered throughout the land.[8]

The *jingi* cult consisted of a broad range of ceremonies. The main aims of *jingi* rituals were securing rain and averting pests to obtain a good harvest; quelling disease among the populace; protecting the state from rebellion and invasion; and guaranteeing the health and safety of the emperor, the palace, and the capital. The establishment of this cult coincided with the adoption by the Yamato ruler of the title of *tennō* (emperor; literally "heavenly sovereign"), and with the renaming of his realm as Nihonkoku ("the land of the sun's origin"). It was a highly political construct, designed to transform the Yamato king into a figure whose position on earth was as universal and undisputed as that of the sun in the sky. Tenmu and Jitō emerge as the main architects of this cult, even though they built on older foundations. The most dramatic among *jingi* rituals were *daijōsai*, marking the investiture of a new emperor, and *kinensai*, a spring ritual in which offerings were distributed in the name of the emperor. The *daijōsai* will be investigated in detail in Chapter 5; here, therefore, we take a closer look at the *kinensai*. The development of this ceremony in the eighth and ninth centuries is a good illustration of the problematic history of *jingi* ritual.

The Shinto historian Okada Seishi (1970: 146–52) argues that the origins of *kinensai* go back to an earlier ritual, in which the Yamato king distributed rice to retainers and provincial chieftains (*kuni-no-miyatsuko*). He further connects this rite with a version of the legend of Ninigi's descent from heaven (recorded as a variant in *Nihon shoki*), in which Amaterasu's gifts to Ninigi include "rice ears from the sacred garden of which I partake on the Plain of High Heaven" (Aston 1972: I, 83). By handing out heavenly rice ears, then, the king signaled that the growing of rice depended on the blessings of the heavenly deities. The rice crop depended on the king's worship of these deities, and, as in the case of Matachi, this gave him a claim on "first ears" from the harvest (*hatsuho*; an early form of taxation).

There is of course no arguing the fact that *kinensai*, whose name means "ceremony of praying for the harvest," was agricultural in nature. Yet it is striking that the actual ceremony, as it was recorded in historical times, moved away from such an exclusive focus on rice. In the sources there are almost no traces of a distribution of rice ears. The earliest source that gives any details on the ritual, *Engi shiki* lists an enormous variety of "offerings" (*heihaku*) to be distributed at *kinensai*, ranging from different kinds of cloth (silk, hemp, bark-cloth, "common cloth") to weapons (shields, spearheads, bows, quivers) and such foodstuffs as sake, dried abalone, bonito, and deer meat; rice is conspicuously absent from the list.

Engi shiki also records the *norito* prayer that was recited at this occasion. Again, this prayer sets out by petitioning the gods for a good harvest, but soon moves on to praising the imperial reign as an institution protected by all the deities of the realm:

> If the mighty gods [of the harvest] grant that the grain will ripen, the first ears of the grain, the thousand, yea, ten thousand ears shall be offered up to them.
>
> May this age of the divine descendant of heaven be an everlasting age, as firm as solid rock, as unchanging as enduring rock. That it may flourish and be a happy reign, we present the choice offerings from the divine descendant to the mighty ancestral gods and goddesses [enshrined at the Council of Kami Affairs] as we offer up our words of praise.
>
> May the land in all directions be governed from the divine palace, and may it be made a peaceful land, a tranquil land by the grace of the mighty gods. (Bock 1972: 68–9, with slight variations)

Despite the fact that *kinensai* clearly was a ritual offering in prayer for bountiful crops, both the goods offered and the prayer intoned in this ceremony celebrated imperial power not in agricultural terms, but rather in economic and military terms. This was, in fact, in accordance with the general tenor of *jingi* myth, where agricultural themes only remain in such traces as deity names, embedded in what is at bottom a tale of subjugation by military force.

Another indication of *kinensai*'s rapid transformation is its changing audience. The earliest extant *jingiryō* laws, included in the Yōrō code of 718, mention *kinensai* as one of five annual occasions which all "hundred court officials" must attend. This host of officials consisted of all the members of various lineages who had been appointed to posts within the imperial bureaucracy. The distribution of offerings was to be witnessed by them, but they were not the intended receivers. Okada Seishi points out that in 702, when it was announced which lineages should serve the court as provincial governors, *kinensai* offerings were distributed among the lineage chieftains who were selected for these new posts (Okada Seishi 1970: 152). By accepting imperial offerings to the deities of their provinces, these chieftains acknowledged that the emperor acted as the supreme priest of all deities in the land, and thus acknowledged their relegation to the position of appointed representatives of the court. In *Engi shiki*, however, more than two centuries later, no mention is made of provincial governors. Here, the recipients of *kinensai* offerings are priests (*hafuri*) of selected shrines from all corners of the land. At the end of the ceremony, the *hafuri* were instructed to "humbly receive these offerings … bear them up and present them [to the gods]" (Bock 1972: 70). In contrast to provincial governors, these *hafuri* were hardly part of the political elite. To most listed shrines the court assigned so-called "kami households" (*kanbe*), households whose tax payments and corvée duties were reserved for the running of those shrines. *Hafuri* were chosen from among these households, and they performed duties directly connected with the worship of the kami. Some listed shrines had no *kanbe*; in that case, the provincial governor appointed *hafuri* from among the "common people." Obviously, presenting offerings to such lowly *hafuri* made for a very different ritual from offering to chieftains-turned-governors.

We do not know when this change happened; nor do we know to what degree it reflected real practice. Already in 775, *hafuri* attendance was so low that the court issued a statement threatening to strip absentees of their priestly status. By 798 the court had given up on its attempt to enforce attendance, and a new law allowed *hafuri* to collect *kinensai* offerings at provincial headquarters rather than in the capital. Even this compromise, though, proved ineffective, and in 875 the court agreed to send offerings to the shrines themselves by special messenger (Nishimiya Hideki 2004: 34–8). The grand description of the *kinensai* in *Engi shiki*, on which later reconstructions of the ceremony have been based, was composed in 927, another 50 years later. Did the *kinensai* ever occur in the form that this classical text prescribes, with the assembled officials witnessing the presentation of enormous amounts of imperial offerings to thousands of provincial priests?

Later Shinto thinkers saw in the *jingi* myths and rites the ancient essence of a pure "Japanese spirit," and at different stages in history drastic steps were taken to impose *jingi* orthodoxy on a very different shrine reality. In this sense the *jingi* cult exerted great influence on the later development of Shinto. Shinto theologians of different ages have had an interest in demonstrating that this ritual system continued to function throughout history without any significant change, and even today *jingi* ritual is regarded as an authoritative blueprint for kami worship. However, a closer look at *jingi* ceremonial reveals that it was in a state of constant flux. Moreover, from a detached perspective it is difficult to agree with the Shintoist vision that construes the *jingi* cult as Japan's indigenous, ethnic creed. *Jingi* myth was far removed from popular beliefs, and *jingi* ritual, in whatever form it actually existed, was not representative of shrine ritual in general. The *jingi* cult did not in any sense advocate a "nativist" or protonationalist ideology, even though it did serve the purpose of establishing the court as the center of a new political regime. Its focus was squarely on the imperial lineage and its allies; the notion of a Japanese people did not yet exist – let alone that of a Japanese spirit. Finally, the *jingi* cult did not pursue an antisyncretic or purist ideal, or reject continental influences. It drew heavily on Tang ritual codes and formalized kami worship by adopting Chinese procedures wherever possible (Naumann 2000). Moreover, as we shall see below, Tenmu and Jitō, who oversaw the creation of the *jingi* system, also invested heavily in Yin-Yang and Buddhist practice, both as a means to position their court as the undisputed center of the nation and to protect it from malign spirits.

The Jingi *Cult and Yin-Yang Ritual*

Yin-Yang divination had been brought to Japan by Korean immigrants long before the age of Tenmu and Jitō. It was an integral part of the Tang model on which these rulers drew. In fact, the title of *tennō* itself was originally a term of Yin-Yang astronomy, referring to the Pole Star as the stationary axis of the rotating universe. In parallel with the Council of Kami Affairs, the court also set up a Bureau of Yin and Yang (On'yōryō) that specialized in Yin-Yang divination, astronomy, calendar making, and time-keeping. The activities of this Bureau staged the emperor as a cosmic being responsible for maintaining the delicate equilibrium between Yin and Yang, and thus securing the safety and prosperity of the realm. The Bureau's diviners allowed the court to detect and mend imbalances that manifested themselves in the imperial body (as illness) and in the world at large (in the form of comets, unseasonal weather, epidemics, local uprisings, or incidents at shrines and temples such as fires or damage to trees). Of course, the kami of heaven and earth were also part of this cosmic balance, and the findings of the Bureau of Yin and Yang had a direct bearing on the activities of the Council of Kami Affairs. Many "interim" rituals addressing the kami at times of crisis were stipulated by this Bureau, and Yin-Yang rites overlapped with *jingi* ceremonial. Yin-Yang thought, then, was an integral part of *jingi* ritual from the start, and it would remain a major theme of Shinto.

Jingi ritual drew most heavily on Yin-Yang expertise in matters related to exorcism and the protection of the emperor and his capital. Yamato kings had sought such expertise among Korean immigrants long before the *jingi* cult took form. Many ancient rites were quite obviously based on the idea that dangerous Yin spirits should be quelled by exposing them to Yang forces. A striking example of this can be found in another eighth-century gazetteer, which explains the origins of the hugely popular horse races at Kamo Shrine:

> During the reign of Emperor Kinmei [sixth century] there were tremendous winds and rain and the people suffered greatly. At that time, Wakahiko of the Iki Urabe was ordered to perform a divination. He determined that the troubles were due to the vengeance [*tatari*] of the deity of Kamo. At this they held a festival on an auspicious day in the fourth month. They hung bells on horses as men rode them wearing lion masks.[9]

This procedure can be traced back directly to Chinese festivals, in which horses and animal masks featured prominently as powerful sources of Yang.

In the eighth and ninth centuries, Yin-Yang-style rituals of pacification (*chinsai*) and purification (*harae*) rose rapidly in importance as the court was shaken by political infighting, natural disasters, and, especially, deadly epidemics on an unprecedented scale. Yin-Yang techniques were soon adapted to serve the private needs of courtiers, and gradually spread further to the population at large, where they must have had a profound impact on shrine cults.

The Jingi Cult and Buddhism

Buddhism was another important ingredient of court ceremonial. Both Tang emperors and Korean kings established extensive networks of Buddhist temples in their territories and employed large numbers of Buddhist monks as protectors of the nation. In Japan, Buddhism had already become established, both at the court and among leading lineages, by the late sixth century. Tenmu, too, repeatedly "did obeisance" at temples, and he even had "orders sent to all the provinces that in every house a Buddhist sanctuary should be provided, and a Buddha image with Buddhist scriptures placed there" (Aston 1972: II, 369). In the sphere of Japanese court ceremonial, then, Buddhism was older than the *jingi* cult, and the latter developed in close dialogue with a pre-existing Buddhist presence.

Yin-Yang ritualists reduced the gods to ethereal forces subject to the rules of a cosmic dynamic, and in that way undermined the individuality and the particularity of locale-specific deities. Buddhism had much the same effect, but its rhetoric was different. Buddhism came with a long tradition of dealing with local spirits that can be traced back all the way to the religion's early dissemination in India (DeCaroli 2004). Throughout east and south Asia, Buddhist deity typologies were applied to local deities, and through this act of classification the individuality and localness of these deities was weakened. Deities were fitted into Buddhist cosmology as nonenlightened sentient beings, superior to man but still caught in the karmic realm of birth and death, and therefore greatly inferior to the enlightened buddhas. The effect of this was that deities who had been regarded as the supreme powers within their territories, or among certain groups of people, were reduced to specimens of universal categories of lesser beings such as *devas* or *asuras*. Stripped of their uniqueness, the deities were no longer all-powerful even in their own ancient domains.

Both the court and local elites cherished Buddhism for its ability to control the violence of deities, spirits, and demons of all kinds, including the kami. Usually, this entailed building temples next to shrines, where monks dedicated themselves to the conversion of the kami by exposing them to the Buddha's benign teachings. By reciting sutras, and other Buddhist practices, these monks created merit or good karma, which was transferred to the kami in the hope that this would, in the words of a source from 788, "increase their power, and thus cause the Buddha-Dharma to flourish, wind and rain to moisten the earth at the right times, and the five kinds of grains to produce good crops."[10] Such temples, called *jingūji* or "shrine temples," were first built in the periphery of the Yamato region in the eighth century, and soon spread throughout the land.

As a result of these developments, a considerable number of the more important shrines were transformed from simple open-air sites into complexes of buildings, often including a temple and a shrine that were closely connected. Buddhism manifested itself in the landscape of ancient Japan as a huge construction project, scattering the islands with temples, pagodas, and sculpted images. Through the *jingūji*, this building boom had a direct impact on shrines. At the same time, shrines' kami came to be seen in ever more human terms. Both the *jingi* cult and the Buddhist *jingūji* cult contributed to this transformation. The shrines of Ise were not of the *yashiro* type: they were not temporary constructions to which deities were invited from some other location for the duration of a ritual. Rather, they were residences of human-like beings. These shrines were called *miya*, "venerable dwellings," and the gods who resided in them were served with food and given clothing and other goods throughout the year. As the residence of the emperor's heavenly ancestor, Amaterasu's *miya* at Ise was a hybrid between the Chinese concept of an ancestral mausoleum (Ch. *zongmiao*, Jap. *sōbyō*) and an indigenous shrine; the layout of its grounds and buildings was closely patterned on that of Japan's earliest Buddhist temples, such as the Yakushiji in Kashiwara and the Hōryūji in Nara (Tamura 1996: 220–7). *Miya*-type shrines appear to have spread to other sites under the influence of the court; we will encounter one example of this at Hie, in Chapter 3 of this book.

When *jingi* ritual went into terminal decline in the ninth century, the court introduced new legislation to shield the last vestiges of the *jingi* cult from being absorbed by Buddhism. In 871 a new code of procedures known as the *Jōgan shiki* banned the performance of Buddhist rites in the palace and in provincial offices in the central Kinai region for the duration of the *daijōsai* enthronement ritual, and prohibited monks and nuns from entering the palace during other *jingi* ceremonies. This artificial separation of *jingi* ritual from Buddhism was more political than religious in inspiration. Court politics was lineage-based: power was hereditary within lineages that traced their origins to (mostly) heavenly deities. Buddhism had the capacity to undermine the legitimacy of lineage prerogatives by including specific deities in general categories of beings that were ultimately subject to the power of the Dharma. The potential threat posed by this property of Buddhism became clear in the 760s, when Empress Shōtoku (r. 764–70) came close to handing the throne to the Buddhist monk Dōkyō (d. 772). After her death, the court took drastic measures to strengthen the ritual foundations of lineage rule. During his years in power, Dōkyō had built a shrine temple at Ise, symbolizing Buddhist supremacy even over the imperial sun cult. After his dismissal this temple was dismantled and steps were taken to isolate Ise from Buddhism. Monks were barred from entering the shrine grounds, and even the use of Buddhist terms was banned on Ise Shrine lands. It was this practice of isolating imperial *jingi* rites from Buddhism that was extended to the court itself in 871.

These events created a dividing line between Buddhism and the *jingi* cult that would retain its relevance until modern times. The principle that worship of the heavenly and earthly deities was the prime task of the emperor was expressed in numerous tangible ways: for example, by banning Buddhist ceremonies in the first week of the year, and by the unwritten rule that emperors received the tonsure only after their retirement. The taboo on Buddhism in connection with the *jingi* cult, especially at Ise, generated much ritual friction and theological reflection. It is perhaps possible to argue that this policy foreshadowed the separation of Shinto from Buddhism that began in the Edo period and culminated in 1868; at the time, however, it was a formalistic measure with little or no impact beyond the narrow confines of Ise and the court. The integration of shrines in Buddhist-dominated complexes deepened, and the marginalization of the *jingi* cult continued. Even at a site like Hie, which had close links with the court, the isolation of *jingi* ritual had no effect whatsoever.

Shrines in Late Classical and Medieval Japan: From Landowners to Pilgrimage Centers

This is not the place to rehearse the political history of Japan, but it may be useful to recall some landmarks. In the ninth century, the imperial apparatus of government was monopolized by the Fujiwara lineage of regents. In the eleventh, the Fujiwara regents were challenged by emperors who retired young and built their own power base from the temples to which they retired. In the twelfth century, warrior groups employed by both regents and retired emperors stepped in to fill the vacuum created by the escalating infighting at the court, resulting in the founding of the first shogunate in 1185. This shogunate, based in Kamakura, fell in 1333, and it was left to the Muromachi shogunate (1336–1573) to restore order. These dramatic changes created both new problems and possibilities for shrines.

By the tenth century, the *jingi* cult and its nationwide network of court-sanctioned shrines existed only in name. A new, much leaner shrine network emerged to replace it. Shrines near the capital with a proven record in controlling rainfall continued to receive court offerings; also favored were recently founded Buddhist shrines in Kyoto, where monks placated disease-spreading spirits. After the final addition of Hie Shrine in the eleventh century, the new network comprised only 22 shrines, all located in the vicinity of the capital – this in contrast to the *jingi* network, whose 2,861 shrines were spread across the country. The 22 shrines were presented with *kinensai* offerings twice a year, and performed interim rituals to deal with crises. With the exception of Ise, all these shrines were part of temple-shrine complexes dominated by monks (Grapard 1988).

In the provinces, *jingi*-type shrine rituals declined even more drastically. Rather than being worshiped in their own shrines, the main kami of a province were gathered in convenient locations called *sōja*, "shrines to the collected kami," and presented with offerings and prayers there. In addition, provincial authorities chose one representative shrine in each province, gave it the title "first shrine" (*ichi-no-miya*) and concentrated their ritual efforts on this single site – although some provinces also had second or even third shrines. These changes marked the final demise of the *jingi* cult. The rites offered at the 22 shrines and the provincial shrines followed predominantly Buddhist procedures of shrine worship, similar to those of the *jingūji*. The same was true of a new network of temple-shrine complexes dedicated to the deity and bodhisattva Hachiman, initiated by the Kamakura shogunate. This deity, with ancient roots in northern Kyushu, won a position of prominence at the Yamato court in the eighth and ninth centuries and then rose to new heights in the medieval period as the protecting deity of the Minamoto lineage that founded the shogunate. A Hachiman shrine-temple complex called Tsurugaoka Hachimangūji served as Kamakura's ritual center, and a network of Hachiman shrines/temples spread across the country as the shogunate expanded its influence. As an alternative to the shrine networks of the court, the Hachiman shrines/temples were less bound by tradition and even more explicitly Buddhist in all respects.

In the same period (the twelfth and, especially, thirteenth centuries), the court lost more and more of its political influence. As court power declined, shrines with ancient privileges were among the first to suffer. Even offerings to the 22 shrines dwindled rapidly and were finally discontinued altogether in the fifteenth century. Initially, Ise was alone in retaining considerable court spending; but even this shrine was increasingly left to its own devices, and by the end of the medieval period it was in ruins.

Some shrines, however, were in a position to profit from the new situation. One effect of the fragmentation of power was that many public lands were turned into private estates. Temples and shrines were ideally suited as holders of such estates. The lands of temples and shrines belonged not to humans but to buddhas and kami, and this fact alone made it more difficult to dispute their ownership. Shrines with connections either at the court or among powerful warrior groups acquired considerable portfolios of tax-exempt land. On the individual estates held by temple-shrine complexes, the kami of the complex was installed in a miniature copy of the main shrine; as a result, a small group of deities achieved regional or even national renown. Hie's "Mountain King" (Sannō) is but one example of a deity whose worship spread across large parts of Japan in this way.

From the fourteenth century onwards, however, it became increasingly difficult for temples and shrines to hold on to their estates. Religious complexes proved unable to compete with warlords, who gradually attained almost complete hegemony over the land at the expense of both the court and the temples. At the same time, economic growth helped local communities to become more robust and take control over their own affairs. As a result, many of the shrines that had once served to control the estates of temple-shrine complexes now became independent village shrines. Their new function was to protect the village and to secure its prosperity. Shrine rites enhanced village cohesion, gave divine sanction to the village hierarchy and to the decisions of the village elite, and displayed the village's vigor and pride to outsiders. Also, shrines served to secure communal assets as "property of the kami" (shinmotsu). Especially in western Japan, many village shrines were run by exclusive groups of landowning families called, in later terminology, miyaza or "shrine guilds." Guild members exerted both political and ritual power over the village as a whole. It is tempting to see at least some structural continuity between the village rites of ancient times and the shrine festivals that developed under this new arrangement.

In the meantime, the larger complexes that were losing their grip on their lands explored new ways to attract income. As their economic and military power dwindled, they used their regional or even national reputation as sites of divine potency to attract pilgrims. Pilgrimages to shrines for personal reasons were not an ancient shrine practice, but emerged first after the incorporation of shrines in Buddhist complexes. Such pilgrimages became popular at the court in the late tenth century; later, the consecutive shogunates followed suit. For the shrines, pilgrimages by powerful courtiers and warriors were of great importance as occasions at which donations (often of land) could be expected. It was not until the later medieval period, however, that pilgrimage grew from an elite undertaking into a popular movement.

The shrines of Kumano are an early example of a temple-shrine complex that built its fame and prosperity on the active propagation of pilgrimage. Kumano was a pioneer in organizing a network of pilgrimage guides (*sendatsu*) and facilitators (*oshi*), and in the use of legends, miracle tales, picture scrolls, and map-like "pilgrimage mandalas" to attract audiences from hundreds of miles away (Moerman 2005). In the long run, the Ise Shrines would be even more successful. The Inner and Outer Shrines of Ise were already engaged in legal procedures about proceeds from the sale of services to pilgrims by the 1330s (Teeuwen 1996: 73–83, 164–70). The Ise *onshi*, as *oshi* were called here, did not typically hold appointments as proper shrine priests, nor did they participate in official shrine rituals. By the mid-fifteenth century, these *onshi* had taken over the running of the towns in front of the gates of the two Ise Shrines. While the shrine priests could not prevent the shrines from falling into disrepair, the *onshi* succeeded in building up large networks of "confraternities" (*kō*), groups of believers who engaged in different kinds of Ise worship under their leadership. The *onshi* had contracts with specific localities, which gave them the exclusive right to provide the Ise *kō* in those places with Ise-related services, from the sale of amulets and calendars in the provinces to accommodation and the performance of rituals in Ise itself.

Confraternities of this kind were of a very different nature from the *miyaza* guilds of village shrines mentioned above. Membership in a confraternity was a matter of free choice, while guilds were by definition closed. Confraternities were informal networks based on a shared faith, cutting across social strata. Membership in a shrine guild was closely tied in with village politics and had little to do with faith (Sakurai 1988: 47–57). Confraternity activities frequently involved the founding of miniature shrines, often in the grounds of the village shrine. As a result, shrine precincts came to include many small shrines dedicated to the region's more famous deities, revered as a matter of personal choice in the shadow of the community's village shrine.

The Emergence of "Shinto"

In the classical and medieval periods there was a string of different networks of shrines (*jingi* shrines, the 22 shrines, *sōja* and *ichi-no-miya*, the Hachiman network), and also a general understanding of shrines and their kami as a discrete category of Japanese practice; but to what degree can we talk of "Shinto" as a distinct tradition at this time? Different perspectives will result in different answers to this question. Shrines were incorporated in the Buddhist worldview that already dominated Japanese culture at the time the *jingi* cult was first institutionalized, to the extent that the distinction between temples and shrines had become blurred. Arguably, the category of kami as opposed to other higher beings, ranging from buddhas to devas, star deities, and powerful animals such as foxes and snakes, was even more fluid. On the other hand, the few vestiges of the imperial *jingi* cult that persisted were sufficient to prevent shrines and kami from being completely absorbed in Buddhism, as was the fate of local deity cults in other Buddhist regions such as Tibet, Sri Lanka, and Southeast Asia (Teeuwen 2007a).

What is beyond doubt, however, is that the concept of Shinto as "Japan's indigenous religion" emerged much later than these networks. Neither the classical *jingi* cult nor the Buddhist *jingūji* cult of shrine temples revolved around a discourse about "Japan." As we have seen, the *jingi* cult aimed to project the authority of local priest-chieftains onto the emperor, and to establish a centered polity in ways that were largely derived from the Asian continent. It did not engage in reflections on the special nature of Japan or on Japan's relationship with India and China – let alone on the relationship between "Japanese Shinto" on the one hand and Buddhism and Confucianism on the other. The Buddhist cult of kami was even less interested in exploring the idea that shrine practice might constitute a Japanese "Way." Neither the *jingi* cult nor the Buddhist *jingūji* cult shared the defining preoccupation of later Shinto with "Japan" as a realm of specific sacredness.

Ideas of Japaneseness first became a significant element of intellectual life in the thirteenth and fourteenth centuries. In these centuries the world had a larger impact on Japan than before, through increased trading with Song China (960–1279), the Mongol invasions of 1274 and 1281, and even more intense dealings with the Yuan dynasty (1271–1368). At least as important, however, were domestic developments. The imperial court leaked power to the warrior governments of Kamakura and Muromachi, and sought to compensate for this by enhancing its prestige in cultural terms. In this setting, courtiers once more stressed the origins of the state in a dynasty of kami and emperors. The emperor, the imperial kami, the imperial regalia, and also court poetry became emblems of a particular Japanese tradition. The significance of these emblems was expanded by Buddhist means. The emperor and his ancestor Amaterasu were conflated with the Great Sun Buddha Dainichi (Mahāvairocana), the regalia were identified with mudras and mandalas that activated Dainichi's powers, and court poetry was equaled with the chanting of esoteric spells that gave instant access to the deepest essence of the Dharma. Taking this new discourse one step further, Japan was contrasted with China and India as the land of Dainichi's Dharma-body, the personified Dharma in which all existence is grounded. Japan, then, came to be seen as the territory in which the Dharma manifests itself in its purest form. Some Buddhist lineages argued that the shortest route to this pure Dharma was through worship of the kami, whom they redefined as the ultimate source of all existence. Lineages that specialized in this Buddhist kami cult began to refer to themselves as *shintō-ryū*, Shinto lineages, in the late fourteenth or early fifteenth century. This was the first time that the term Shinto was used in a "sectarian" sense, referring to a distinct teaching and practice.

From its first instance of use in *Nihon shoki*, the word that we today read as "Shinto" had had clear Buddhist connotations. In Japan, it was used almost exclusively in the context of Buddhist kami worship, most likely in the reading *jindō*, to refer to the kami as objects of Buddhist sublimation (Teeuwen 2002, 2007a). In the *shintō-ryū* of the fifteenth century, however, the kami were understood to represent the raw, original essence of Dainichi's enlightenment, made manifest in the form of the emperor, the Ise Shrines, or even the Japanese territory as a whole. The *shintō-ryū* transmitted a range of rituals in which the emperor, the kami, the regalia, and the ancient texts of kami myth (notably the *Nihon shoki*) were transformed into conduits that gave direct access to the very foundations of the Dharma, the roots from which the buddhas themselves arise.

These Shinto lineages were a rather marginal phenomenon in the landscape of medieval Japanese religion. Yet they were important as pioneers of the idea that Japan had a distinct Way that was called "Shinto." In this sense, they prepared the stage for an even more radical notion: that Shinto is not part of Buddhism.

Yoshida Kanetomo and the Invention of One-and-Only Shinto

In the 1480s, there took shape on Mount Yoshida in Kyoto, northeast of the imperial palace, an extraordinary site. It was unlike any other in Japanese religious history, and its uniqueness articulated a new understanding of the cosmos and a new religious endeavor. The Yoshida site, known as the Saijōsho or "ritual space," was testament to the extraordinary imagination of one man, Yoshida Kanetomo (1435–1511). Kyoto had been devastated by the Ōnin wars of 1467–77, leaving the Ashikaga shoguns powerless and the imperial court destitute. Fighting quickly spread to the provinces, and a hundred years of military conflict ensued. Such was the turmoil in society at large that contemporaries often wrote of *gekokujō*, that is, of "those below overthrowing those above." Kanetomo's endeavors in the religious realm were very much of this subversive order.

Kanetomo was head of the Yoshida family, whose forebears had been employed by the Council of Kami Affairs as diviners. Subsequently, they had served the Yoshida Shrine in Kyoto as priests. In fact, however, neither the Council of Kami Affairs building nor the Yoshida Shrine had survived the Ōnin wars. The centerpiece of Kanetomo's new Saijōsho was the Daigengū, or "shrine of the great origin." Its striking octagonal shape attests to Kanetomo's ambition, for eight was a number intimately related to imperial power and its cosmic reach. The very center of the Daigengū comprised eight wooden pillars reaching from floor to ceiling, surrounding a thicker pillar of bamboo. The bamboo pillar cradled a jewel at its top, and affixed to it at eye level was an octagonal plaque of wood drawing ritual participants' attention to the kami enshrined therein. Here it was that, amongst others, the great kami Kuni-no-Tokotachi was worshiped (Scheid 2001: 183). The Daigengū was the ritual center of what Kanetomo referred to variously as "one-and-only" or *yuiitsu* Shinto, and "origin of the source" or *sōgen* Shinto. The Daigengū stood in a courtyard surrounded by a wall, lined with shrines dedicated to all Japan's kami. Either side of it were two more shrines, one for Amaterasu and one for Toyouke, the kami of Ise's Inner and Outer Shrines. To the rear of the courtyard was yet another shrine. This was the Hasshinden, the name given to the ritual center of the state's Council of Kami Affairs, dedicated to the eight kami protectors (*hasshin*) of the imperial line. The original had been destroyed in the civil wars, and Kanetomo had taken it upon himself to construct here his own version. The Saijōsho was clearly designed as a new sacred center for Japan, with Kanetomo its guardian.[11]

The Saijōsho was the most important of three sites within the Yoshida mountain complex. The Yoshida Shrine was another, but this was resurrected only after the Saijōsho was completed on a site immediately adjacent to the north. Yoshida Shrine owed its historical significance, to the fact that it venerated Ame-no-Koyane, the tutelary kami of the great Fujiwara court family. For this reason it had been long understood as the Kyoto branch of the Kasuga Shrine in Nara, but its importance, to Kanetomo at least, was now secondary. On Kanetomo's death a third structure was erected on the Mount Yoshida site, between the Saijōsho and the Yoshida Shrine. This was the Shinryūsha, a shrine entirely conventional in appearance, but extraordinary in implication, for it was built on the very site where Kanetomo's body was buried. It enshrined his spirit as a kami, and subsequently too those of his descendants. The Shinryūsha thus confronted head-on long-held shrine taboos of death, and in so doing opened the way for two historic developments: the posthumous veneration of great men as kami, and the institution of Shinto funeral rites. To these matters we shall return below.

If Kanetomo's Daigengū was entirely egregious in structure, his Shinto thought was suitably subversive. His achievement was to create a Shinto that turned the traditional medieval worldview on its head. For all its Buddhist influences, Kanetomo understood one-and-only Shinto to exist before and beyond Buddhism. The clearest articulation of this idea appears in his *Shintō taii*, "The great truth of Shinto," of 1476 (Nishida 1978: 249).[12] What strikes the reader first perhaps is the Japan-centeredness of this text. Japan is the center of the cosmos, because the light of the kami first shone on Japan. Japan is thus rightly designated the land of the kami (*shinkoku*), and the Japanese Way as the kami Way (*shintō*). It is immediately clear that Kanetomo's kami are no longer the raw, original essence of Dainichi's enlightenment that we encountered in medieval Shinto lineages. Kanetomo imparts special significance to Kuni-no-Tokotachi, who in the *Nihon shoki* metamorphosed out of a reed-shoot after the creation of heaven and earth (Aston 1972: 2–3). Kanetomo reimagines Kuni-no-Tokotachi as a creator kami with "the shape of no-shape" and "the name of no-name." From him sprang "the one-great-three-thousand realms" (a term which, it might be noted, is Tendai Buddhist in origin). In other words, all creation began with this kami's beginning. Here Kanetomo's subversion of the medieval worldview is clear: "The teachings of Confucianism and Buddhism are streams, flowing from the source of the limitless law which is this kami's heart. Buddha and Confucius draw their life from heaven and earth [as created by this kami], and thus owe to this kami their virtues" (*ST* Urabe 1: 3–4). Kanetomo's cosmos is thus entirely kami-determined. His summoning of the myriad kami into the Saijōsho was intended, it is now clear, to redeem them from their centuries-old identification as Buddhist avatars.

Of special interest are Kanetomo's *Shintō taii* appendices. The first is a genealogy charting the 12 kami generations as listed in the *Nihon shoki*. Kuni-no-Tokotachi and the sun-goddess Amaterasu are located as supreme among the heavenly and earthly kami respectively, but Kanetomo's commentary on the twelfth kami, Hiko Nagisatake Ugaya Fukiaezu, hints at his deeper purpose. This kami began his rule more than a million years after Amaterasu, who herself emerged eons after Kuni-no-Tokotachi. It was only in the latter years of Hiko Nagisatake's 800,000-year rule that Amaterasu finally "softened her light and mingled with the dust [of samsara]" to effect the birth of Śākyamuni in India; 2 million more years passed before that birth took place (*ST* Urabe 1: 28–9). This genealogy rendered absurd, of course, the medieval insistence that kami were "traces" of the Buddha's true substance. A second appendix dates the origins of the Saijōsho to Mount Atago in 905, the fifth year of Engi. In that year, Kanetomo explains, Emperor Daigo ordered 3,132 kami be enshrined there before dispersing them once more to shrines throughout the 60 provinces (*ST* Urabe 1: 29–30).[13] There is, however, no historical record of any such imperial orders, nor any evidence of the Saijōsho existing before Kanetomo created it in the late fifteenth century. Kanetomo's last appendix cites Prince Shōtoku (573–621) to the effect that "Shinto is the source of Confucianism and Buddhism, and the origin of all creeds." Thus it is that Shinto is known as *sōgen*, "the source of the origin" (*ST* Urabe 1: 31–2). It is perhaps superfluous to note that no such statement is anywhere else attributed to the Prince.

The most audacious of Kanetomo's claims for one-and-only Shinto concerned Ise. In the tenth month of 1489, Kanetomo informed Emperor Go-Tsuchimikado (r. 1464–1500) that a bright celestial light had illuminated the Saijōsho. On investigating, he had found in the courtyard between Daigengū and Hasshinden a sacred object. This he had duly enshrined in the Daigengū and worshiped. There had been a similar incident a few months before, too. Kanetomo now invited the emperor to confirm that these objects were, indeed, the sacred treasures of Ise's Outer and Inner Shrines. Kanetomo was well aware, of course, that the Outer Shrine at Ise had been destroyed in 1486, and its temporary replacement burned to the ground in 1489. The gullible emperor saw these objects, was filled with wonder, and duly gave his confirmation. Ise priests were quick to denounce Kanetomo as a fraudster, but his purpose was clear. The shrines in Ise undermined his claims for the cosmic centrality of the Saijōsho; the Ise kami had to be accommodated and rescued, too, from their Buddhist identification. Here lay Kanetomo's purpose. We might note too that Emperor Go-Tsuchimikado was himself shortly to receive initiation into one-and-only Shinto (Hagiwara 1962: 638–40).

We saw earlier how the Council of Kami Affairs had served as the ritual center of the *jingi* cult in the seventh century, binding regional shrines to court and capital. Kanetomo aspired now to replicate that system, with his Saijōsho replacing the Council as the center (Hagiwara 1962: 647). Increasingly he referred to himself as *Shintō chōjō* or "superintendent of Shinto." This was the title that appeared on the Shinto licenses that Kanetomo began to issue to shrines in the 1480s. His strategy was to intercede with the emperor on behalf of local and regional shrines, and have the emperor issue certification of court rank. A shrine's purchase of a license invariably meant that an erstwhile avatar or *gongen* was transformed now into a *myōjin* or "light-emitting" kami, a referent that had a distinctly Yoshida resonance. It was not until the time of Kanetomo's mid-sixteenth-century successor, Yoshida Kanemigi (1516–73), that these licenses were distributed far and wide. Kanemigi traveled extensively, gaining the trust of local warlords, and offering licenses of different types to local shrines, though increasingly without imperial sanction. The *Shintō saikyojō* confirmed a priest as belonging to Yoshida Shinto and determined the ritual garments he would wear. Closely related were *Shintō denju* or initiation certificates, which were conferred on those undergoing one of multiple rites, from the introductory *Nakatomi harae* to the advanced *jūhachi Shintō* (18 rites of Shinto).[14] Kanemigi distributed amulets, too, to those who commissioned his ritual performances, and he did a brisk business selling scrolls bearing oracles from the three great shrines of Ise, Hachiman, and Kasuga (Bocking 2001).

A final comment is called for here on the issue of fabrication. Kanetomo was a fabricator of stories of objects flying in from Ise, of the origins of his Saijōsho, and of his family's lineage, too (Hagiwara 1975: 618). Early modern critics were not far off the mark when they attacked the foundations of Yoshida's one-and-only Shinto as entirely fraudulent. We must not lose sight, however, of Kanetomo's endeavor. He set out at a time of great political and social upheaval to give substance to a radically new worldview. His achievement was to conceive of kami, shrines, and their priests as constituting a new religion called one-and-only Shinto, distinct from, superior to, and the very source of Buddhism, Confucianism, and Daoism, even as it accommodated those creeds. The fact of accommodation may have given Yoshida Shinto an unmistakably combinatory character, but such a Shinto had never before existed. This was Kanetomo's vision, and it demanded legitimizing. In a society totally dominated by a Buddhist worldview, Kanetomo perhaps had little choice but to fabricate. Anyway, as we shall see, for leaders of the early modern state who entrusted to the Yoshida family a major political and social role, the truth or otherwise of Yoshida claims was never the issue.

Early Modern State Shinto

The combined endeavors of the warlords Oda Nobunaga, Toyotomi Hideyoshi, and Tokugawa Ieyasu restored order to sixteenth-century Japan, laying the foundations of the early modern state (1600–1867). It is testament to the characters of Yoshida Kanemi (1535–1610) and his brother Bonshun (1553–1632) that they won the trust of these great men.[15] Evidence of this trust is to be found in their involvement in the posthumous cult of Hideyoshi. Hideyoshi's body was buried on the top of Mount Amida-ga-mine in Kyoto, and his cult was practiced in the Hōkokusha Shrine, where he was venerated Yoshida-style as Hōkoku Daimyōjin, the "great kami illuminating the abundant land."[16] Kanemi's grandson served the shrine as its priest, Bonshun performed Buddhist rites there, and the cult endured until it was destroyed by the Tokugawa in 1615.

The intimacy of these men with Hideyoshi did not initially condemn them in Tokugawa eyes. Indeed, they so impressed Tokugawa Ieyasu that, in 1601, he granted to the Kyoto Saijōsho official status as "substitute Council of Kami Affairs." Later, when the court resurrected the practice of dispatching emissaries to the Ise Shrines, the emissaries set off from the Saijōsho. Ieyasu had Kanemi lecture him on the *Nihon shoki*, and he may even have been initiated into Yoshida Shinto secrets after his abdication in 1605. There were in Ieyasu's inner circle, however, men resentful of Yoshida influence; of these none was more articulate than the remarkably long-lived Tendai monk Tenkai (1536–1643). Bonshun and Tenkai contained their mutual animosity till Ieyasu's death in 1616, but then they clashed over interpretations of his will. Briefly, Ieyasu demanded posthumous veneration as a kami, but his will left unclear what sort of kami that should be. As a consequence, Ieyasu was first buried on Mount Kunō, near today's Shizuoka, and venerated there as a Yoshida *daimyōjin* like Hideyoshi before him; after the burial, however, Tenkai argued that a grave mistake had been made. Surely, it had been Ieyasu's intention to entrust his cult to Tendai Buddhism, and to be worshiped as a great avatar? Such was Tenkai's influence over Ieyasu's son and heir, Hidetada, that he had Ieyasu's body disinterred, transferred east to Mount Nikkō, north of Edo, and reburied there with Buddhist rites. Tenkai constructed in Nikkō a massive mausoleum, and Ieyasu was worshiped there as Tōshō Daigongen or the "Great avatar illuminating the realm from the east." In Tendai Buddhism there were of course no kami who were not avatars.

Tenkai's appropriation of Ieyasu's cult was a major setback for the Yoshida family, but their connection to the early modern state was by no means over. Yoshida priests maintained and cultivated contacts with regional shrines, and Tokugawa Ietsuna (r. 1651–80), the fourth shogun, was persuaded to deploy the Yoshida family to establish control over all shrines in the land. Ietsuna and his closest advisors, such as Hoshina Masayuki (1611–72), lord of Aizu, were obsessed with developing enduring systems for the maintenance of social stability. A Shintoist with Yoshida connections called Yoshikawa Koretari (1616–94) earned Masayuki's confidence, and this connection helps explain why the Tokugawa government now moved to entrust supervision of shrines across the realm to the Yoshida family (Hashimoto Masanobu 1997: 289–90). The publication, in 1665, of the Shrine Clauses or *jinja jōmoku* was critical. The clauses gave to the Yoshida the sort of authority that the fifteenth-century Kanetomo could only have dreamed of. Article 1 speaks not of Shinto but of *jingidō*, recalling the *jingi* cult of ancient Japan, and demands that priests "know their kami" and perform traditional rites. There is no explicit Yoshida reference here, nor in Article 2, which concerns procedures for shrine priests' procurement of court rank. Nonetheless, *jingidō* was interpreted to mean one-and-only Shinto, and the Yoshida were hereby effectively sanctioned to mediate with the court to procure rank for priests at shrines across the land. Article 3 alone refers to the Yoshida: shrine priests, it says, should wear garments "determined in the licenses issued by the Yoshida family [to confirm court rank]"; those without rank should wear white. It was never the intention that great shrines like Ise and Izumo be included in this arrangement; they after all had their own court connections. But this was left ambivalent, prompting priests at the great Izumo Shrine to protest that they would never accept Yoshida authority (Nishioka 2004: 65–8).

Authorized by these Shrine Clauses, the Yoshida brought thousands of provincial priests under their supervision. These priests displayed Yoshida-mediated court rank, wore Yoshida garb, and performed Yoshida rites. These rites also increasingly included the entirely new phenomenon of Shinto funerals. Shrine priests' performance of funeral rites was actively promoted by the Yoshida, who prepared texts outlining Yoshida-style procedures (Endō 1998: 1–15). In several domains, Aizu in the north, Mito in the east, and Okayama in the west of Japan, Yoshida authority was established virtually overnight; elsewhere it took longer. In Aizu, for example, the aforementioned Hoshina Masayuki compelled seven major shrines to attach to the Yoshida. These shrines he repaired, and deployed as Yoshida training institutes. To them he gave authority over all other shrines in Aizu, which he then reduced to one per village. The Yoshida family benefited in Aizu, Mito, and Okayama from the powerful anti-Buddhist inclinations of those domain lords (Inoue Hiroshi 2006: 193–6). Outside these select domains, however, the Yoshida encountered sustained challenges to their new authority. One source of challenge was the Shirakawa court family. The Yoshida had risen to prominence at the expense of the Shirakawa, who had played a vital role in the ancient Council of Kami Affairs and all court rituals, from the emperor's daily worship to the *daijōsai*. The Yoshida were in origin only court diviners, and as such subordinate to the Shirakawa in every sense. The reinstatement of numerous court rites in the seventeenth century, and their entrustment to the Shirakawa, gave new vigor to that court family. Increasingly they contested

Yoshida influence over provincial shrines (Mase 1985: 67–74).[17] In the 1750s, the court allowed the Shirakawa to construct their own Hasshinden in the family residence. This was belated recognition that they, and not the Yoshida family, had been responsible for rites at that shrine in the ancient state. Emboldened, the Shirakawa began now to dispatch followers to regional shrines in numbers. By the end of the early modern period, the Shirakawa had recruited some 400 priests to their cause, including some at major sites, such as Matsunoo in Kyoto.

In the 1750s the Yoshida faced another challenge, this time from adherents of what became known as Suika Shinto, the creation of Yamazaki Ansai (1618–82). Ansai, a one-time Zen monk who then trained in Neo-Confucianism, was initiated into Yoshida secrets in 1671 and received the "kami name" of *suika reisha*, meaning "shrine of the Suika spirit." The word *suika* derived from the characters for "bestow" (*sui*) and "protection" (*ka*) as they featured in an oracle attributed to the legendary founder of the Ise Shrines, Yamato-hime.[18] Ansai's Suika Shinto inherited much from one-and-only Shinto, even as it departed from it in important ways. For example, Ansai was, notwithstanding his Buddhist training, uncompromisingly anti-Buddhist. Again, his Shinto had a solid ethical core, which drew on Confucianism and was directed toward the imperial institution. Moreover, Ansai was influenced by Neo-Confucian metaphysics. This is evident in his proposal of "the essential unity of kami and humankind" (*shinjin yuiitsu*), which implied that kami-nature inhered in all creation, including humankind. It was to manifest this belief that Ansai built a shrine to the kami within his own heart, and had it located in the Shimo Goryō Shrine, near the imperial palace in Kyoto. Suitably enough, he gave to this shrine his own kami name, Suika Reisha, (Katō 1931: 54–6). For Ansai, all men were duty-bound to discover the kami within, and the strategy demanded was "steadfastness." Steadfastness in turn demanded *tsutsushimi*, essentially a vassal's unswerving loyalty to his lord. This brings us on to a further defining feature of Suika Shinto, namely its imperial focus. For Ansai, Prince Toneri, the eighth-century compiler of the *Nihon shoki* myths, was the paragon of this virtue. The Prince's faithful recording of the acts of the heavenly and earthly kami, and of sovereigns from Jinmu to Jitō, was the ultimate in *tsutsushimi*. Was it not the Prince's endeavors alone that had ensured that the mysterious truth of the imperial line was known today? The virtue of the founder of that line, the sun-goddess, was for Ansai beyond compare, but her descendants, the emperors, were also truly kami, and their virtue, too, was hardly inferior. Ansai's reflections on the imperial line clearly had subversive potential in a realm ruled by the Tokugawa, and Ansai's disciples were to explore this aspect of his thought after his death (Maeda Tsutomu 2006: 207–24).

Ansai never exerted an influence over local shrine priests comparable to to that of the Yoshida or Shirakawa families, but some of his followers did attach themselves to the Shirakawa, and Ansai won a following among priests in Kyoto, in Edo, and in Izumo, too (Hatakama 2007; Nishioka 2004: 102–6). It was in the imperial court, though, that Suika Shinto had its most profound impact. Before his death in 1682, Ansai entrusted Suika Shinto's future to the courtier Ōgimachi Kinmichi (1653–1733), and as a result of Ōgimachi family patronage, courtiers of all ranks, and emperors too, were captivated. Kinmichi initiated regent Ichijō Kaneteru, and he so earned the trust of retired emperor Reigen that Reigen, like Ansai before him, had his living spirit venerated in the Shimo Goryō Shrine.[19] Suika Shinto's influence reached its zenith at court during the tenure of Kinmichi's youngest son, Sanetsura (1720–1802).[20] Most noteworthy was the role of Takeuchi Shikibu (1712–68) in these years. Shikibu opened a Suika school in Kyoto, where he taught young courtiers, frustrated with the court system that restricted advancement to members of just five families of pedigree. Shikibu, in his *Nihon shoki* lectures to these men, stressed the right of emperors to rule their own realm, querying as he did so the legitimacy of Tokugawa rule. Shikibu was an unmistakable advocate of imperial restoration: "The people of the realm, overwhelmed by [imperial virtue], will devote their hearts to the emperor. The shogun will then return to him the administration." When the regent, tipped off by the head of the Yoshida family, learned that Emperor Momozono (r. 1747–62) was himself a Suika Shinto student, he launched a purge of Suika adherents. He had 27 courtiers disciplined, and dispatched Shikibu himself into exile (Tokutomi 1926: 375–6). Suika Shinto never recovered the influence it enjoyed in the 1750s.

Popular Practices

An understanding of kami, shrines, and rites in early modern Japan overlooks at its peril popular practice. Popular practice constituted a dynamic realm that owed nothing at all to the influence of the Yoshida, Shirakawa, or Suika schools of Shinto. From the outset one point needs stressing: there is no suggestion that, when early modern Japanese engaged with the kami at shrines, local or remote, they understood their actions to constitute something called "Shinto"; the word has simply no explanatory value for popular kami practice in early modern Japan.

Much of this popular activity took place at pilgrimage sites removed from local shrines. Ise, Ōyama, and Konpira were perhaps the best known among the countless pilgrimage destinations of this age; of them all, though, the Ise Shrines were the most popular.[21] The statistics for Ise pilgrimage are staggering: 3.5 million pilgrims headed to Ise in 1705, 2 million in 1771, and as many as 4.5 million in 1830. These were exceptional years, but the annual average was around 400,000. Great pilgrimages followed abundant harvests and were known as *okage mairi*, "thanksgiving pilgrimages." People headed for Ise out of belief in the miraculous power of the Ise kami, of course, and reports of Ise amulets falling miraculously from the heavens were often the stimulus for pilgrimage booms. But itinerant Ise priests played an indispensable role. As we have already seen, the *onshi* priests of Ise had been active in medieval Japan; but early in the seventeenth century their clientele diversified from warriors and merchants to commoners. *Onshi* numbers increased correspondingly, so that by the mid eighteenth century, 600–700 *onshi* and their assistants were criss-crossing Japan, servicing some 4 million households, or 80 percent of Japan's population. *Onshi* were entrepreneurs, the most successful of whom accumulated great wealth as they catered for "parishes" of up to 200,000 households.

Each year, for a fee, they distributed Ise amulets and Ise calendars; they served as guides, too, overseeing pilgrims' travel arrangements to Ise. *Onshi* encouraged villagers to organize themselves into confraternities, whose members paid into a communal fund to ensure that one member at least might head to Ise each year.

Outer Shrine *onshi* were more numerous than those of the Inner Shrine by a factor of five to one, and their shrine received far more pilgrims, not least because *onshi* persuaded pilgrims that their shrine, too, venerated the sun-goddess. Pilgrims' travel diaries reveal, inevitably enough, that Ise pilgrimage had as much to do with travel, adventure, and entertainment as it did with worship. It seems, too, that it was not primarily Ise's imperial connection that attracted pilgrims; more important by far was the sun-goddess's function as a numinous agricultural kami, who bestowed on supplicants and their communities abundant harvests and many other this-worldly benefits besides. There is an important slippage, then, between pilgrims' understanding and that of, say, the Arakida and Watarai priestly families who served the Inner and Outer Shrines. Even as these priests catered for the masses, they maintained a privileged connection to the imperial court in Kyoto. The shrine–court link was provided by the Fujinami family of court ritualists who, from 1647, were dispatched to Ise as imperial emissaries each year in the ninth month. There they performed rites in celebration of the sun-goddess as imperial ancestress (Takano 2003: 284).

The kami of the Ise Shrines, however they were understood by pilgrims, featured in the great imperial mytho-histories of the eighth century, but much popular practice revolved around kami with no such connections. The kami of other great pilgrimage centers such as Ōyama and Konpira were of this order, but so too were those of minor pilgrimage sites. Take for example the Hakami Shrine located within the great Shitennōji temple in Osaka. Hakami was a tooth kami whose cult required toothache sufferers to make a paste of soy beans and bury it in shrine ground. Supplicants prayed to Hakami to release them from pain, at least until those pasted beans sprouted. Or again, consider the cults of Inari, a rice kami quite unconnected to the imperial myth. Inari was associated with the fox and was the object of veneration for centuries throughout rural Japan. In the early modern period, belief in both Inari and fox possession spread to the great urban centers. In the 1830s, for example, a shrine appeared in Ichigaya ward of Edo dedicated to the so-called "bush Inari," promising to cure eye complaints. Shrine legend had it that Inari in his foxy guise had poked his eye out on the branch of a tea bush when walking in the mountains. Accordingly, if the supplicant abstained from tea for 27 days and made suitable offerings, "bush Inari" would cure the eye complaint (Miyata 1972: 141). The cult of the kami Kōshin, widely practiced in early modern Japan, was different again. In origin, Kōshin refers to a moment in the Chinese calendrical cycle when metal clashes with metal to herald dramatic, inauspicious change. In Japan, this calendrical moment was apotheosized as the kami Kōshin. On Kōshin days it was the practice to stay up all night praying to that kami lest heaven vent its wrath on the community. Kōshin became associated with Saruta-hiko, a long-nosed kami with distinct imperial connections, as well as with the Buddhist Vajrapāṇi. Early modern almanacs advised their readers, though, that Saruta-hiko and Vajrapāṇi were none other than guises adopted by the kami Kōshin (Breen 2007b: 72–3).

In the early nineteenth century an entirely new phenomenon emerged, enriching further still the kami-scape of early modern Japan. Kurozumi Munetada (1780–1850), Nakayama Miki (1798–1887), and Kawate Bunjirō (1814–83) exemplify this phenomenon since all three, born into impoverished families in rural Japan, became kami, and, as kami, established mass followings across Japan. The kami into which they transformed were distinct from one another, but they all promised salvation, a concept alien to the cults we have seen thus far (Kozawa 1988: 302–4). Here it must suffice to discuss only Kawate Bunjirō, who in 1855 was first possessed by, and subsequently became, the kami Konjin. Konjin was the most ferocious of the many kami whose image appeared on the front of early modern calendars, striking fear into the hearts of rural Japanese (Breen 2007b: 66–7). In the 1850s, Bunjirō lost two young sons and a daughter in quick succession, and then two of his livestock died, threatening his family's livelihood. Bunjirō then collapsed with an incurable throat disease. He was convinced his misfortunes were due to his having unwittingly offended Konjin, perhaps by transgressing a directional taboo. At his bedside, his brother-in-law was possessed by that kami, who declared that, sure enough, an offence had been committed. When Bunjirō apologized profusely, Konjin pardoned him and promised divine help. Bunjirō duly recovered, opened up a shrine in his home, and devoted his life to doing Konjin's will, which involved "interceding [with Konjin] for those who suffer." In 1868, that tumultuous year in which the early modern yielded to the modern, the kami Konjin confirmed that Bunjirō was after all Konjin in fleshly form. Henceforth, Bunjirō was known to his disciples as *ikigami Konkō Daijin*, the "great living kami of golden light" (Suzuki 2003: 218–20).

Kurozumi, Nakayama, and Kawate all founded national movements; they built shrines that became national religious centers, where solemn rituals were performed for the kami that had possessed, inspired, and transformed them. All three were of common stock and shared a concern for the salvation of the common man or woman. There is no evidence, however, that they understood their activities as constituting "Shinto"; even Kurozumi, who was a shrine priest, never used that word in his writings. In their orientation, they offered a striking contrast not only to Yoshida Shinto but also to a major intellectual movement, dominated by kami concerns, which gathered pace even as Kurozumi, Nakayama, and Kawate were active in rural Japan. This intellectual movement was "nativist," since the men involved were obsessed with Japan and its uniqueness. That uniqueness, they agreed, inhered in the kami of the myths and in the imperial institution. Their nativism manifested itself further in their keen and critical interest in foreign thinking and foreign ways.

The Nativists and their Kami

Not until the publication of the *Kojiki-den* (*Kojiki* commentary) by Motoori Norinaga (1730–1801) in the early nineteenth century did the *Kojiki* become widely known in intellectual circles and beyond.[22] Prior to this masterwork, knowledge of the kami and the myths was drawn almost exclusively from the *Nihon shoki*. As we have already seen, the stories narrated in these two works of mytho-history were rather different. To take but one example, the *Kojiki* narrative, unlike the *Nihon shoki*, does not accord a creator-role to Kuni-no-Tokotachi, the kami who inspired both Yoshida and Suika Shinto. Motoori's work anyway revitalized intellectual interest in the kami and the myths, especially of the *Kojiki*, and it is possible to identify two fairly distinct kami-approaches amongst the nativists active in the last decades of the early modern era. Representative of one approach were Motoori himself and Aizawa Seishisai (1781–1863); typifying the other was Hirata Atsutane (1776–1843). These nativists attracted followers of different social classes from across Japan, but they were thinkers not priests, and none created a "Shinto" school. Indeed, where possible they eschewed the word "Shinto," probably owing to its Yoshida associations. Their thought was, however, to have deep political and social reverberations, shaping Shinto in its modern guise.

Motoori and Aizawa were of quite different social backgrounds; they lived a generation apart in different regions of Japan. Motoori was of a merchant family in Matsusaka near Ise, Seishisai a samurai intellectual from Mito domain, east of Edo. They shared, however, a conviction that the sun-goddess was the most important of all the kami by far. Motoori wrote thus in the opening lines of his *Naobi-no-mitama* (The spirit of the rectifying kami) of 1790:

> The great imperial land is the great land wherein resides the great goddess of the sun, the divine ancestress. Japan is superior to all other countries, since all other countries receive her plentiful benevolence. The goddess held the sacred symbols in her hand … the three sacred treasures transmitted by the court through the generations. She decreed Japan was the land where her descendants would reign forever. Thus, in the beginning, the imperial throne was established here in Japan along with heaven and earth.[23]

In his focus on the sun-goddess, Motoori is offering his own spin on the *Kojiki*. In the *Kojiki*, Amaterasu is goddess of the sun, to be sure, but in the narrative she reflects mirror-like, rather than generating, the sun's light, and she is definitely subordinate to Takami-musubi (Mizubayashi 2005: 8–10). The *Kojiki*, after all, identifies Takami-musubi as the greatest of the heavenly kami, the first sun kami who generates all life. Motoori does acknowledge the creative power of Takami-musubi, but he has only the slightest interest in the *Kojiki*'s account of the cosmogony. He finds his inspiration in the sun-goddess, in her foundation of the imperial line, and perhaps, above all, in the spontaneous, emotionally pure "Way" of ancient Japan which her descendants oversaw (Isomae 2000b: 20). For Motoori, each human emperor is descended from the sun-goddess, and so the emperor's heart and the emperor's commands are those of the sun-goddess. In ancient Japan, therefore, "the realm was ruled in peace, and emperors' succession to the heavenly throne continued uninterrupted." The *Kojiki*, Motoori claims, reveals the Japanese Way that resulted, but that Way neither arose naturally, nor was it man-made; it was created rather by Takami-musubi and then nurtured by the sun-goddess. In *Naobi-no-mitama* Motoori constantly contrasts Japan with China, where wise men invented "Ways" as techniques to restore order which never worked. As a result, Chinese history was one of violent overthrow of successive dynasties. Japan's own problems began, indeed, when Chinese influence infiltrated the imperial court. Motoori's writings were not, in a narrow sense, political. The ancient Way as he understood it was rather one of spontaneity and emotion, and his concern was to spread knowledge of it to all classes of Japanese. Motoori had no program for radical social or political reform, and it is here that he differs most from Aizawa Seishisai and his text *Shinron* (New theses) of 1825.

This opening passage from *Shinron* resonates unmistakably with Motoori's thinking:

> Our divine realm is where the sun emerges. It is the source of the primordial vital force sustaining all life and order. Our Emperors, descendants of the sun-goddess Amaterasu, have acceded to the imperial throne in each and every generation … Our divine realm rightly constitutes the head and shoulders of the world and controls all nations. (Wakabayashi 1986: 149)

Aizawa penned his political treatise *Shinron* as a solution to Japan's impending crisis, the first cause of which was the appearance of Russian and British vessels off the Japanese coast, threatening Japan's isolation. Where Motoori was scathing of Chinese "Ways," Aizawa saw the solution to lie in the revitalization of Confucian ethics. This is where for him the sun-goddess and the emperor assume their importance. For Aizawa, Amaterasu is the progenitor of loyalty and filial piety; her descendants, the emperors, are paragons of these virtues. "Each emperor strives to recompense Amaterasu's blessings by personifying filial devotion, honoring the tombs of imperial forebears, and revering her prescribed set of religious rituals" (Wakabayashi 1986: 158). The ancient Way idealized by Aizawa could hardly have been further removed from Motoori's. It was essentially a Confucian Way, where social order constructed upon loyalty and filial devotion obtained, forever invigorated by the emperor's exemplary performance of ritual acts in the presence of his ancestress, the sun-goddess.

A quite different nativist "take" on the kami is typified by Hirata Atsutane in his voluminous writings. Amaterasu is hardly unimportant for him, but her presence is only relative. In Hirata's first major publication, *Tama-no-mihashira* (The august pillar of the soul) of 1813, he wrote of the need to understand the soul and its fate in the afterlife. This in turn entailed an appreciation of the division of the universe into heaven, earth, and the nether realm, and of the divine virtues that informed creation. Only when Japan's role in creation is made clear does its superiority over all other lands become apparent. Motoori had argued that all the dead, good or bad, are destined for the polluted realm of Yomi, but Hirata begged to differ. He understood the souls of the dead to stay in Japan, gathering at shrines where propitiation ensures they rest in peace. These concerns of Hirata explain his emphasis on kami which, for Motoori and of course for Aizawa, were of no consequence at all (Endō 2008: 27–8). The first such kami is Ōkuninushi who, in the *Kojiki*, rules the earth before ceding it to Amaterasu's offspring, the emperors; he then disappears. Hirata, however, rereads Ōkuninushi as sovereign of the invisible realm which is inhabited by the dead. "When His Majesty's subjects die, their souls become kami and return to the invisible realm. There they are subject to the rule of the great kami Ōkuninushi" (Sasaki 1998: 143–4). Elsewhere, Hirata writes that Ōkuninushi not only rules the invisible realm, but stands there as judge, determining whether souls proceed to heaven or to hell. He also gave new importance to the kami Ame-no-Minakanushi who becomes a dominant presence in his writings (Sasaki 1998). In the *Kojiki* this kami appears after the heavens are created and plays no further part in the narrative, fading into invisibility (Philippi 1969: 47). Hirata effects an important switch when he writes: "Since this great kami exists *without a beginning*, it is only appropriate he be called the ultimate, first deity. [N]o words possibly exist to describe the heights and depths of his virtuous power" (emphasis added). In other words, this kami is not created; he is the creator. Hirata is elsewhere explicit on this point: "[This kami is] furnished with the quality of producing all things within heaven and earth," and is "sovereign over all existence" (Sasaki 1998: 138–40). What is particularly striking in Hirata's writing is his accommodation of foreign knowledge. He read Copernican theory, and was familiar with the biblical story of creation, and there is evidence, indeed, that his theories of the soul, the afterlife, and the cosmogony developed under biblical influence.[24]

In the first half of the nineteenth century, the writings of Motoori, Aizawa, and Hirata spread to every corner of Japan. Motoori had a network of some 500 disciples in his lifetime, who published his works and ensured a wide dissemination. Aizawa's *Shinron* was not published for a generation, but it circulated amongst activist samurai in the 1850s and 1860s, and was read by all the men who carried out the Meiji Revolution of 1868. It may be that Hirata had the widest audience of them all. His disciples came from all backgrounds, shrine priests, merchants, and wealthy peasants alike (Walthall 1998). After his death their numbers rose exponentially; his books, too, sold in their thousands. Ten thousand copies of *Tama-no-mihashira* were sold before 1868.

These, then, were the blocks out of which Meiji leaders built modern Shinto. The most influential architects were Ōkuni Takamasa (1792–1871) and his disciple Fukuba Bisei (1831–1907). Takamasa was an admirer of Motoori and a disciple of Hirata; he also enjoyed cordial relations with scholars of the Mito domain in the circle of Aizawa. Ōkuni and Fukuba were recruited by the Meiji leadership to construct an ideological system that would proclaim the emperor's descent from the sun-goddess, and so legitimize the imperial Restoration even as it united the hearts and minds of all Japanese. Ōkuni and Fukuba adopted Aizawa's views on imperial ritual, claiming all shrines in the land as sites for state rites. In the process, they freed Ise from the control of the Arakida and Watarai lineages of priests, and ended the nominal control of the Yoshida and Shirakawa families over all other shrines. These men were the authors of the Shinto–Buddhist clarification edicts of 1868 that expelled Buddhist influence from shrines, transforming them into dedicated Shinto spaces.[25] The Shinto they championed was the Amaterasu-centered version proclaimed by Motoori and Aizawa, although in the early Meiji years Hirata's ideas about Ōkuninushi and Ame-no-Minakanushi found fleeting favor. As for the popular kami practice of early modern Japan, Fukuba Bisei was of the view that much of it belonged to the distinctly unmodern, uncivilized realm of superstition.[26]

Here ends our general survey of the pre-Meiji history of shrines and Shinto. In Chapters 3, 4, and 5 our focus becomes thematic. We discuss first a single sacred site, namely the Hie Shrine complex at the foot of Mount Hiei, near the shore of Lake Biwa in Shiga Prefecture; next the enduring myth of the sun-goddess and the rock-cave, and, finally, the ritual known as the *daijōsai*. Our purpose is to pin down dynamic aspects of the pre-Shinto history of these several "Shinto" phenomena, and to shed light on the vital and complex processes of Shintoization that impacted on each in turn.

Chapter 3

The History of a Shrine
Hie

The train leaving Kyoto in an eastward direction passes through two tunnels to reach the city of Ōtsu, on the southern shore of Lake Biwa in Shiga Prefecture. Here, it swings to the north onto a narrow plain that stretches from the lakeside to the wooded slopes of Mount Hiei, which now separate us from the old imperial capital. (Hiei, incidentally, is a classical, sinified reading of the older Hie, retained in the name of the shrines.) Only some 15 minutes after boarding the train we reach the small town of Sakamoto, an almost bucolic place of narrow streets interspersed with small fields. Shrines are scattered across the town in conspicuous numbers, and enough Edo-period structures have survived to earn the upper part of the town the status of a conservation zone. The main street leads away from the lake towards the mountain. Where the road begins to slope gently upwards, it broadens into a promenade stretching beyond a huge torii gate. This promenade guides the visitor to the right, under a second torii, across a modest brook, and into a bewildering complex comprising seven major shrines and a host of minor ones. Some are large and elaborate, others modest and worn-looking. Together, they are known today as Hiyoshi Taisha, the Great Shrines of Hiyoshi; prior to the Second World War they were called the Shrines of Hie (see Maps 1 and 2).

Some of these shrines have histories that stretch back more than a millennium, while others are much more recent additions. Over the centuries this sacred site has undergone countless transformations, both in its physical appearance and in its religious identity.

From the classical through the medieval periods, Hie grew from a ritual site without any permanent buildings into the country's largest assembly of shrines. Since then, Hie has gone through two major spates of destruction and restoration. In 1571, during the wars of reunification that ended the medieval period, warlord Oda Nobunaga (1534–82) reduced the entire complex to ashes. In 1868, Hie freed itself from the control of the Buddhist monks of Mount Hiei, and the shrines went through a phase of violent anti-Buddhism that involved the abandonment of most of its traditions. Hie may not be a "typical" shrine, if such a thing exists at all; but its dramatic saga illustrates some of the twists and turns that marked the history of shrines in most corners of Japan.

Hie in Ancient and Medieval Japan

Origins

How did this remarkable site come into being, and why did it rise to such prominence? The catastrophe of 1571 utterly destroyed the buildings, images, and documents pertaining to Hie, and much of the site's early history can only be gleaned from the re-collections of the Hie priest Shōgenji Yukimaru (1512–92), who barely survived the onslaught, and from the scattered shrine traditions that he managed to reconstruct. Beyond Yukimaru's work, we have little more than fragmentary references in other records, a few medieval doctrinal texts that survived away from Mount Hiei, and some scarce archaeological findings.

In its present form the Hie complex consists of two compounds centered on the Eastern and the Western Main Shrines (Higashi- and Nishi Hongū), located less than 300 meters apart. The eastern compound contains four major shrines, the western three. The ancient origins of Hie lie in the eastern compound, which itself consists of two separate sites: two shrines near the top of Mount Hachiōji (381 m), and two more at the foot of the mountain. The two shrines on the top are built up against a large slab of stone known as the "golden rock." Today, they are believed to enshrine the "violent spirits" (*ara mitama*) of a male and a female kami, while the shrines at the bottom of the hill accommodate the "gentle spirits" (*nigi mitama*) of the same divine couple.

In order to reconstruct the original significance of this setup, the historian Kageyama Haruki, himself a native of Sakamoto, analyzed the structure of Hie's spring festival, *Sannō matsuri*, the main event at the shrines to this day (Kageyama 2001 [first published in 1971]). Nowadays, two *mikoshi* (palanquins for transporting deities) are carried up to the two upper shrines on March 1, and from this day onwards, fires are lit on Mount Hachiōji every night. Some six weeks later (at present, on April 12), the *mikoshi* are rushed down the precipitous mountainside to the Eastern Main Shrine. Here, the male and female *mikoshi* are symbolically united in a rite called the "tying together of hips" (*shiri-tsunagi*). The next day, April 13, they are carried down to a third site, an open pavilion on the lower border of the Hie compound called the Ōmandokoro, or Great Office. Offerings of many kinds are presented at the Great Office; among them, colorful children's toys stand out. Then, in the dark of night, the *mikoshi* are rocked back and forth violently for up to two hours, displaying the vigor both of the deities they carry and of the young men who manipulate the *mikoshi*. In front of the Great Office is another small shrine, called the "Birth Hut" (Ubuya). Nowadays it is understood to enshrine a god of thunder called Kamo Wake-ikazuchi, identified as the son of the two deities of the eastern compound. On April 14 the *mikoshi* bearing the kami of all seven Hie Shrines are transported through the town of Sakamoto, all the way down to the harbor, from where they are ferried out onto Lake Biwa on boats. They receive more offerings at various locations, and finally make their way back to the shore and their respective shrines in the late afternoon.

Stripping the symbolism and geography of this festival down to its bare essentials, Kageyama Haruki reconstructs an ancient mountain cult. This cult was spread over three sites: the golden rock, the shrines at the foot of the hill, and finally the site on the plain, the Great Office. Kageyama surmises that the spring festival would have begun with a lengthy period of interaction, perhaps by female shamans, with the male and female deities on Mount Hachiōji, culminating in the descent of the deities to the site at the foot of the hill. This would not have involved *mikoshi*, which were first introduced in the twelfth century; rather, the deities would have been transferred from the rock into branches, perhaps of the evergreen *sakaki* tree. In this phase of the festival, the deities of the uninhabited mountains beyond the limits of the village were first wooed and placated within their own sacred domain, and then invited down to the borders of the human world. Here they played out their powers of fertility. A ritualized intercourse took place at this liminal site, and subsequently the pregnant deities were taken even further into the village, to the place where rice is grown and children are born. There the gods gave new powers of fecundity to the world of humanity, blessing their worshipers with another prosperous spring season.

Kageyama's Hie, then, was a peaceful place where boisterous but ultimately benevolent deities bestowed blessings on an ancient Japanese community. We will soon find, however, that his analysis of the Sannō festival does not reflect premodern or even early modern understandings of its proceedings. In fact, little is known about the structure of the Hie festival before the Edo period. It is likely that it has undergone profound changes in the course of its history. There is, for example, no record that the "tying together of hips" was performed even in the Meiji period, and what is more, the oldest sources do not in fact make any mention of a male and a female deity. The extent to which Kageyama's interpretation is based on modern, post-Meiji innovations will become increasingly clear towards the end of this chapter. Kageyama's assumption of at least structural continuity between prehistorical and modern Hie reflects Shinto's self-image as an indigenous tradition that has remained unchanged, at least in its deeper structure, since ancient, sacred times. His emphasis on agricultural fertility rites is based on an equally modern thesis about the genesis of Japanese culture as the product of local communities of rice growers. Of course, rice culture was indeed a major factor in the political and economic life of ancient Japan, but a closer look at ancient kami cults, including that of Hie, reveals a range of other themes. In fact, the single kami that appears in the earliest source on Hie (*Kojiki*, 712) was not so much a generous god of rice as a threatening and violent force. Moreover, this kami's cult appears to have been based less on a changeless native culture than on a dynamic interaction between the expansionist politics of the Yamato kings on the one hand, and ritual specialists with continental skills and backgrounds on the other.

This is what the *Kojiki* has to say about Hie's deity:

> Ōyamakui, also named Yamasue-no-Ōnushi: this deity dwells on Mount. Hie in the land of Chika-tsu-Ōmi, and also at Matsunoo in Kazuno. This is the deity who holds the humming arrow. (Philippi 1969: 118)

Ōyamakui figures here among the many children of Ōtoshi-no-Kami ("the kami of great harvests"), one of Susanowo's numerous sons. This places the kami of Hie in the lineage of earthly deities from Izumo that ultimately culminated in Ōkuninushi, that earthly deity who "built the land" before handing it over to Ninigi, the heavenly ancestor of the imperial dynasty. Ōyamakui means "the great mountain peg," and Yamasue-no-Ōnushi "the great lord of the mountain's end."[1]

Beyond this brief note the sources are silent about ancient Hie, but the link with Matsunoo is telling. Matsunoo, in the area where the capital of Kyoto was to be founded in 794, was the ancestral shrine of the Hata, a lineage of immigrants of Korean origin who served the Yamato kings not only as weaving experts and managers of estates but also as skilled ritualists. The deity of this shrine features also in the founding legend of the neighboring Kamo Shrines. According to this legend, a daughter of the Kamo chieftain found a red arrow in the Kamo river, which she took home and kept in her bedding. Soon, she gave birth to a son. Nobody knew who the boy's father might be, and when he had grown up, he was asked to serve sake to his real father at a drinking feast. Without hesitating the boy offered the sake to heaven, transformed himself into a kami, and disappeared, piercing the roof on his ascent. Like the red arrow that had fathered him, he turned out to be a deity of thunder.[2]

This is but one instance of a motif that appears in many variants: deities who appear as snakes, arrows, and thunderbolts and who father semidivine children by impregnating young virgins. Hie's Ōyamakui, with his "humming arrow," clearly belongs to this category. There is much to suggest that the Yamato court attached great importance to this type of cult. At least until the reign of Tenji (r. 626–71), the hill of Miwa at the eastern edge of the Yamato basin was a major site of court kami worship. The deity enshrined there was Ōnamuchi or Ōmononushi – identified with Ōkuninushi, Ōyamakui's distant relative and the undisputed leader of the earthly deities. This deity shared many of Ōyamakui's characteristics. In *Kojiki* and *Nihon shoki* (720), the kami of Miwa emerges as the prototypical earthly deity: a violent force that Yamato's heavenly dynasty struggled to control. One episode relates how the kami of Miwa transformed into a red arrow and impregnated a beautiful maiden while she was defecating in a ditch. The child that was begotten from her union with the arrow deity was chosen to become the wife of Jinmu, the first human emperor and Yamato ancestor. Nine royal generations later, when Yamato was plagued by a mortal epidemic, the kami of Miwa appeared to Emperor Sujin in a dream. The deity declared that the disease was his doing and demanded that his spirit be served by a certain Ōtataneko. Soon it became clear that this Ōtataneko was a child of the Miwa deity himself, who had entered the sleeping quarters of Ōtataneko's mother in the guise of a snake by way of the keyhole (Philippi 1969: 201–4). Another 11 reigns later, Emperor Yūryaku dispatched one of his vassals of Korean stock to seize the Miwa deity. It turned out to be a large snake that cracked thunder at the emperor, forcing him to flee (Aston 1972: I, 347).

Ōtataneko was the ancestor of the priestly lineages of both Miwa and Kamo. The priests of Hie, in their turn, claimed the same ancestry as the priests of Kamo. This suggests that they were part of an extensive network of intermarrying priestly lineages who controlled a category of earthly deities that threatened the heavenly rule of the Yamato kings with the help of techniques that were, at least in part, of continental origin.[3] Like the Matsunoo area dominated by the Hata lineage, Hie was located in a stronghold of immigrant groups. In the very precincts of the shrine there are more than 70 grave mounds of a distinctly Korean type, dated by archaeologists to the sixth or seventh centuries. Just south of Sakamoto is a large complex of more than 500 mounds associated with various immigrant groups (Mizuno 1992: 253–5).

Hie, then, was not an archetypical indigenous cult that flourished in an apolitical, harmonious setting of rice-growing natives. Rather, it emerged in the context of the establishment of the Yamato kingdom, as one of a range of sites where the dangerous deities of the earth were subdued with the help of immigrants who possessed special knowledge of continental rites.

Court vicissitudes transform Hie

After a catastrophic defeat of Yamato forces waging war in Korea (in 663), Tenji decided to move his court out of the Yamato plain to the more secluded site of Ōtsu on the southern shore of Lake Biwa. In 667 he built a new palace only 5 kilometers south of Hie, which now suddenly became the ritual site closest to the court. In 671 Tenji died and was succeeded by his son, but in the following year, 672, Tenji's brother Tenmu (r. 673–86) rebelled and took the throne after heavy fighting in the Ōtsu/Hie area. After his victory, Tenmu moved the capital back to Yamato, where he ascended the throne in 673. All this made for a brief but intense incursion of Yamato power into the direct vicinity of Hie. These dramatic events marked the beginning of a new phase in the site's development.

There is no hard evidence as to the date of the founding of the western compound at Hie, but it is clear that this event had its origins in Yamato. The main kami enshrined in this compound is none other than Miwa's Ōnamuchi. It appears that by medieval times there were two legends about the appearance of this deity at Hie. One group of sources claims that the Miwa deity was moved to Hie at the initiative of the monk Saichō (767–822), who (as we shall see below) turned Mount Hiei into a stronghold of Tendai Buddhism. However, it is hard to see why Saichō would have made such a move, since by Saichō's time Miwa had lost its position as the foremost protector of the imperial court to the Ise Shrines. Other sources, however, point at the years of Tenji's rule in Ōtsu. In ancient poems written shortly before the move to Ōtsu, courtiers lamented that they would now no longer be able to savor the familiar shape of Mount Miwa.[4] If we take this as proof that Miwa was still important to the Yamato court at this time, it appears reasonable to assume that Tenji had the Miwa deity installed at Hie, where a related cult already existed.

This new arrival marginalized the pre-existing cult of Ōyamakui. The new shrine came to be known as "Great Hie" (Ōbie), while the Ōyamakui compound was demoted to become "Lesser Hie" (Obie). It appears that Great Hie was the only shrine on the site to receive court offerings in the classical period, and it was accorded a much higher court rank than its older companion.[5] It is no surprise, then, that the priestly lineage of Hie traced its origin to the arrival of the Miwa deity. This lineage, called the Hafuribe, claimed descent from a certain Kotomitachi-no-Ushimaru, who was said to have moved to Karasaki, the harbor of the Ōtsu court on the shore of Lake Biwa, from the northern province of Hitachi. One day, legend tells us, a stranger appeared who wanted to borrow Ushimaru's boat. After some time Ushimaru asked to have his boat back, and then found that it had suddenly materialized in the high branches of a tree in his yard. The stranger lifted the boat down to the ground and revealed himself to be a kami. He gave Ushimaru the lineage name of Hafuribe, meaning "priest,"[6] and ordered him to build a shrine hall at a "favorable site to the northwest" of Karasaki, where his descendants were to serve as priests. This tale, recorded in various versions in a Hie record called *Yōtenki* (Record of bright devas; c. 1223?), is mirrored in the final stages of the Sannō festival, which re-enacts the arrival of the Miwa deity by boat from Karasaki (*ST* Hie: 44–5, 59–60).

The Hafuribe, then, attributed their original appointment as Hie priests to the deity of Miwa at the new Great Hie. The significance of the legend that traces their origin to northern Hitachi is not at all clear; it is significant, however, that this new legend did not displace the connection with Kamo. In *Yōtenki*, the tale of Ushimaru is concluded with the remark that the Kamo and Hafuribe are "identical in origin." Links with Kamo and Matsunoo were also expressed in ritual. *Yōtenki* notes, for example, that as a part of the rituals of Great Hie, a branch from the *katsura* tree that grew in front of the southern gate was offered to the Matsunoo Shrine, which in its turn sent it on to the Kamo Shrine – all according to "ancient precedent" (*ST* Hie: 53).

Reconstructing the Hie traditions after the disaster of 1571, Ushimaru's descendant Yukimaru noted:

> This shrine complex was begun with the construction of Ōmiya [i.e., Great Hie]. Ninomiya and Hachiōji are older, but they had no shrine buildings. Kotomitachi [that is, Ushimaru] was the first to construct a shrine hall here [at Hie]. This happened during the reign of Emperor Tenji. (*ST* Hie: 331)

If there is some truth to this Hafuribe tradition, it suggests that, with the arrival of Ushimaru and the Miwa deity, a new type of kami cult came to Hie. A permanent, palace-like hall was built to accommodate Ōnamuchi, implying that he was believed to reside there throughout the year. In the Ushimaru legend, the Miwa deity figured as a human being; only when he returned Ushimaru's boat in a superhuman manner did it become clear that he was not a mere "stranger." The deity of the new shrine, then, was a supremely human-like figure, closely associated with the court, who lived in a "palace" much in the manner of a court aristocrat, and who demanded the permanent care of a full-time priest. The contrast with the old cult of Ōyamakui could hardly be greater.

Already at this stage, then, Hie was a complicated site where dissimilar forms of worship existed side by side. The cult of Ōyamakui, focusing on a rock and a "peg," was overshadowed by that of the Miwa deity in its permanent "palace" (*miya*), imported during the court's brief stay at Ōtsu. Even in the earliest sources, a priestly lineage called Hafuribe (which later divided into two sublineages, Shōgenji and Juge) was in charge of both cults, and both are reflected in the main celebration at the Hie complex, the Sannō festival.

Hie and the Tendai temples on Mount Hiei

The founding of Great Hie was soon followed by equally drastic changes. A new period of transformation began in the ninth century, when Hie was annexed by the most successful branch of Japanese Buddhism, Tendai. As a result, Hie would expand to become the largest shrine complex of the land; its deities would be given radically new identities; and the Hafuribe priests would be joined by numerous Buddhist ritualists. Soon they would be reduced to a subordinate role as the Tendai abbot assumed authority over the shrines.

At the beginning of all this was Saichō, the founder of the Japanese Tendai school. Saichō's biography, *Eizan Daishi den* (Biography of the Great Master of Mount Hiei; c. 830), recounts that his father, Momoe, had been a devout Buddhist from the Hie area. Because he was childless, Momoe climbed Mount Hiei in search of an appropriate spot to practice "repentance" and pray for a son. After a few days, he arrived at a place "to the right hand of the [Great Hie] shrine, on the left slope of the mountain," where after four days and five nights of practice, a well-shaped son appeared to him in a dream; the next day, Saichō was born. Thus, in this most authoritative of all Saichō biographies, written soon after his death, Saichō was presented as a gift from the Hie deities (Sagai 1992: 106).

Saichō practiced austerities on Mount Hiei as part of his early training, staying on the mountain for 12 years from 785 onwards. Already in 788 he founded a small temple there that would eventually become known as Enryakuji. In 794, when Emperor Kanmu moved the capital to Heiankyō at the southwestern foot of Mount Hiei (today's Kyoto), Saichō's small group suddenly found itself in a very strategic position. Saichō gained the confidence of Kanmu and was selected as a member of a mission to China in 804–5, where he received ordinations in a number of Buddhist traditions, including the Tiantai school (Jap. Tendai). Upon his return Saichō transformed Enryakuji into the head temple of Tendai in Japan. In 822, a week after Saichō's death, the court finally permitted the founding of an ordination platform at Enryakuji, enabling the Tendai school to break free from the Buddhist establishment in the old capital of Nara. With hindsight, this laid the foundation for the development of Enryakuji into the largest and most powerful Buddhist institution in the land.

The transformation of the remote Mount Hiei into a Buddhist powerhouse affected the Hie Shrines profoundly. The shrines were on the wrong side of the mountain, far from the new capital; yet they were soon drawn into the orbit of Enryakuji, and through Tendai they emerged on the center-stage of court life. The shrines were gradually incorporated in the temple complex and remained so until 1868.

There are few sources to tell us how this process of incorporation developed. In 806 the court allowed Saichō two "annual ordinands" – that is, permission to have two monks ordained every year – and in the same year the court also awarded the "kami of Hie" 10 deity households, meaning that the taxes paid by these households were reserved for the shrine.[7] Ten households was a very modest grant, but this was the first time Hie had received any court support at all since the abandonment of Ōtsu in 672. It is hardly a coincidence that these awards of ordinands and deity households were made simultaneously. Tendai clearly offered Hie a new chance to make itself relevant to the court.

There is early evidence of Saichō's involvement with Hie. *Eizan Daishi den* mentions that Saichō's father Momoe had built a small "thatched retreat" on the mountain, which had since developed into a small temple called Jingū Zen'in, the "shrine meditation hall." Another reading of the sources suggests that there had already been a "shrine temple" (*jingūji*) on the mountain before Momoe's time, and that Momoe sent his son to this temple to complete the Buddhist services that he himself had broken off when Saichō was born (Sagai 1992: 106–9). *Eizan Daishi den* also records that Saichō found a Buddha relic in the ashes of the incense burner while he was praying at this shrine temple, and that he built Enryakuji for the purpose of accommodating this precious treasure (Sugahara 1992: 14).

Whatever the historical facts, it is clear that, from the very start, the Tendai community on Mount Hiei associated itself closely with the Hie deities, and that the Hie Shrines benefited from this new relationship. Now, Hie became part of the court's national shrine cult. This meant that the shrine priests were transferred from the register of tax-paying peasants to that of priests (*hafuribe*), and that they henceforth were under the jurisdiction of the Council of Kami Affairs, the court office in charge of official deity worship. Also, Hie was now expected to send representatives to this Council each spring for the *kinensai* ceremony, where they were to receive public offerings from the court priests. Hie was ranked as a "major" deity, which implied that its offerings were to be placed on top of the offering tables – in contradistinction to minor shrines, whose offerings were presented below these tables, on matting. This rank signaled that Hie was regarded as a site with intimate links to the court. Also after the Council's decline in the tenth and eleventh centuries, Hie became part of the new, more modest network of 22 court-sponsored shrines.

In the meantime, Hie's deities were receiving ritual treatment of a radically different type than before, and as a result their identities were once more changing rapidly. In at least one instance, Saichō dedicated his practice of the Lotus sutra to the salvation of "the deities of heaven and earth, the eight Great Deities, and the Mountain King of Hiei" (Sugahara 1992: 17). Here, Saichō described the Hie deities collectively as the "Mountain King" (Sannō), after the deity of that name who served as the protector of the Tiantai head temple of Guoqing-si where he had studied in China. In the same document, read on the occasion of a Lotus ritual, he stated his hope that these deities may overcome the evil karma that had caused them to be reborn as kami, that they may serve as protectors of the monks' practice hall, and that they may bring their innate seeds of buddhahood to maturation by listening to the preaching of the Lotus.

In this dedication document Saichō echoed Chinese rhetoric on the Buddhist "taming" of local mountain deities. Chinese biographies of eminent monks (*Gaosengzhuan*) refer frequently to the submission of hostile and violent deities who seek to obstruct the building of temples in their domain. By demonstrating the superiority of the universal Dharma over local "demons," Buddhist monks proved both the truth of their religion as well as their ability to apply it for useful purposes. Throughout the Buddhist world, monks faced local deities by defining them as deluded beings subject to the eternal laws of karma. By means of Buddhist procedures, such as copying, reciting, and depositing Buddhist scriptures or erecting stupas containing Buddha relics, dangerous deities and demons could be transformed into faithful allies of the Buddha and his supreme protector, the king. In classical Japan such skills were especially welcome. Deadly epidemics, fires, and other disasters constantly threatened the court and the populace, and the control of "wrathful spirits" (onryō) was at the top of the political agenda.

In Japan this Buddhist approach to local deities took many forms. One was the founding of shrine temples, where sutras were read for the deities at some distance from their shrines. Slightly later, shrines themselves were decked out with Buddhist paraphernalia and the deities themselves were depicted as human-like sponsors or practitioners of the Dharma, or as emanations of Buddhist divinities (Teeuwen and Rambelli 2003: 7–31). The founding of the Jingū Zen'in, which was described as Hie's "shrine temple" in later sources, and perhaps even of Enryakuji itself, followed this pattern. The court supported the Buddhist taming of Hie by allowing the annual ordination of two Tendai monks with the specific task of reciting sutras for the benefit of the deities of Greater and Lesser Hie (in 886). The next year, a stupa containing a copy of the Lotus sutra was erected in front of the Great Hie Shrine. In subsequent centuries, the Hie Shrines themselves became the main scene of Buddhist rites to the kami, and the Jingū Zen'in gradually lost its significance (Sagai 1992: ch. 5).

In the centuries after Saichō the Tendai community on Mount Hiei grew into a bewildering complex of competing Buddhist centers. The interest in Hie of this expansive monastic community took the form of a proliferation of shrine buildings. By the late ninth century, the Ninomiya Shrine (that is, the old Ōyamakui compound of Lesser Hie) had been furnished with a permanent shrine building, like Great Hie. By this time, Hie had in fact been expanded to include three main shrines: Ōmiya or the Great Shrine, Ninomiya or the Second Shrine, and the new Shōshinshi Shrine. It is unclear where this last deity came from; we know only that he had been enshrined in the grounds of Ōmiya before he was moved to a separate site. The shrines were also given new identities: Ōmiya was now known as Ōmiya Gongen, associated either with Miwa or with Kamo in the capital; Ninomiya was restyled Ninomiya Gongen, associated with Kuni-no-Tokotachi, the first deity of the cosmogony according to Nihon shoki; and the new Shōshinshi Shrine was identified as the great bodhisattva of Usa Hachiman, or the spirit of the ancient Emperor Ōjin.[8] The title *gongen* means "avatar" and characterizes deities as local emanations of Buddhist divinities. All three deities, then, were identified both in Buddhist terms as avatars or bodhisattvas, and in terms of Japanese myth as Miwa, Kuni-no-Tokotachi, and Ōjin. In the new shrine buildings they were represented in the form of statues, Ōmiya Gongen as a man in Chinese-looking aristocratic attire, and the other two as monks.

More shrines were added in the tenth and eleventh centuries, until the number of seven was reached by the 1120s at the latest. In subsequent centuries, these "upper seven shrines" were joined by 14 more: the "middle" and "lower" seven shrines. Eventually, the list grew to include 108 lower and 108 upper shrines. These numbers were not random; they were chosen to reflect Tendai ceremonies and doctrines. The number seven referred to the stars of the Big Dipper, which was the focus of the most important ritual performed in the imperial palace by the Tendai abbots in prayer for the emperor's health and longevity (*Shijōkō-hō*), and 108 referred to the 108 types of afflictions or karmic bonds.

In most cases it is impossible to reconstruct the circumstances that led to the founding of this multitude of shrines, but the following tale about the origin in c. 1030 of Marōdo, Hie's fourth shrine, lifts a tip of the veil:

When the Tendai abbot visited Hie to worship, he noticed this [Marōdo] shrine and asked: "Since when has this shrine been worshiped?" The shrine priests said: "We have heard that the shrine monk [*miya-komori*] Kōshū worships here." The abbot said: "This is improper. If shrine monks were allowed to start worshiping shrines as they see fit, there would soon be an innumerable mass of shrines. It must be dismantled." When the shrine priests were about to take the shrine apart, the abbot said: "No, let us wait just one day. I will pray tonight and make a decision tomorrow." The next day, he went to the shrine precinct. As he worshiped in front of the Marōdo shrine, a foot of snow piled up on its roof. This was in the seventh month. The abbot asked whether the other people present also saw this snow, but they did not. The abbot sensed a miracle, and decided that henceforth his disciples would worship only this shrine. (*Yōtenki, ST* Hie: 49–50)

The same entry also notes that Kōshū had previously made pilgrimages to Mount Hakusan, a major site of mountain practice in what is today Ishikawa Prefecture, but had now grown too old to make the journey. In a dream, he had received divine permission to worship the goddess of Hakusan at Hie instead.

This tale shows the power of the Tendai abbot over Hie, and illustrates the activities of low-ranking "shrine monks" (*miya-komori*) there. A more literal translation of this term would be "monks who seclude themselves at the shrines." These were not proper, ordained monks; rather, they were vagrants who stayed at sacred places and dedicated themselves to various kinds of religious practice there. According to a source from the early fourteenth century, "shady beggars and outcasts called *miya-komori* flock together in the space underneath the Hachiōji [Shrine], refusing to leave the shrine precincts day or night."[9] It would appear that the dark "basements" underneath the elevated shrine floors served both as living quarters for all kinds of marginal religious figures and also as ritual sites. All of the seven Hie Shrines had such basements, known as *geden* or "lower halls" in contrast to the shrines proper. Fragmentary evidence suggests that, in at least at some of the shrines, the deities were enshrined in their Buddhist guises in these cellar-like spaces.[10] The same Buddhist "originals" of the kami (Śākyamuni at Ōmiya, Bhaiṣajyaguru at Ninomiya, Amitābha at Shōshinshi, and so forth) were also displayed on large circular boards with a diameter of ca. 1 meter, exhibited high up under the eaves of the shrine buildings and known as "hanging buddhas" (*kakebotoke*). These boards displayed each shrine's Buddhist identity, flanked by the protective "kings" Acala and Vaiśravaṇa (Sagai 1992: ch. 9). Each shrine, then, combined different cults conducted by different people, and the priests who traced their roots to the ancient Hafuribe now shared the shrines with many others.

The *miya-komori* appear to have had overall control over the shrines' "lower halls." Similar shrine monks existed also at the Buddhist shrine of Gion (today's Yasaka Shrine), which served as an outpost of the Hiei complex in the capital. Here the *miya-komori* performed various lowly tasks, serving as cleaners, guards, and bullies who put force behind the various petitions and demands made by the monks of Mount Hiei in the capital. They also had a ritual role in Gion, performing *kagura* dances, for example, during the Gion festival.[11] It is likely that the *miya-komori* performed similar roles at Hie.

Yet another group of religious figures was a type of "shaman" known as *rō-no-miko* ("children of the corridor") and *yorikidono* ("mediums"). They appear to have been based at the eastern compound, or, to be more precise, in the corridor between Jūzenji and neighboring Daigyōji Shrine.[12] The *yorikidono*, described in one source as the "daughters" of the *rō-no-miko*, acted as mouthpieces of the gods, pronouncing oracles that could scare even the most powerful. In 1012, for example, the famous imperial regent and hegemon Fujiwara-no-Michinaga succumbed to an illness that, according to rumor, had been called down upon him by a Hie deity, as announced by a Hie medium.[13] In later literature, not least the warrior epic *Heike monogatari*, the oracles of Hie often hover over the greatest political and military battles of the age. Clearly, despite the Buddhist rhetoric of domestication, the deities of Hie were still designed to inspire fear as much as salvation.

Both the *miya-komori* and the *rō-no-miko* were figures of ambiguous status. On the one hand they were little more than beggars, living off offerings presented to the shrines where they were staying, no doubt in very primitive shelters. On the other hand they enjoyed semidivine status and exerted considerable power. The *rō-no-miko*, for example, would later trace their origin to a liaison between the imperial prelate Jien (1155–1225) and a manifestation of the child-god of Jūzenji. According to legend, "spirits of love" (*saiai-no-mono*) were born from their sexual encounters; these "spirits" were then abandoned in a Hiei valley where they transformed into children.[14] These children were eventually adopted by the Jūzenji deity and supported by Jien's temple, the Tendai-connected imperial cloister of Shōren'in. This legend reflects sexual practices between elder monks and young novices, and it documents the presence of outcasts who claimed spiritual powers at the fringes of the shrines (Faure 1998: 254–8).[15] If one accepts Kageyama's thesis that the ancient Ōyamakui cult involved sexual symbolism, the legend can be read as a new variation on that ancient theme. Its immediate purpose, however, was to secure both imperial and divine status for the lowly shamans of the Jūzenji corridor. The fact that there were *rō-no-miko* at Hie until the end of the Edo period attests to this legend's legitimizing potential.

Hie as an economic power

The Tendai establishment did not hesitate to use the divine powers of Hie to further its multifarious interests. It was for this purpose that the shrines first acquired the *mikoshi* palanquins that are so prominent in today's Sannō festival. One of the earliest sources to mention "seven palanquins" relates to an incident that took place in 1123 (Sugahara 1992: 134–5). The Tendai abbot of the time noted in his diary:

> *Seventh month, fifteenth day*:
> The great assembly of monks descended the western slope [of Mount Hiei] while shaking the *mikoshi* of Hachiōji, Marōdo, and Jūzenji. Warriors rushed to the defense of the capital and prevented them from entering the city.

> *Eighteenth day*:
> Again the assembly of monks descended from the mountain, carrying the *mikoshi* of Ōmiya, Ninomiya, Shōshinshi, and Sannomiya [the Third Shrine], and did battle with forces sent by the court. Many monks fell, and in the end they abandoned the seven *mikoshi* by the riverside and fled.

Another source adds that the "mountain monks" fled to Gion, where they were attacked by Taira and Minamoto warriors sent by the court. Here "many lost their lives inside the main sanctuary, and afterwards the deity was moved so that the shrine could be rebuilt." The move, no doubt to an existing or a temporary hall, was necessary to ensure that the Gion deity would not be provoked into violence by this exposure to the impurities of blood and death.[16]

These events in the early twelfth century marked the beginning of a new age. They reflect two watersheds in Japanese history: the emergence of warriors as an increasingly organized power bloc, and the collapse of court control over agricultural land. Classical law, introduced in the seventh and eighth centuries, had established that all land was public and taxable to the imperial court, but by the eleventh century this basic principle was rapidly being undermined. As central control collapsed, more and more land was privatized and granted exemption from taxation, often at the initiative of court-appointed provincial governors. Donations to the buddhas and kami for special blessings were a much-used justification for privatization, and temples and shrines frequently served as holders of such tax-exempt estates, called *shōen*. For local elites, it could be advantageous to hold these estates in the name of a temple rather than as court-appointed caretakers. Donation to a powerful temple, arranged through a noble or a provincial governor, afforded more security than continued dependence on the fickle favors of the court.

Both Enryakuji and Hie were already among the largest holders of estates in the country during the earliest stages of this privatization process. The *mikoshi* attack of 1123 was directly related to this new function of the temple-shrine complex. This incident appears to have been connected with a struggle between two factions within the Hiei temple system over an estate in the mountains of Mino. At the time, this kind of attack was rapidly becoming an established procedure to put pressure on the court in matters related to estates or appointments. By 1160 the Hie *mikoshi* had already crossed Mount Hiei four more times. After the decision to proceed, monks would gather at the Hie Shrines, where the deities were transferred to *mikoshi* of up to 5 meters long, decorated with mirrors and topped with a golden phoenix. These *mikoshi* were then carried up to Enryakuji's central hall, from where they descended down the western slope of Mount Hiei to the capital. The vigorous rocking of the *mikoshi* still observed in the Sannō festival may once have served as a visual expression of the deities' fury in the context of such *mikoshi* attacks. When the *mikoshi* arrived in the city, they were abandoned at strategic locations so that the presence of Hie's angry deities could induce fear of divine punishment in the court officials. Only a safe return of the *mikoshi* to Hie could solve the conflict that had caused their descent.

Similar tactics were also used by other temple-shrine complexes, most famously Kōfukuji in Nara, which used the deity of Kasuga for the same purpose. Mikael Adolphson, who has made a detailed study of this kind of "deity attack," has shown that the *mikoshi* were perceived as a very real threat by the court (Adolphson 2000: ch. 6). As in the case of Fujiwara-no-Michinaga, illness and misfortune confirmed the reality of the deities' curse, and courtiers went to great lengths to satisfy, or at least compensate, the temple monks. It has been estimated that the court had to deal with some 300 deity attacks between the late eleventh and the sixteenth centuries, more than a quarter of which involved Hie (Adolphson 2000: 5). This demonstrates both the effectiveness of these attacks and the difficulty of pacifying the great temple complexes in the capital region.

The new function of Hie as a landholding institution gave rise to a new type of building that soon dominated the shrine compounds. Called "equinox halls" (*higansho*), these structures were much larger than the quite modest shrine halls that contained the kami themselves. According to Kuroda Ryūji, the first equinox halls appeared in the late eleventh century; by the fourteenth, there were at least 20 of them (Kuroda 1999: 25–47). Their official purpose was the performance of Buddhist services for the deities at the spring and autumn equinoxes (*higan-e*). Similar equinox services were also performed at the shrines of other temple-shrine complexes such as Kōfukuji and Tōdaiji, and they soon developed into one of the most popular Buddhist observances, which they remain today (*o-higan*). At the Hie equinox halls, low-ranking Hie monks known as *dōshu* performed a variety of rites, including Lotus penances, *nenbutsu* chanting, and *kagura* dances. Groups of such monks were stationed permanently in these halls, forming yet another category of Hie ritualists. Each equinox hall was linked to a monks' quarters on Mount Hiei, which dispatched *dōshu* monks to staff them. Apart from ritual tasks, these *dōshu* had important economic and military roles. Each equinox hall had a portfolio of estates from which it extracted so-called equinox contributions (*higanryō*). The equinox halls, then, served as holders of estates in the name of the various monks' quarters on the mountain. The equinox contributions provided the monks' quarters with capital that they lent to merchants and others against interest. Such loans were backed by the powers of the Hie deities and the Tendai monks, ensuring that few forfeited on them. Therefore, many preferred to channel excess funds through the equinox halls, which developed into important financial institutions. It is no wonder, then, that the equinox halls architecturally outshone the shrine sanctuaries themselves, and on occasion served as the lodgings of Tendai abbots, visiting emperors and shoguns, and, when the times demanded it, entire armies. These halls may be seen as a symbol of Hie's medieval power; their absence from the new Hie as it was rebuilt after 1571 was a sure sign that Hie's age of glory was now over.

Through its estates, the Hie cult expanded beyond the capital area. Typically, estates linked in some way to the temples and shrines of Mount Hiei (either directly or through a branch temple) were furnished with a small Sannō Shrine, from which the deities asserted their powers over the land and its produce. Through this process, the deities of central temple-shrine complexes spread across the land. Even when Hie lost control over most of its estates in the later medieval period, many of these shrines survived as village shrines. This is one reason why there are still some 3,800 Sannō Shrines spread over most of Japan today, although most of these originated later, in early modern times.

Through their estates the Hie Shrines now made themselves relevant to a much larger constituency. Considerable numbers of the cultivators on these estates were designated by the holding temple or shrine as *jinin*, "deity people" (Nakamura 1988: ch. 1; Toyoda 1982: 248–67). *Jinin* were exempt from "public" taxation, and even legislation; their status was that of "private" service people attached to a specific temple or shrine. They served the temple-shrine complex as producers of goods, as managers, as laborers, and as foot-soldiers tasked, for example, with carrying the *mikoshi*. In return, they enjoyed special freedoms guaranteed by Enryakuji and could count on temple protection in the case of conflicts. *Jinin* came in many different forms and shapes. Some were little more than shrine serfs, feared for the mystery that their contact with the deities cast over them, but otherwise despised as social outcasts. Others were elite landowners and merchants who used their connection with the shrines to protect and expand their businesses. Some had ancient roots in the deity households assigned to shrines in the ancient period; others became *jinin* almost on a contract basis, as the result of a deal that was beneficial both to themselves and to the shrines.

In the case of Hie, the most established *jinin* group was located in Ōtsu. According to legend, the residence of their leader marked the site where the Miwa deity had first manifested himself, and the *jinin* of Ōtsu contributed to the Sannō festival by re-enacting the move of this deity to the Ōmiya Shrine. These *jinin* had an ancient connection with the Hie Shrines and were directly involved in shrine rituals. Other *jinin* groups would also play some role in the Hie cult, but usually a more passive one: as purveyors of special offerings, as contractors of labor, as the managers of tollgates run by the shrines, and so on. On Hie's many estates, the local Sannō Shrines were staffed by *jinin*. The historical record contains quite a few complaints against *jinin* who terrorized local peasants with threats of divine wrath, often by planting a divine *sakaki* branch in a strategic place. It appears that *jinin* did not hesitate to use the strategy of "kami attacks," if on a much smaller scale, in settling local affairs. Today, there is hardly a shrine festival without a *mikoshi* parade; this spread of *mikoshi* over the whole of Japan is a legacy of the *jinin* of medieval times.

While some *jinin*, then, functioned as local priests, their basic function and official *raison d'être* was as purveyors of goods and offerings to the shrines. The economic and military powers of Mount Hiei made the status of Hie *jinin* attractive for many producers and merchants, while the Hie Shrines benefited from the increase of their *jinin*. These forces of push and pull caused the number of Hie *jinin* to grow rapidly. Especially in Kyoto, Hie *jinin* dominated the world of trade and finance. As purveyors of sake and oil to the shrines, they formed guilds (*za*) that held trade monopolies in the capital. At the height of Hie's influence in the late thirteenth century, some 80 percent of Kyoto's sake brewers and moneylenders were Hie *jinin*.

New images of the deities

The late thirteenth and early fourteenth centuries were a time of great theological creativity. A string of new texts integrated Hie's Sannō cult ever more intimately into the Tendai complex on Mount Hiei, while elevating Sannō's status to that of the greatest among the gods of Japan, and, in fact, of the entire universe. Scrolls depicting the shrines set in a highly idealized landscape sent the same message by representing Hie as a sacred Buddha-land.

This new discourse on Hie appears in three main texts: *Yōtenki* (Record of bright devas), *Sanke yōryakki* (Abbreviated records of the houses of Mount Hiei), and *Keiran shūyōshū* (Collected leaves from hazy valleys). The oldest among them, *Yōtenki*, is usually dated to c. 1223, but almost half of the text is taken up by an exposition on Sannō that must have been added later in the thirteenth century. Here, Hie's Sannō is contrasted with the other kami of the land as the Japanese manifestation of Śākyamuni himself. It appears, says *Yōtenki*, that some people believe that Japan became a "land of the gods" because the kami of Ise, Kamo, Matsunoo, and Sumiyoshi protect its kings and bestow blessings on its people. However, these people do not understand Śākyamuni's true intentions. Śākyamuni decided to manifest himself at the foot of Mount Hiei as the "Mountain King" (Sannō) in order to bring benefits to sentient beings both for this life and the next (*ST* Hie: 73, 81). Since Japan is an extremely small and undeveloped country, inhabited by foolish people unable to understand the teachings of the Buddha, Śākyamuni changed his appearance and manifested himself at Hie as the deity of the Ōmiya Shrine. In this guise he chastises the impure, the impious, and the indolent, while rewarding those of good faith by answering their prayers. All the other "13,700 deities" of Japan also have their "original ground" (*honji*) in buddhas and bodhisattvas; this is the true reason why Japan is a "land of the gods," and this is why shrines are so important there. In other words: Japan is a divine land because Śākyamuni (that is, Sannō) made it so. Moreover, this is not because Japan is superior to China and India, but because it is inferior. Only in Japan is the Buddha compelled to teach the people in the guise of shrine deities.

In *Yōtenki* the deities no longer appear as unenlightened beings who need to be saved by Śākyamuni's Dharma; they are the essence of the Dharma itself, made manifest on the distant islands of Japan. This new vision was developed further in *Sanke yōryakki*, a collection of doctrinal information on the essence of Sannō and his relationship to a range of other divine figures. In this text, *Yōtenki*'s negative image of Japan has disappeared. Sannō is the protective deity of Vulture Peak in India and of Mount Tiantai in China (*ST* Tendai Shintō ge: 6–7); also, he is identical to the imperial kami of Ise (ibid. 26). Sannō, then, is the foremost deity of India, China, and Japan alike. Accordingly, Hie is no longer "merely" Śākyamuni's base in Japan but a site of truly cosmic dimensions. According to *Sanke yōryakki*, the three main shrines of Hie (Ōmiya, Ninomiya, and Shōshinshi) represent the sun, moon, and stars of heaven, and the seven Hie Shrines are the stars of the Big Dipper, which determines the life spans of both the son of heaven and all other sentient beings (ibid. 10, 107). By numerological means, the Hie Shrines are interpreted as manifestations of central concepts of Buddhist doctrine, such as the "three virtues" (*santoku*) of the Buddha: the merits of compassion, severing affliction, and wisdom (ibid. 18). In this way, a dazzling web of significations and associations is spun around Hie, which, taken together, have the effect of placing Hie's Sannō at the very center of the Buddhist universe.

Some of these associations are also reflected in the iconography of so-called Hie mandalas. Such mandalas were painted in considerable numbers in the thirteenth and fourteenth centuries. They were probably used primarily for Buddhist Hie rituals away from Hie, as a substitute for a visit to the shrines themselves. Some of these mandalas simply display the deities of Hie in their Buddhist guises; others focus on the landscape of Mount Hachiōji with the shrines of Hie at its foot. In the latter, gold is used to give the landscape of Hie a luminous aspect, suggesting that the mountain itself is a Buddha-land on earth (Arichi 2006). Similar mandalas were also created at other shrines, most famously at Kasuga.[17] Here too, shrine mandalas displayed the Buddhist identities of the kami and depicted the shrine grounds and the shrine mountain as Buddhist paradises.

While *Yōtenki* appears to be based on Hafuribe traditions, *Sanke yōryakki* and *Keiran shūyōshū* originated among a special group of monks known as *kike*, "recordkeepers." These monks collected, created, and transmitted knowledge of all kinds, ranging from Lotus doctrine and esoteric initiations to medicine; but their true speciality was the documentation of information on the sacred sites and buildings of Mount Hiei, including the Hie Shrines. The scope of their "records" can be gleaned from the surviving volumes of *Keiran shūyōshū*, a truly encyclopedic work finished by the recordkeeper Kōshū (1276–1350) in 1348.[18] Strikingly, the recordkeepers claimed that knowledge about Mount Hiei and its divinities, and especially Hie's Sannō, constituted the very essence of the Dharma. *Keiran shūyōshū*'s section on Sannō is even more expansive than *Sanke yōryakki*'s. Here, too, Sannō is discussed as a figure of cosmic stature. Sannō is superior to all other kami because he is the only true manifestation of Śākyamuni; all the others are mere "helpful means" (*upāya*) established by the buddhas and bodhisattvas to prepare the land for Sannō's appearance. In fact, on an even deeper level, Sannō is the "ultimate source of all existence, including the buddhas" (*ST* Tendai Shintō ge 2: 414). In other words, Hie represents the raw force of primal enlightenment from which the entire universe arises.

Here, the recordkeepers tied in with the notion of "original enlightenment" (*hongaku*) that was central to medieval Tendai (Stone 1999). Original enlightenment refers to the idea that all sentient beings, and in some texts even the insentient beings, are enlightened just as they are. They do not only possess the innate potential to attain buddhahood; they are made up of the physical stuff of buddhahood, and are therefore perfect manifestations of "true suchness" in their present, karmic state. It is this primal, innate buddhahood that makes the Dharma-methods of the buddhas possible, and for that reason it is even more fundamental than the "acquired enlightenment" attained through the practice of those methods. The roots of this notion of original enlightenment can be traced back all the way to Chinese Tiantai, but it was in medieval Japan that it became a dominant theme in Buddhist thought and practice. What began as a doctrinal argument within Tendai ended up as an influential theme also in other schools, and even in medieval literature and theater. It appears that the identification of kami with original enlightenment was first pioneered in Ise. At Hie, this notion was imported by way of the identification of Hie with Ise, quoted both in *Sanke yōryakki* and at the very outset of the Sannō section of *Keiran shūyōshū* (*ST* Tendai Shintō ge 2: 405). In this vision of the kami as the primal foundation of Buddhist practice, we may recognize a first step towards the later idea that "Shinto" is older and more fundamental than Buddhism itself.

It is important to note that this new vision of the kami as a primal force did not mean that they had now become mere symbols of abstract, meditative serenity. Quite to the contrary, the "nondual" nature of the kami elevated them above notions of good and evil and served to mystify their violent actions as pure, enlightened energy. The kami were in many ways similar to Tantric demons. In essence, *Keiran shūyōshū* tells us, all kami are snakes: physical manifestations of the supreme powers (*siddhi*) of the three poisons (craving, anger, and ignorance) that form the karmic foundation of all existence (*ST* Tendai Shintō ge 2: 451). Exactly because of their venomous nature, it is the kami rather than the buddhas who embody the ultimate insight of Buddhism, namely that the afflictions of the karmic world are identical to the wisdom of nirvana. In a more direct manner than the benign teachings of the buddhas, the kami acted out the Dharma in the karmic realm that we inhabit. In a sense, then, the Hie deities had remained their old selves, in spite of the Buddhist idiom in which they had now been cloaked. Even to the recordkeeper monks of medieval Hiei, the Hie deities were at heart "violent spirits," rife with antinomian powers.

The demise of Hie's medieval power

By the fourteenth century, the power of Mount Hiei and the Hie Shrines as a major landowner and center of *jinin* trade had begun to wilt. The monks and priests of Mount Hiei shared this fate with most other temple-shrine complexes (Adolphson 1997). In the late Kamakura period, and even more strongly in the subsequent Muromachi period, temples and shrines gradually lost their grip on their estates. As a result, many of their *jinin* also slipped from their control, and with them the wealth and military power that they had represented disappeared. Guilds lost interest in maintaining ties with shrines and broke loose, or their monopolies were challenged and undermined by new competitors and warlord rulers. To make matters worse, the established Buddhist sects, including Tendai, lost influence to a new network of Zen temples, actively promoted and controlled by the Ashikaga shoguns of Muromachi who took over the capital from c. 1340 onwards.

In the mid fifteenth century the situation deteriorated further when shogunal authority all but collapsed and Kyoto descended into the catastrophe of the Ōnin war (1467–77). This marked the beginning of a period of political fragmentation and endemic fighting. These dramatic changes were disastrous for most of the established religious centers. The Hiei community lost its traditional sponsors as the court descended into obscurity, and it failed to hold on to its estates and its *jinin*. Even so, Hie appears to have fared better than, for example, Ise, which became completely dilapidated in the century after Ōnin. Yet by the sixteenth century the Hie complex had weakened beyond recognition.

In the ninth month of 1571 the warlord Oda Nobunaga sent his massed armies up the eastern side of Mount Hiei. They razed all in their path to the ground, killing not only monks but laymen, women, and children as they went. Nobunaga obliterated all traces of Enryakuji's medieval power from the mountain. Tendai monks in the Enryakuji complex had sided with Nobunaga's enemies and refused his invitation to declare neutrality. In the onslaught, the Hie Shrines at the eastern foot of the mountain were not spared, but neither did Nobunaga's men slaughter the shrine priests and their families. Evidently, it was not they who had offended him. After Nobunaga was slain in 1582, the Hie priest Shōgenji Yukimaru set about soliciting funds to resurrect the shrines. Meanwhile, the Tendai monk Tenkai assumed responsibility for reviving Enryakuji; the two rebuilding projects were pursued entirely independently. Thanks to the support of Nobunaga's successor, Toyotomi Hideyoshi (1537–98), Yukimaru saw Ōmiya Shrine emerge from the rubble in 1586. The full reassembling of the seven Hie Shrines took another 15 years; it was completed when Hachiōji Shrine stood ready in 1601. The reconstruction of the huge Enryakuji was much more demanding, and in spite of equally generous contributions from Hideyoshi construction work was finished only in the 1660s.

The Hie Shrines and Early Modern Japan

Ordering the early modern

In 1601, then, exactly 30 years after Oda Nobunaga had laid Hie waste, all seven shrines were finally restored. The tireless campaign led by Yukimaru, the moral support of the imperial court, and the sponsorship of the great overlords Toyotomi Hideyoshi and then Tokugawa Ieyasu had been essential to this resurrection. Of especial importance to the future of Hie was Ieyasu's donation of land to the Enryakuji temple in spring 1601. Ieyasu, who had just defeated his foes in the great battle of Sekigahara (1600) and was now the undisputed military overlord, granted to that temple 5,000 *koku* worth of land, much of it in the villages of Upper and Lower Sakamoto.[19] The relevance of this donation is that 402 *koku* were set aside for the upkeep of the Hie Shrines, for the sustenance of the shrine priests, and for their performance of rites, including the great Sannō festival (Shibuya 2000: 491–2). The implications were immediately clear. The Hie Shrines would survive, but they would not recover the vast tracts of land they had owned in the medieval period. Indeed, unlike the Gion, Kamo, or Matsunoo Shrines in Kyoto with which Hie was closely linked, Hie would possess no land of its own. Hie and its priests were to be financially dependent on Enryakuji, and this situation endured throughout the Tokugawa period. Enryakuji quickly understood its authority over Hie to extend beyond the economic. What makes Hie's early modern history of special interest is that Yukimaru's descendants did not accept the subordinate position they were allotted in this early modern order. They resisted, and the nature of their resistance merits attention.

There was one other feature of the early modern settlement that impacted on the fortunes of Hie. The Tokugawa government was officially established in 1603 when Tokugawa Ieyasu received from the imperial court the title of shogun, and it very quickly set out a series of religious policies. It would suffer no interference in the politics of the realm from temples like Enryakuji, but their thriving would be sanctioned within the state's clearly defined, legitimizing parameters. Those parameters were set down in law, and underwritten by the threat of violence. The Tokugawa government duly followed up the 5,000-*koku* benefaction to Enryakuji with "Regulations on Tendai" (1608). In this way Enryakuji and other great temple complexes were quickly accommodated. Led by the redoubtable Tenkai, Tendai monks responded in a quite distinctive fashion, forging for themselves a unique and privileged role in Tokugawa Japan. Tenkai gained access to the innermost circles of the first three Tokugawa shoguns, Ieyasu, Hidetada, and Iemitsu, and his legacy was the construction and dissemination in the years after Ieyasu's death of that great warrior's posthumous cult.[20] Briefly interred on Mount Kunō, Ieyasu's body was then removed east to Nikkō, where it was reburied and venerated as "the great avatar who shines from the east" (Tōshō Daigongen), according to the rites of what Tenkai called Sannō *ichijitsu* Shinto.[21]

Sannō *ichijitsu* Shinto, which was Tenkai's creation, thus became the guardian of Ieyasu's cult, and it guaranteed Tendai Buddhism the most privileged linkage with the early modern state. Yoshida Shinto, represented by Bonshun in the dispute over Ieyasu's will, now lost influence in the political realm as Tenkai moved to consolidate.[22] Having constructed Ieyasu's Tōshōgū mausoleum in Nikkō, Tenkai built a Tōshō Shrine in the heart of Edo castle. In Ueno, northeast of the castle, he constructed the magnificent Kan'eiji temple, modeled closely on Enryakuji. This construction work represented a momentous shift of the center of Tendai away from Mount Hiei in Kyoto, east to Edo and beyond. But Tenkai's institution of the office of Rinnōji *monzeki* was decisive here. *Monzeki* is the title given to a temple whose incumbent priest is a member of the imperial family, and Tenkai duly had a prince appointed to this new office, who resided alternately in Kan'eiji and in Nikkō. He then located the Rinnōji *monzeki* at the pinnacle of early modern Tendai. So, for example, the five Tendai *monzeki* temples in Kyoto, Enryakuji itself, and, of course, the Hie Shrines were all now subject to the Rinnōji *monzeki*, whose authority in Edo, it was said, was second only to that of the shogun.

These developments impacted directly on the Hie Shrines in 1634, when Tenkai built a new Tōshōgū on land adjacent to the shrine compound. It was modeled closely on Nikkō, and it transformed the nature of the Hie site. Tokugawa Ieyasu's spirit now displaced the kami of Ōmiya as Enryakuji's chief protector. Tendai maps of Sakamoto from the latter half of the seventeenth century are typically drawn around Tōshōgū as the center; guides to the site penned by monks invariably begin with the history and powers of the Tōshōgū before introducing Ōmiya. The Hie Tōshōgū symbolized the birth, then, of a new, early modern Enryakuji to which the Hie Shrines were now of very much subordinate importance. At precisely the same time, the Tokugawa appropriated a Hie Shrine in Edo, founded in the fifteenth century, as protector of the shogun's castle; that shrine's annual Sannō festival in Edo quickly became the greatest in the land. The point is that in the Tokugawa settlement there was no role for the "original" Hie Shrines at the foot of Mount Hiei. As far as the Enryakuji temple, Tendai Buddhism, and indeed the early modern state were concerned, the Hie Shrines in Sakamoto offered nothing of value. The challenge for the Hie Shrine priesthood was to find meaning in early modern Japan.

The folly of Hie

Tensions between the shrine priests and the Tendai monks surface in the historical record for the first time in the 1660s. The immediate stimulus appears to have been the Tokugawa-sponsored rebuilding of the seven Hie Shrines at that time, dilapidated after 60 years of service. On completion of the work, the sacred objects representing the kami were ritually returned to the sanctuaries of each of the seven shrines in a rite known as *sengū*, but the priests objected to the monks' behavior on this occasion. They complained to the senior Tendai prelate that the monk Shunkai had insulted the reinstalled kami by placing before them not the water and rice they needed, but carvings of wood (Myōhōinshi 1976: 349). It is, indeed, impossible to imagine the same monk placing wooden offerings before the spirit of Ieyasu enshrined at the Hie Tōshōgū. For good measure, the shrine priests also filed a complaint that the monks had for years now been stealing *their* firewood from the woodland on Mount Hachiōji. In the 1670s trouble resurfaced. In 1674 Tendai monks tried to enter the Ōmiya sanctuary to place three wooden statues of monkeys there. The three monkeys had their origins in the Sannō cult, and the monks were presumably seeking to assert their dominance over the shrine and rile the priests. The priests barred their way, insisting the sanctuary was off limits to Buddhists, and fierce arguments ensued. In the following year, monks repeatedly arrived in Ōmiya to perform one religious rite or another. Tensions continued to simmer, and matters reached a head towards the end of 1683. The monks' persistent encroaching on Hie's spaces prompted the priests once more to file complaints with the senior Tendai prelate. When the prelate refused to listen, the Hie priests decided on drastic action.

That action began one morning in the late autumn of 1683, when priests from both the Shōgenji and the Juge lineages gathered by the main gate of the Ōmiya Shrine. They proceeded to each of the seven shrines in the complex, Ōmiya, Shōshinshi, Marōdo, Ninomiya, Jūzenji, and finally up the mountain to the Hachiōji and Sannomiya Shrines. At each shrine, they entered the sanctuary, forced open the tabernacle doors, and removed the sacred objects contained therein. These were mostly Buddhist statues, which represented the "original ground" (*honji*) of the seven Hie kami. The priests replaced these with boxed *heihaku*, wands with strips of paper attached representing a kami. One of their number gathered the statues in a cart, wheeled them off to Kyoto and burned them to cinders (Satō 1993: 122–3). This action was anti-Enryakuji and anti-Tendai, and obviously designed to challenge the wisdom that the Hie kami all had an original Buddhist "grounding." It is tempting to see here an early modern precursor of the Shinto–Buddhist violence that was to strike the Hie Shrines in the revolution of 1868, but this was different: it was an act of priestly defiance against their allotted place in the early modern order. Some time after the burning of the statues, the Hie priests headed off to the capital Edo to complete their strategy. They filed a complaint with the Tokugawa magistrate for temple and shrine affairs (*jisha bugyō*) about the interfering behavior of the Tendai monks. The priests explained to the magistrate the history of the Hie Shrines and the nature of their sacred objects, and informed him that the seven shrines had never accommodated statuary that identified kami with buddhas. There was, therefore, no reason why they should be subject to Tendai Buddhist authority. They themselves had never worshiped buddhas for the simple reason that the shrines were, and always had been, attached to Yoshida Shinto (Satō 1993: 122). The magistrate was not fooled by this extraordinary assertion, but the whole episode is a testament to the Hie priests' desperation. In 1665, as we have already seen, the Tokugawa state had commissioned the Yoshida family to exercise control over regional shrines. Hie and other shrines of illustrious pedigree were from the start, however, placed outside Yoshida control. Nonetheless, the Hie priests evidently saw in the Shrine Clauses the tantalizing possibility of liberation from Enryakuji control and the assumption of a new, Yoshida Shinto identity.

It is not clear what connections the priests actually established with the Yoshida family. There is some concrete evidence of personal contact.[23] From the 1660s there were certainly rumors aplenty that Hie priests were cultivating the Yoshida or being cultivated by them. A senior Tendai prelate wrote as much in his diary in the 1660s. He made the same assertions to the Kyoto magistrate once more in the 1670s. Then, in 1683, when their disputes with the monks got out of hand, the Hie priests began to proclaim openly their allegiance to one-and-only Shinto. To a senior Tendai prelate, they insisted : "It states in the [Yoshida text] *Myōbō yoshū* that Saichō the founder of Mount Hiei, Enchin, and Ennin were all initiated into the secrets [of one-and-only Shinto]. Are the monks ignorant of this fact?" As this assertion makes clear, Hie priests were familiar with one of the basic Yoshida texts, but they also acquired Yoshida ritual manuals. In the Shōgenji archives, for example, is a collection styled *Gyōjiki* (Ceremonial records), which contains abundant illustrations of multiple Yoshida rituals, such as the *Sangen jūhachi Shintō shidai* (Ceremony of eighteen Shinto contained in the three foundations).[24] Nonetheless, the priests' destruction of Buddhist statues as a way of "proving" their allegiance to one-and-only Shinto was, of course, unrealistic; moreover, the mighty Tendai would hardly allow an association with the Yoshida, their arch-enemy. The Rinnōji *monzeki* quickly assumed responsibility for handling the incident, and meted out harsh punishments. The heads of the Shōgenji and Juge families were sent into exile, and 10 other priests involved were barred from the shrine's environs. The *monzeki* then issued a clutch of regulations confirming Hie priests' subordination to Tendai monks in all matters. Monks, they stipulated, were at liberty to enter the inner sanctuaries of the Hie Shrines whenever they pleased. For posterity, the regulations made clear that the Hie Shrines belonged, after all, to Sannō *ichijitsu* Shinto, "the very origin of [the combinatory system that identifies all kami with buddhas]" (Satō 1993: 133–5).

The end to the episode and, indeed, the start of the early modern period for the Hie Shrines, can be dated to a ritual performance that took place at Hie on New Year's Eve 1689. This was the re-enshrinement of Hie's seven sacred icons, necessitated by the priests' act of immolation. The performance, which featured a multitude of senior Tendai monks, an imperial emissary, and, of course, the new heads of the Shōgenji and Juge lineages, unfolded around the Ōmiya worship hall and sanctuary. A procession of monks approached, chanting and ringing bells. They bore a *miko-shi* containing the new statue of Ōnamuchi, the kami understood by the monks to be Śākyamuni, and they were followed by Hie priests, bearing incense and gifts. The procession filed through the worship hall to the sanctuary. The monk Keisan entered the sanctuary and placed Ōnamuchi within a tabernacle there. Before the kami, he formed mudras with his hands and intoned mantras. Shrine priests presented offerings of wine and cakes; a *norito* prayer was recited and *kagura* dancing performed. The entire rite of re-enshrinement concluded with the assembly of monks chanting and ringing bells in the shrine's incense-filled worship hall.[25] The historical significance of the performance is that it established once and for all that the seven shrines of Hie, their kami, and their rites belonged to the monks of Enryakuji and to Tendai Buddhism. The priests of Hie had thought and acted otherwise. For the briefest moment they had seized the shrine and claimed it for one-and-only Shinto. The extent of their folly was clear. In a real sense, it was only now that the place of the Hie Shrines, their kami, and their priests in the early modern order was established.

The Hie Shrine and the early modern Sannō festival

Shrines are first and foremost ritual sites. Shrines and their priests exist for no other reason than to perform rites before the kami; rites and festivals are their lifeblood. This was as much the case with Hie as with any other shrine in early modern Japan. A first question about Hie rites and festivals is prompted by the foregoing discussion. To what extent did Tendai monks determine and dominate them? The ritual calendar at Hie answers the question. The Hie year turned on eight ritual events, spread from the first to the eleventh months. On these special occasions, the doors of the innermost sanctuaries of Ōmiya, Ninomiya, and the other shrines were opened, and offerings placed directly before the kami.[26] Although the monks kept the sanctuary keys and were authorized to enter the sanctuaries at will, their ritual duties did not require them to do so. For example, every year in the third month they recited sutras before the kami, but this they did in the Ōmiya worship hall rather than in the sanctuary (the kami hall) itself. A key ritual moment of the Sannō festival in the fourth month was also incorporated into the Hie program of eight annual rituals, and while shrine priests and temple monks were both in attendance on this occasion, only the priests entered the sanctuary. It is clear, then, that the monks by no means dominated ritual proceedings in early modern Hie. In the discussion that follows, the focus falls uniquely on the Sannō festival.

Table 1 lists the main phases of the festival, as set down by the Tendai monk Kakushin in 1688. It is clear there were two spatial foci: the Ninomiya Shrine on the days of the horse and sheep,

Table 1 The early modern Sannō festival: main events

		Events	Site
4th month	Day of the horse	*Events centred on Mount Hachiōji*	
		The *mikoshi* from the Hachiōji and Sannomiya shrines are brought down the mountain and placed in the Ninomiya worship hall	Hachiōji, Sannomiya, Ninomiya
	Day of the sheep	*Events centred on Ninomiya shrine*	
		The *mikoshi* of the Ninomiya, Sannomiya, Hachiōji, and Jūzenji shrines are transferred to the Great Office (Ōmandokoro) building	Ninomiya → Ōmandokoro
		Tea and offerings from the Gion Shrine in Kyoto are placed before the four *mikoshi*	Ōmandokoro
		Lion dancing and *dengaku* drama are performed before the *mikoshi*	Ōmandokoro
		All four *mikoshi* are transferred to the Ōmiya worship hall, where they join the *mikoshi* of the Ōmiya, Shōshinshi, and Marōdo	Ōmandokoro → Ōmiya
	Day of the monkey	*Events centred on Ōmiya Shrine*	
		Priests open the inner sanctuary and make offerings	Ōmiya
		Monks enter pavilions	Banba promenade
		The Tendai prelate makes offerings; branches of *katsura* are offered to each *mikoshi*	Ōmiya
		A great branch of *sakaki* arrives from the Ōtsu Shinomiya Shrine	Shinomiya → Ōmiya
		All seven *mikoshi* are transported down to Lake Biwa	Ōmiya → Banba → Lake Biwa
		Mikoshi are transferred to boats and feted with offerings on Lake Biwa before returning to Ōmiya	Lake Biwa → Banba → Ōmiya

Source: Kakushin, *Hie Sannō sairei shinki*, 1688 (*ST* Hie: 205–20).

and the Ōmiya Shrine on the day of the monkey. Shrine priests were involved with all three, while the monks' involvement was confined to the monkey-day events. In his studies of Japanese festivities, the great folklorist Yanagita Kunio proposed a critical distinction between "sacred rite," or *matsuri*, and "public and festive event" or *sairei* (Yanagita 1969: 176–92). We might begin by suggesting that the events of the days of the horse and sheep corresponded to Yanagita's category of "sacred rite" or *matsuri*, while those of the monkey day were "public and festive events," or *sairei*. For Yanagita, the critical distinction between the two was the presence of the spectator's gaze. Whereas sacred rites (*matsuri*) are performed by ritual specialists and take place within the sacred confines of the shrine, often at night, the festival (*sairei*) is defined by public spaces, daytime, and above all the spectating presence of men and women not connected to sacred ritual performance. At the heart of festivals in Yanagita's sense are processions. Most feature those kami-bearing palanquins known as *mikoshi*, but what typically draws spectators is *furyū* or "style": creatively and colorfully constructed floats, dancing, music, and other forms of entertainment originating in the local community. The architecture of the typical festival also often includes pavilions, or *sajiki*, which afford a privileged view of proceedings. We might usefully confirm first of all the extent to which the events on the day of the monkey were, indeed, public and festive in Yanagita's sense.

Seventeenth-century illustrations of the Sannō festival typically depict the *mikoshi* procession heading down the Banba promenade in the afternoon of the day of the monkey. They are of a kind.[27] The torsos of the semi-naked porters can be seen straining under the weight of the 2-ton *mikoshi*. Conspicuous too are armor-clad men, some shaven-headed, running, shouting, and brandishing swords around the *mikoshi*; they are the Sakamoto *kunin*. Here it will suffice to note that the *kunin* were responsible for organizing the festival, and also for administration of the town of Sakamoto. They were low-ranking monks attached to the Enryakuji temple, but were allowed to marry and, like many senior Tendai monks, lived in Sakamoto. These illustrations all feature the pavilions along the promenade with monks clearly visible within as they gaze out on the *mikoshi* passing by. There

Figure 1 Extract from Akisato Ritō, *Ise sangū meisho zue* (Illustrated guide to famous sites for Ise pilgrims). The text reads "Sannō sacred rite: the transport of the great Sakaki on the day of the monkey." The great branch of *sakaki* cut from the forests of Mount Hachiōji was taken to the Shinomiya Shrine (renamed in Meiji as the Tenson Shrine) in Ōtsu on the first day of festivities. It is returned to the Shinomiya Shrine on the day of the monkey.

are clusters of spectators along the roadside, too, and then, of course, there are those, including ourselves, who are privy to the pictorial representations of the event. At least 20 paintings of the Sannō festival from the seventeenth century and early eighteenth century are extant, and most focus on this *mikoshi* procession as it heads down to Lake Biwa. It clearly constituted a major high- light for seventeenth-century artists and their sponsors. Late in the eighteenth century, however, it seems the representational mold was broken. The author of at least one popular travel guide drew his readers' attention to the earlier procession which heads *up* the Banba promenade. Figure 1 from the *Ise sangū meisho zue* (Illustrated guide to famous sites for Ise pilgrims) shows that pro- cession, led by a man holding a *gohei*, a wand with paper stream- ers purifying the path ahead. There follows the *sai-no-hoko* or pike of good fortune, and then the main feature: the huge branch of *sakaki* tree being carried up to Ōmiya. As in the paintings, the artist of this print captures the procession as it passes in front of the monks' pavilions and the spectators scattered along the route.[28] This too is quite clearly a festive moment.

Compared to other festivals of early modern Japan, there is, however, something very distinctive about these processions up and down the promenade that links the Hie complex to the shores of Lake Biwa, and that is the complete absence of what Yanagita termed "style" or *furyū*. Examples of festivals dominated by concerns with "style" abounded in the towns and villages around Lake Biwa; the great Ōtsu festival was a case in point.[29] The Sannō festival crowd is especially revealing in this regard. The print shows the vast majority of spectators seated; they are, moreover, clearly subject to some form of discipline. In the top right-hand corner, a man armed with a split-bamboo stick is striking a seated spectator; at the bottom left are men striking or poised to strike others. These men are the aforementioned *kunin*. Akisato Ritō, the author of the pilgrims' guide featuring this print, wrote not only of the solemnity with which the procession passed up the promenade, but also of the remarkable frequency with which spectators were hit. "This," he conceded, "is entertainment of sorts" (Akisato 1944: 373–5). Samukawa Tatsukiyo, the samurai author of the mid eighteenth-century *Ōmi yochi shiryaku* (Ōmi province: an abbreviated gazetteer), was less forgiving about the violence meted out by *kunin*. "The *kunin* are out of control and wound people with impunity. They [excuse themselves saying] the Hie *mikoshi* will not continue on their way till they have seen blood flow … Why would the Hie kami delight to see people suffer? If the *mikoshi* must witness blood, someone should take hold of a *kunin* each year and bleed him!" (Samukawa 1733: 216).

In other words, the events of the day of the monkey are only festive in a very restricted sense of the term. They were produced principally for the benefit of the Tendai monks, and it is evident that the monks did not approve of the men, women, and children of Sakamoto innovating, competing, or celebrating. Rather, they favored a disciplined, still, and respectful crowd. As a result, these Sannō processions were as restrained as festive processions could be.

The character of the whole festival began to change, however, in the early nineteenth century, and the reasons appear to lie in the changing structure of power in Sakamoto. The *kunin* had overall charge of the town's day-to-day affairs, and the key to their authority was the Elder system. The 31 wards (*chō*), comprising Upper and Lower Sakamoto, were each overseen by Ward Elders; these men were in turn responsible to the four Senior Sakamoto Elders, each of whom was a *kunin*. First among their administrative responsibilities was ensuring that farmers, who made up at least 75 percent of Sakamoto's working population, paid their annual dues and that law and order were kept. The problem faced by the *kunin* was that they received no stipend for running the town, so they had also to work as farmers and woodcutters.[30]

When Samukawa compiled his gazetteer in the 1730s, there were some 150 *kunin*; in the 1790s, when Akisato Ritō drew Ise pilgrims to Hie with his travel guide, *kunin* numbers had plummeted to 90 or so. In the first decades of the next century they continued to drop, so that by the 1840s *kunin* resident in Sakamoto numbered no more than 25 or 26 (Takashima 1978: 22). In 1803, *kunin* were complaining bitterly to the monks about the insufferable burden of supervising work at harvest time, of waiting on the senior Tendai prelate whenever he ventured into Kyoto, and of staging the Sannō festival, all in addition to their need to earn a living. In 1819 the *kunin*, who were now desperate, pleaded with the Tendai monks to release them from all occasional duties, so they might on the monks' behalf reassert control of Sakamoto's administration. "We are now effectively at the beck and call of Sakamoto farmers," they complained (Takashima 1978: 24). The single privilege that attached to the *kunin* office was the right to wear armor and bear arms at the Sannō festival. It is little wonder that numbers declined. In this context of the loosening *kunin* grip on Sakamoto's affairs, a striking innovation appeared in the festival. It was one that for the first time accorded to the events of the day of the sheep a genuinely "festive and public" character.

The 1820s transformation to which I refer can be seen in Figure 2, taken from a scroll dated 1822.[31] It shows a procession of flowers. The sprays of flowers are held high by children. In attendance are

Figure 2 One-panel extract from *Hie Sannō sairei emaki* (Ancient map of the Sannō festival), 1822. Author unknown. *Reproduced with the permission of Hiyoshi Taisha.*

men who are not priests, monks, or *kunin*. The flowers, artistically arranged and quite distinct from one another, surround a platform-like structure featuring different sorts of displays. On one can be seen a rabbit; on another a man stands beneath a willow tree; on a third, a rope co-joins two rocks. These are evidently festival floats, albeit of a very primitive kind. They are, however, both individualistic and creative, and no doubt represent the interests and aspirations of people of different Sakamoto wards. This scroll was apparently composed as a visual prompt for *kunin*, instructing them where they were to take up position as the procession got under way; as a result, it fails to convey a sense of the festive. A later scroll (Figure 3), by an unknown artist probably from the early 1850s, places the new flower procession in context. Evident in Figure 3 are seven extravagant flower sprays, each of differing colors and designs, borne by throngs of people walking up the Banba promenade.[32] Armor-clad *kunin* are in evidence, but they are not waving sticks or swords. They appear in fact to be motionless, observing the procession pass by. Most interesting of all perhaps is the crowd. It extends up the promenade as far as the eye can see, three or four deep on either side. No spectators are seated. Many stand jostling, their eyes fixed on the spectacle

Figure 3 One-panel extract from *Hie sairei tenkō byōbu* (Panels depicting the Hie festival), 1850s. Author unknown. *Reproduced with the permission of Mr. Yamada Naokazu.*

unfolding before their eyes. Still more appear to be walking alongside the procession as it makes its way to the four *mikoshi*-borne kami waiting in the Great Office.

Exactly when this flower procession was initiated is unclear, but it features in no pictorial or textual record prior to 1822 and is mentioned frequently thereafter. A cautious evaluation is in order given this absence of evidence, but it seems the flower procession was the idea of the people of Sakamoto, and that it materialized at a time when the *kunin* grip on the town was significantly loosened. The flower procession connected those sheep-day events to the local community and its imagination and, by the same token, accorded the people of Sakamoto a first opportunity to create, entertain, and be entertained. It is tempting too to read into this innovation Sakamoto defiance of the Enryakuji monks. In the early decades of the nineteenth century there were reasons enough to defy. Sakamoto was hit time and again by typhoons, floods, and drought, and even by an earthquake. On each occasion, the Tendai monks' response was slow, grudging, and altogether inadequate (Oketsume 1981: 132–5).

The 1850s scroll, taken in its entirety, suggests a greater transformation was under way. It depicts throngs of people standing, mingling at all the different events that make up the great Sannō festival. "Festive and public," suggests the scroll, is now applicable to all four days and nights. It is noteworthy that there is not a single depiction here of armor-clad *kunin* intimidating or striking out at spectators. Instead, stalls are set up along the Banba promenade selling snacks to men and women who amble by. The flower procession, for its part, was now firmly established, and it remains to this day one of the great highlights of the Sannō festival.

It was, then, only at the start of the nineteenth century that the common people of Sakamoto began to engage dynamically with the Sannō festival, but we should note finally two points about popular participation with the shrine and its festival. The first is that members of Sakamoto's two communities of so-called *eta*, the "much-defiled," were not included in these developments; to their history we must turn below. Secondly, we know very little at all about the engagement of the common people with the Hie Shrine at non-festival times of the year. There existed in premodern Sakamoto multiple confraternities known as Sannō-*kō*, whose members convened in the first, fifth, and ninth months of the year to intone sutras before a Sannō mandala. As far as we can tell, however, these associations were set up by the *kunin* for the *kunin*, and there is no clear evidence of participation by the common people. After all, they were anyway parishioners of one or other of the 16 shrines scattered throughout Upper and Lower Sakamoto.[33]

The end of an era

The priests of the Hie Shrine naturally enough had a keen interest in the kami they served, but none was more important to them than the Ninomiya kami, Kuni-no-Tokotachi. Kuni-no-Tokotachi was not only "the first kami of the universe," he was venerated as the ancestral kami for priests of both Shōgenji and

Juge lineages. In the 1830s, however, the shrine priests made a disturbing discovery. They encountered indisputable evidence that the Ninomiya kami was not in fact Kuni-no-Tokotachi after all, but an entirely different kami called Ōyamakui. They owed this discovery to the diffusion of new knowledge about the kami myths in the early nineteenth century. In medieval and early modern Japan, the ultimate textual authority on kami affairs had been the *Nihon shoki*. The older *Kojiki* was much less known and used. This all changed in the early nineteenth century with the publication of Motoori Norinaga's *Kojiki-den*, and its citation in an increasing number of nativist works. As we noted above, the *Kojiki* spoke, albeit briefly, about Hie and its kami, identifying him as Ōyamakui. The discovery was made by the Hie priest Shōgenji Kiyo sometime in 1836, it seems. At least, he was the one inspired to pen a short study of Ōyamakui in that year, called *Ōyamakui shinden* (A biography of the kami Ōyamakui). The nativist Sugawara Natsukage also found inspiration in these *Kojiki* revelations in 1836, but his delight at learning the truth was complicated by bitterness. After all, was it not the case that the Tendai monks had deliberately concealed the truth of the Hie kami for a millennium and more?

In the short term, this revelation about the Ninomiya kami seems to have had no wider impact; in the longer term, as we shall see, it did. In the 1850s, however, there was a second, quite unrelated, development of consequence at Hie; it arose out of the national crisis of those years. In 1854, the US Navy commodore Matthew Perry anchored his squadron off the coast of Kanagawa, determined to secure from the Tokugawa military rulers a "friendship treaty." In that dreadful year, Emperor Kōmei commanded priests and monks at seven temples and seven shrines across Japan to seek the assistance of the buddhas and kami in expelling the barbarian presence. Heedless of the emperor's wishes, the Tokugawa signed the proposed treaty in March. In July 1858 the Tokugawa shogun yielded further and agreed to commercial treaties with the Americans, the British, and other foreign powers, opening up Japan's ports to foreign trade. As diplomatic negotiations proceeded, Kōmei once more mobilized priests and monks. Enryakuji was one of the seven temples, but Hie was not included among the seven shrines. The emperor nonetheless contacted the senior Tendai prelate on four separate occasions to have Hie priests perform 17 days of prayers.[34] Details are obscure, but it seems the emperor had learned of the keen loyalist leanings of the Hie priest Shōgenji Kiretsu (1784–1862).

These two unrelated developments, the revelation about the true nature of the Hie kami and the burgeoning proximity between Hie priests and the imperial court, enabled shrine priests like Shōgenji Kiretsu and Juge Shigekuni (1816–84) to imagine a future entirely divorced from the present. It was a future that drew its inspiration from the remote past when Ōyamakui was venerated as the kami of Hie, and when the priests were devoted uniquely to Ōyamakui and the imperial court. In that future, there could be no place for Tendai or any other form of Buddhism. After all, Buddhism had not existed in Japan when Ōyamakui was first venerated in Hie. Only a revolution could transform that imagining into reality.

The Hie Shrine and Modern Japan

The Meiji Revolution, 1868

The Meiji Revolution arrived in Sakamoto on April 23, 1868. It did so in the person of Juge Shigekuni, presently employed by the fledgling Meiji government in Kyoto. He arrived with some 40 armed men who called themselves the Band of Divine Authority (Shin'itai). This was a fitting name, since many members were in fact shrine priests drawn from across central Japan. When they reached Sakamoto, they were joined by other priests and a gang of local peasants. Led by Juge, these men fell upon each of Hie's seven shrines in turn. They ripped out and then smashed, burned, or stole anything that was Buddhist. A partial inventory of the treasures lost from the Ōmiya Shrine alone reads as follows: a Śākyamuni statue; a bronze bell; 14 boxes containing the assembled Buddhist sutras and commentaries; the Prajñāpāramitā sutra in five boxes; the Lotus sutra in 10 volumes; golden Buddhist ritual implements; a statue of Dainichi (Mahāvairocana); and an altar used in a Buddhist fire rite (*goma*). All in all, more than 1,000 treasures were lost in the April frenzy at Hie (*SBSa*: 686–700).

It is clear from Juge's own account that he was inspired partly by deep resentment towards the Tendai monks. He referred to the incident 200 years before, when his forefathers were exiled for their own immolation of Buddhist statues.[35] But the immediate prompt was government legislation. On April 20, the fledgling government had issued an edict ordering shrine priests across Japan to do precisely what Juge had done: remove all Buddhist statuary from their shrines. This came in the wake of an earlier edict banning Buddhist monks from serving the kami (Miyachi 1988: 425). Collectively, this legislation was known as "clarification" (*hanzen*), its purpose being to clarify what was of the kami and what of the Buddha; what was a shrine and what a temple; what, in short, was "Shinto" and what "Buddhism." The stripping of shrines that went by the name of clarification impacted on Hie first, but it spread quickly the length and breadth of Japan. It is difficult to exaggerate the effect. "Clarification" marked out new, exclusive time-spaces for shrines, their kami, and their priests, separating them off from temples, buddhas, and monks. Clarification laid the foundations for Shinto as we know it today, an autonomous religion, entirely distinct and independent from Buddhism (Breen 2000).

The new government was a "Restoration" government that took shape around the young sovereign known to history as Emperor Meiji. Its samurai leaders transformed Japan into a modern nation-state with remarkable speed and clarity of vision. At the end of 1867, Japan was still ruled by the Tokugawa, teetering though they were on the brink of collapse, undone by diplomatic crisis and domestic unrest. A military coup in January 1868 dealt the final blow. Young samurai from the domains of Satsuma and Chōshū, along with some forward-thinking court nobles, swiftly erected a new imperial, civilian government. The peasants and merchants, not to mention the samurai, of early modern Japan became imperial subjects, governed now by imperial decrees. The most pressing task accorded the emperor was legitimizing the new regime and the coup that brought it into being. It was to this end that he and government leaders now invested in the imperial myth. The mythical narrative was a simple but arresting one: the sun-goddess established the imperial line in mythical time; she dispatched her grandson Ninigi to earth to rule Japan on her behalf, and his descendant, Jinmu, was then enthroned as the first human emperor. All subsequent emperors were direct descendants of Jinmu and so of the sun-goddess.

This narrative was hardly new; we have seen its clearest articulations in the writing of the nativists Motoori Norinaga and Aizawa Seishisai. However, the 1868 Restoration and the construction of the modern nation-state demanded it be made manifest and resonate throughout Japan. In the orchestration of the myth, shrines like Hie were accorded a vital role. No shrine, of course, was more important in this endeavor than Ise, which, as we have seen, was the most popular of many "national" pilgrimage sites in early modern Japan. In 1869 the new Meiji emperor made his own historic pilgrimage to Ise, en route to the new capital of Tokyo from Kyoto. It was historic, since no emperor had ever before worshiped there.[36] The emperor's visit transformed Ise from a popular pilgrimage site into the modern nation-state's most sacred center, and it was critical too in animating the imperial myth. It was dramatic proof, after all, of the most intimate relationship between emperor and sun-goddess. The imperial pilgrimage was preceded by a thorough stripping away of all Buddhist symbols from the shrine's vicinity. Temples in Ise were either destroyed or screened from view; sutras were banned from sale. For Buddhism, far from clarifying the imperial narrative, offered a threateningly alternative view of history, in which Amaterasu was none other than the Sun Buddha and the emperors that Buddha incarnate. Clarification was imposed on all shrines in 1868 for the same reason. It was essential to the process of priming shrines in preparation for the articulation of the imperial myth. Much other change was implicit in shrines' new myth-bearing role.

In 1868, government leaders ended the authority of the Yoshida and Shirakawa Shinto families, and placed all shrines and their priests under nominal control of the revived Council of Kami Affairs. In 1871, the government banned the practice of hereditary succession at shrines, dispatching priests of its own choosing to the most important sites like Hie. At the same time, it declared all shrines to be "sites for the performance of state rites," and a national shrine pyramid structured beneath Ise began to take shape (Miyachi 1988: 437). In 1873, the Meiji government laid down in law the annual cycle of rites which shrine priests were to perform: the spring *kinensai* and autumn *niiname-sai* rites, both involving rice offerings to the sun-goddess; the New Year *genshi* rite, a celebration of the imperial line's mythic origins; and *kigensetsu*, which commemorated Emperor Jinmu's ascent to the throne. There were also rites for the new emperor's birthday and the anniversary of his father's death (Miyachi 1988: 450, 452, 457). Where shrines in early modern Japan were defined by their diversity, uniformity would be the order of the day in Meiji.

Hie's modern spaces

Juge Shigekuni, as it turned out, was both perpetrator and victim of change in Meiji. Tendai monks protested vigorously at his stripping of the Hie Shrines, which eventually elicited a response. Local government launched an investigation that led to the interrogation and arrest of Shigekuni and a fellow priest; the two men spent a full year in Ōtsu prison for their vandalism.[37] Juge Shigekuni was released from prison in 1870, and the 1871 ban on heredity then effectively removed him and his family, as well as the Shōgenji priests, from the positions of power they had craved at Hie. In the same year, Hie was accorded elite status in the national shrine pyramid. It became Kanpei Taisha Hie Jinja ("State-funded great shrine Hie"), one of only 29 shrines in the land to occupy the rank. Hie received 2,500 yen per year from the government, with other disbursements available for ritual performance and shrine repairs (Kanpei Taisha Hie Jinja shamusho 1942; Miyachi 1988: 437–9). In 1872, the government appointed Matsuda Inari, erstwhile priest at the Kasuga Shrine in Nara, as Hie's first non-hereditary chief priest. He was a state employee, charged with the vital task of implementing a new annual ritual cycle dedicated to proclaiming the uniqueness of Japan's imperial line. The storm of "clarification" in 1868 proved to be but the violent start of Hie's accommodation into the modern nation-state.

Juge Shigekuni may have been sidelined from the Hie Shrines, but far from retiring in disgrace he quickly found employment in the Imperial Household Ministry in Tokyo, while a decade later Shōgenji Kitoku, in fact, returned to Hie as chief priest. These men were well aware of their debt to the government, for it had liberated Hie from Buddhism and from Tendai control. Before his arrest in late 1869, Shigekuni found the new authorities amenable to several other proposals for change. For one thing, he was deeply offended by the shape of the Hie torii gate. The triangular structure that sat atop the crossbar, distinguishing it from all other torii in the land, symbolized the oneness of the kami and the buddhas, and so with the permission of the Ōtsu authorities he had it removed. Juge also took offense at the names of three of the Hie Shrines, Hachiōji, Shōshinshi, and Jūzenji. To him they smacked of Buddhism, and he renamed them Ushio, Usa, and, intriguingly, Juge Shrine respectively.[38] For the Juge and Shōgenji priests, however, these acts of "clarification" were but one aspect of recovering Hie's past. A task no less pressing was to secure government recognition for the discovery that the priests had made in the 1830s, namely that the Ninomiya kami was not Kuni-no-Tokotachi after all, but Ōyamakui.

Sometime in 1869, Shigekuni penned a notice for Ōtsu prefectural authorities styled *Saijin oyobi kanjō nenki* (On the Hie kami and the dating of their enshrinement).[39] Here he cited the *Kojiki* passage on Ōyamakui, but also adduced new evidence. The kami enshrined in Ninomiya, he insisted now, was "the gentle spirit" of Ōyamakui. "Emperor Sujin in the seventh year of his reign ordered the gentle spirit to be venerated at the foot of the mountain" by Kamo priests. There is no evidence, in fact, of any such imperial order, but what is more interesting still is the linkage Shigekuni went on to establish between the different Hie kami. He wrote next of the Ushio Shrine at the top of Mount Hachiōji: "The kami of this shrine is [also] Ōyamakui. When the ancients spoke of Hie, they referred to this shrine." The point he makes is that the Ushio kami and the Ninomiya kami are one and the same. Shigekuni then explained that Ōyamakui's "princess" is venerated "alongside." "Alongside" referred of course to Sannomiya, the second of the two mountain-top shrines

Table 2 The Hie kami

Tokugawa period	Meiji (1869)
Kami name (shrine name)	Kami name (shrine name)
Kuni-no-Tokotachi (Ninomiya) →	Ōyamakui: gentle spirit (Ninomiya)
Kuni-no-Satsuchi (Hachiōji) →	Ōyamakui: violent spirit (Ushio)
Ninigi (Jūzenji) →	Tamayori-hime: gentle spirit (Juge)
Kashikone (Sannomiya) →	Tamayori-hime: violent spirit (Sannomiya)

and, indeed, Shigekuni wrote of the Sannomiya Shrine that its kami was Princess Tamayori-hime, or rather the "violent spirit" of Tamayori-hime. He also informed the Ōtsu authorities that the "gentle spirit" of the same princess was venerated in the Juge Shrine at the foot of the mountain.

In Shigekuni's reading of the interconnection between these four kami, two principles can be identified. The first is that of gentle and violent spirits, or *nigi* and *ara mitama*. Ōyamakui and Tamayori-hime both have these contrasting yet complementary "facets," which bind the mountain-top shrines with those at the foot. The second principle is that of betrothal. Ōyamakui's violent spirit is betrothed to Tamayori-hime's violent spirit, and the gentle spirits of each kami are similarly betrothed. What is important to note is that neither the relationships nor the principles sustaining them are to be found anywhere in pre-Restoration sources. These are quite simply Juge Shigekuni's creation, the full extent of which is most easily grasped in the tabulation in Table 2.

A most striking transformation was effected on Ninigi, the grandson of the sun-goddess, reimagined by Shigekuni as Princess Tamayori-hime. There was of course no historical evidence to suggest Tamayori-hime was venerated at Hie at any time in its history, nor that the kami of the Hachiōji Shrine was understood to be Ōyamakui. It is tempting to dismiss *Saijin oyobi kanjō nenki* as a mere fabrication, but it is possible, too, to see here a creative act in the reimagining of Hie's past. At least, Shigekuni's fashioning of this new Hie pantheon provided an answer to at least one vital question: why at the Sannō festival the two kami descend the mountain to spend the night together in the Ninomiya worship hall, and why the four kami move to the Great Office (Ōmandokoro), there to be feted with offerings. For Shigekuni, it is betrothal that makes sense of the night the kami spend together. His interpretation also made some sense of the small Ōji Shrine located next to the Great Office. The shrine was, as its name suggests, dedicated to a divine prince. Was this prince not born of the coupling of Ōyamakui and Tamayori-hime? In early Meiji, presumably at Shigekuni's urging, this shrine was duly restyled Ubuya Shrine, the "birth hut" of the newborn prince.

The problem for Juge Shigekuni was proof; how to counter the inevitable accusations of fabrication. That Ōyamakui and not Kuni-no-Tokotachi was the original Hie kami was evident from the *Kojiki*, but the rest was Shigekuni's imagining which may, or may not, have reflected Hie's original form. So Shigekuni decided to create proof where none existed. The fruit of his labor was a text styled *Hie sha negi kuden shō* (A digest of oral transmissions of the Hie priesthood) (*ST* Hie: 1–7). That this was not the recording of ancient oral traditions by a medieval priest but, indeed, a Meiji fabrication has been demonstrated conclusively by the historian Satō Masato (Satō 1989). The fabrication was, however, a highly successful one. Its validity appears never to have been questioned in the nineteenth or twentieth centuries, until Satō analyzed it in the 1980s. Of course, the Hie Shrine priests reiterated the truth of Ōyamakui and Tamayori-hime on countless occasions; even the press helped publicize it.[40] But what removed the possibility of doubt was that the space of the shrine was transformed, and indeed the Sannō festival reinterpreted, to accommodate Juge's imaginings as they appeared in *Hie sha negi kuden shō*.

In 1873 the Meiji government appointed Nishikawa Yoshisuke (1816–80) as chief priest of Hie. He was a man of impeccable loyalist credentials, a disciple of the great nativists Hirata Atsutane and Ōkuni Takamasa. The early 1860s had even seen him arrested and imprisoned for involvement in an infamous anti-Tokugawa plot. Nishikawa was typical of the men the government was now dispatching to major shrines across Japan, and he left a deep impression on Hie. Nishikawa began where Juge Shigekuni left off with a second round of shrine renaming. He gave to the Marōdo Shrine the new name of Shirayama-hime, or "White mountain princess"; Shirayama is a Japanese reading of the name of Mount Hakusan from which this kami originated. More importantly he restyled the Ōmiya Shrine "Ōmiwa" or Great Miwa. This was in deference to the fact that its kami, Ōnamuchi, had originally been summoned to Hie from Miwa in Nara. This renaming amounted to a demotion for the shrine, which throughout Hie's history had been the most prominent among the seven. Nishikawa now accorded pride of place to Ōyamakui's shrine, and changed its name from Ninomiya, which meant "Second Shrine," to Hongū or "Main Shrine." He then declared all other six shrines to be subordinate branch shrines (sessha). As a consequence, "State-funded great shrine Hie" in Japan of the Meiji period and beyond referred uniquely to Ōyamakui's restyled Hongū. In all this, of course, Nishikawa sought, and swiftly received, central government permission. It was likewise with government sanction that Nishikawa now effected a radical reordering of ritual space at Hie. The shrine newly designated Hongū was less impressive in appearance, more awkward to approach, and less spacious than Ōmiwa; after all, it had been very much secondary in importance for more than a millennium. Nishikawa now effected a spatial swap. In a solemn rite in September 1875, he transferred Ōyamakui to what had been the Ōmiwa site, and Ōnamuchi to the former Hongū site. He transferred the names of the shrines along with the kami. In order that Ōyamakui might not be parted from his princess, Tamayori-hime was also transferred to what had been the Shōshinshi Shrine. The implications of this reordering for the modern Sannō festival will be discussed below. First, though, it will be instructive to reflect on another aspect of Nishikawa's tenure as Hie's chief priest.

Priests and propaganda

Nishikawa's arrival at Hie coincided with a major upheaval in Meiji government religious policy. In 1872, as we have seen, the government created a new Ministry of Edification (Kyōbushō), with administrative responsibilities for Shinto shrines and their priests, Buddhist temples and monks, as well as the new religions founded by such as Kawate Bunjirō, Nakayama Miki, and Kurozumi Munetada.[41] The Ministry was specifically charged, though, with planning and executing a nationwide propaganda campaign. The campaign was to harness the energies of priests, monks, and other religionists. For this doomed initiative the impoverished government provided almost no funding, but it did promote research into Shinto theology; it encouraged shrine priests to perform new Shinto funerals; and it sponsored, too, the dissemination of amulets from the Ise Shrines throughout the land. For the likes of Nishikawa, this meant the assumption of an entirely new role. No longer simply charged with performing state rites at Hie, Nishikawa now became a "national evangelist." In all of this endeavor, the government was motivated by a dread of Christianity. Prohibition and persecution were no longer options for a leadership craving international recognition; the combined efforts of shrine priests and temple monks might yet offer an ideological bulwark.

Nishikawa assumed his propagandist role with urgency and enthusiasm. He invested his own funds in the creation of Shiga Prefecture's Chūkyōin (Teaching Institute) and trained up some 25 Shinto propagandists, whom he dispatched across the prefecture. Though few in number, they nonetheless claimed considerable successes. Nishikawa wrote in July 1875 of the "wonderful response" that greeted his own sermons (Inoue Suguru 2000: 69–70). Six months later he planned to invest in a permanent "preaching station" in Kashiwara, given the keen interest in nearby villages (Yamamoto 2002: 35–6). At the Hie Shrine, he created a discussion group with some 400 members, and other propagandists set up similarly popular groups elsewhere (Yamamoto 2002: 29). In 1879, Nishikawa reported with satisfaction that commoners all over the prefecture were gathering in good numbers to listen to his lectures, and making generous financial contributions as well (Yamamoto 2002: 41–2). This apparent optimism explains his disappointment later that year on learning of his transfer to the Ikutama Shrine in Osaka. Nishikawa declined to go; in March 1880, at the age of 64, he died before matters came to a head.

Nishikawa reported good news from the mission field against a background of deep frustration with the imperial government he was so anxious to serve. He waited desperately for some lead on propaganda. The bureaucrats in the Ministry of Edification had opted for a theology that drew heavily on Hirata Shinto. They located Hirata's three creator-kami as the core of the theology; they also specified a list of topics to be addressed, such as the creation of the universe, the fate of the soul, and patriotism. What exactly, though, was Nishikawa to say about these topics? Nishikawa was an erstwhile Hirata disciple, but even he lamented that Hirata's writings were not fit for purpose (Yamamoto 2002: 29). He waited, too, for funeral guidelines, even as he observed that people in Shiga Prefecture showed little interest in abandoning the Buddhist habits of generations. In 1877, Nishikawa greeted with relief news that the government had closed the Ministry of Edification, and he hoped, in vain as it transpired, for greater efficiency from the bureaucrats in the Home Ministry, which now assumed responsibility for shrines and temples.

Nishikawa's personal fear of Christianity gave impetus to his endeavors. In January 1876 he heard that a Christian church had been built in Kyoto, and reflected: "The great enemy has now encroached to within three *ri* of us; danger is ever-present" (Yamamoto 2002: 35). Later in the year, he learned that a French missionary was now resident in Ōtsu and went to meet him, only to find to his delight that the Frenchman professed an understanding of the "great Japanese Way."[42] At the end of the following year, Christianity put down its first, very tentative, roots in nearby Ōtsu in the form of a private school advertising lectures on the teachings of Jesus. Nishikawa was shocked to discover that an erstwhile nativist disciple of his, one Takada Yoshinami, was the school's founder. (Inoue Suguru 2000: 50). In fact no Christian church was built in Shiga Prefecture during Nishikawa's lifetime, but his anxiety was real. He was already persuaded that Shinto priests could not cope alone; they had to work alongside True Pure Land Buddhists, increasingly active in Shiga. This conviction was tempered only by fear that in terms of finances and theology, not to mention training and intellect, Shinto priests were no match for Buddhists.

A few months before the Ministry of Edification was shut down in 1876, Tanaka Tomokuni, former Hie priest and now Justice Ministry bureaucrat, wrote to Nishikawa articulating an idea that was gaining currency in Tokyo. It was that Shinto be reimagined not as a religion of the Buddhist or Christian variety but as "non-religious," as a set of ethical teachings and ritual practices transcending religion. The implication of this idea was clearly that priests like Nishikawa would no longer preach about creation and the afterlife, or perform funerals; they would once again dedicate themselves uniquely to the performance of myth-sustaining state rites. That Nishikawa expressed sympathy with Tanaka's ideas suggests his labors as national evangelist were exacting their toll (Yamamoto 2002: 25–6). Shortly after he died in 1880, the Home Ministry reconfigured religious policy, precisely to render Shinto and shrines "non-religious." In January 1882 the Ministry banned priests at all 29 great state shrines from engaging in propaganda activities; no more were they to conduct Shinto funerals. What lay behind this dramatic reversal were the experiences of shrine priests across Japan; a Buddhist-led campaign for the separation of religion and state; and a theological controversy that split the fledgling Shinto community.

The controversy concerned the state pantheon, specifically those kami to be venerated in the shrine of the Shinto Office (Shintō jimukyoku), a new semi-official organ created in Tokyo after the Ministry of Edification's demise. Priests from the Izumo Shrine were insistent that their kami, Ōkuninushi, be included in the new pantheon as the lord of the netherworld. Priests from Ise were equally determined to keep that kami out. The government became concerned lest these increasingly bitter disputes embroil the sun-goddess; and it intervened in support of the Ise position, before taking more radical action. It ordered priests wishing to preach about theological matters or perform funerals to leave their shrines and form their own religious sects; and many did. The remaining priests were now to dedicate themselves exclusively to the task allotted them back in 1871, namely the preservation and promotion of the imperial myth.

Festivals and fights

The one possibility for shrines like Hie to pursue their own distinctive path amidst the uniformity of Meiji was the annual festival. Yet even here government intervened. At the end of 1872 the Meiji government legislated a distinction between shrine rites.[43] "State rites" (*kansai*) would be funded by government and attended by government officials, but "private rites" (*shisai*) would receive neither funding nor patronage. In the "state" category were of course the many rites articulating aspects of the imperial myth, but also shrines' annual festivals. "Private" referred to all other ritual activity. What this meant in the case of Hie's Sannō festival was that government funded the offerings made to Ōyamakui on the morning of the third festival day, but for the rest – the descent from the mountain by the two *mikoshi*, the offerings in the Great Office, the processions up and down the promenade, and the offerings on Lake Biwa – these activities were all redefined now as "private." If they were to survive, they would need funding by the townspeople of Sakamoto. And lest "private" be interpreted as a license for merrymaking, the government in 1873 ordered *mikoshi* processions everywhere to exercise restraint and avoid "being rough, bumping into houses or impeding passersby" (Miyachi 1988: 457).

The first point to make about the modern Sannō festival is that it did survive. In the new solar calendar, festival dates were quickly fixed as April 12, 13, 14, and 15. The second is that, in its modern manifestation, it yielded entirely new meanings. The discovery and enshrinement of the kami Ōyamakui, and the reordering of Hie space around that kami, displaced the pre-Meiji interpretation promoted by priests like Shōgenji Yukimaru. For Yukimaru, the descent of the mountain by the two *mikoshi*-borne kami, and then the departure of the seven *mikoshi* from the Ōmiya compound, were most replete with cosmic meaning. These were joyous moments marking the entrance of the kami into the human world. For Yukimaru, their significance was akin to Amaterasu's stepping out of the heavenly cave, restoring light to the world (*ST* Hie: 161–85).[44] The passage of the seven *mikoshi* under the three torii gates of Hie as they headed down the promenade to the lake had a different, mystical significance for him. This represented the essential oneness of the kami and the buddhas (*ST* Hie: 315–78). Yukimaru, for one, never doubted the truth of Tendai claims about the Buddhist nature of all kami.

The modern Shinto-style Sannō festival yielded a different order of interpretation. It became an enactment of a mythical drama featuring the kami Ōyamakui and his princess Tamayori-hime. The two kami descend the mountain together, spend the night in the Hongū worship hall, and are joined by their "gentle spirits" the following day in the Great Office, where all are feted with offerings before the princess kami gives birth. This tale of a divine birth was made explicit in at least one mid-Meiji commentary. In his *Hie jinja korei saiki* (The ancient rites of the Hie Shrines), Shōgenji Kitoku explained that "the festival, which is of the greatest antiquity, serves to recreate the birth and the subsequent ascent to heaven of [the divine child] Wakamiya." Kitoku understood Wakamiya to be enshrined in the Ubuya Shrine. There is a moment in the festival, in its Meiji manifestation, when a priest, having presented offerings of rice wine to the four *mikoshi*, throws the wine cup high into the air. This, insisted Shōgenji, represents the divine child's flight up into heaven. Deeper readings of the Sannō festival had to await the postwar historian Kageyama Haruki, whose interpretation we encountered at the start of this chapter. Kageyama found explicit sexual meaning in the placing of the two *mikoshi* side by side in the Hongū worship hall, and read the violent shaking of the four *mikoshi* in the Great Office on the night of April 13 as Tamayori-hime's birth pangs (Kageyama 2001: 52, 60). It is worth stressing that neither interpretation is to be found in prewar writings on the shrine by priests or other observers.

Of the festival as it was performed in the early Meiji years, history records very little. A decade after the Restoration, the first signs emerged that all would be well. So many visitors descended on Sakamoto in 1879 that local inns could not cope.[45] The 1880s saw further growth, apparently owing to transport provided by Lake Biwa ferry companies. In 1887, the local newspaper *Chūgai denpō* recorded crowds of unprecedented size at the festival, but it also reported on an "extraordinarily huge fight" which erupted on the night of April 13. The fight left 60 men with serious injuries.[46] The paper reminded its readers that the Sannō festival had a reputation as a "blood-fest" (*chimatsuri*) even in Tokugawa times, but this incident was of a very different order. Among the villages comprising Sakamoto was Hagiyama, occupied by families stigmatized for their dealing with leather and carcasses. Despised as *eta* ("the much-defiled") prior to the Restoration, Hagiyama villagers became imperial subjects in the new Japan, the equals of others in every way. The distance of theory from reality surfaced when villagers sought participation in the 1873 Sannō festival. The Sakamoto headman, responsible for apportioning roles, agreed Hagiyama villagers might carry the heavy iron spear and the boxes of offerings in the procession up the Banba promenade on April 14, but refused their request to carry a *mikoshi*. Vigorous Hagiyama appeals to the prefectural governor bore fruit in 1874. They were allowed to carry the Sannomiya *mikoshi* on its journey down to the lake, but others would carry the same *mikoshi* up and down the mountain, and on the stretch from the Hongū to the Great Office. The fights of 1887 began, it seems, with youths from Hagiyama and other Sakamoto villages taunting each other. Such fights became a regular feature of the festival until, in 1894, the Sakamoto headman banned Hagiyama. "In recent years [Hagiyama youths] have been the cause of much disobedience and unrest, obstructing the conduct of this ancient festival."[47]

When the Sannō festival resumed in 1906 after the Russo-Japanese war, Hagiyama residents were still excluded, but now they took action. A party ambushed the Sannomiya and Ushio *mikoshi* as they were carried up the mountain on March 1; others intimidated the district governor and, on March 11, 500 villagers surrounded the Sakamoto headman's residence, showering it with rocks and stones. Police were deployed and made arrests, but conceded that order would never be restored until Hagiyama villagers were accommodated in the festival. Details are obscure, but Hagiyama villagers now secured the right to bear the Sannomiya *mikoshi* on all three days of the festival; they were also allotted a role in the flower procession of April 13.[48] At the 1906 festival, the *Asahi* newspaper reported that the thousands gathered in anticipation of fights were disappointed. The only bloodshed was that of a man crushed to death by one of the *mikoshi*.[49]

Violence never disappeared from the Sannō festival, but Hie Shrine and the Ōtsu city authorities were keen to advertise the festival in other ways. Early in the twentieth century it was reinvented as an occasion for cherry blossom viewing. This was partly fortuitous since the solar calendar had realigned the festivities with the cherry season; it was partly planned. Ōtsu authorities planted cherries in many public places after the Sino-Japanese war of 1894–5, and in Sakamoto scores of Yoshino cherries were set either side of the Banba promenade. This variety takes just 10 years to mature and transformed the promenade in the first decade of the twentieth century. The press quickly caught on, proposing visitors use the afternoon of April 13 for cherry-viewing and picnics, before the drama of the night-time "*mikoshi* shaking" and the processions the next day.

The shrine and its festival in the twentieth century

The year 1906 was a significant one in the shrine's modern history for another reason. It marked an end to a long period of financial uncertainty. Back in 1887, Home Ministry bureaucrats had come up with a radical plan to reduce the cost of supporting shrines, even though the government now supported only Ise, Yasukuni, and some 140 other major sites. The scheme was called the "shrine preservation fund" (*hozonkin seido*). In the financial crisis of the 1880s, some bureaucrats regarded shrines more as a burden than a blessing. Their plan was to sustain all 140 shrines for a period of 15 years only. The expectation was that shrine priests would invest a portion of their income and survive on the interest, their wits, and, of course, worshipers' contributions. Ise and Yasukuni were exempted, and would be funded in perpetuity (Miyachi 1988: 483). A greatly reduced 1,654 yen per year was set aside annually for Hie under this scheme; chief priest Shōgenji Kitoku was to invest 950 yen, with the remainder covering all the shrine's annual expenses. In 1890, the Home Ministry relieved some of the pressure by announcing funding would continue for an additional 15 years. The emperor had bestowed the

Constitution on his subjects in the previous year in a heady atmosphere of intense ritual activity designed to promote the truth of his mythical origins. It was shrines' essential myth-bearing role that won them a stay of execution. In 1906 the government decided to sponsor the elite shrines ad infinitum, and abandoned the preservation scheme. Japan had fought and won wars against China in the 1890s and most recently against Russia. Victories meant Japan had now emerged as a world power, but the international environment remained menacing, and there were worrying signs too of domestic unrest. The government needed its imperial myth, and the shrines which ensured it resonated across Japan. Indeed, from 1906 the government issued a flurry of regulations directed increasingly now at *all* shrines in the land, relating to ritual performance, offerings, and especially the moral conduct of priests.

Shrines like Hie, however, remained a category apart. This is evident in the realm of patronage. From the 1870s through till 1945, Shiga Prefecture's governor or one of his deputies attended the Sannō festival and all Hie's state rites. Hie was graced with imperial emissaries to commemorate major events like the 1889 Constitution, the funerals of emperors Meiji and Taishō in 1912 and 1926, their successors' enthronements, and the great festivities in 1940 to mark the 2,600th anniversary of Jinmu's accession to the throne. Imperial princes and princesses were also frequent visitors in the 1920s and 1930s and Empress Teimei, Taishō's wife, paid Hie a historic, if fleeting, visit in 1922. The first decades of the twentieth century saw Hie and other shrines acquire a status in national life higher than at any time since the Restoration. In the case of Hie, this coincided with an interesting reappraisal of Hie's modern form. In 1915, in celebration it seems of the Taishō emperor's enthronement, the priests obtained Home Ministry permission and restored the triangular structure to the top of the main *torii* gate. Then in 1928, for reasons that remain frustratingly obscure, the Home Ministry ordered that Hie end its ritual subordination of Ōnamuchi to Ōyamakui.[50] The kami were to be regarded as equal, and their equality was to be manifest in new referents for their shrines: Ōyamakui's shrine was to be known as Nishi Hongū, and Ōnamuchi's as Higashi Hongū, that is the Western and Eastern Main Shrines respectively. An imperial emissary attended the Sannō festival in 1929 to present his own offerings to Ōnamuchi, and thus mark the restoration of that kami's status. If there was after all no status distinction between the two kami, there could no longer be any justification for the reordering of Hie's ritual space which Nishikawa had effected back in the 1870s. In 1942 Ōyamakui and his princess were returned in solemn ceremony to their original sites in the eastern compound; Ōnamuchi too was removed to what was once known as the Ōmiya Shrine.[51] This is the situation that prevails today: Hie is imagined as comprising western and eastern compounds, each dominated by two great kami whose divine virtues are in every measure equal.

Japan endured multiple crises, domestic and foreign, during the first half of the twentieth century, but the Sannō festival was carried out every year even if, sometimes, it was abbreviated. During the China crisis in the late 1930s, for example, and then after the Pacific war began in 1941, the seven *mikoshi* were often substituted with seven *sakaki* branches. In these difficult years the festival was less about betrothal and birth than beseeching all the kami to help "secure success in the Great Asian War and rouse the martial spirit."[52] At the 1943 festival, the grounds of Hie were "swollen with people praying for the destruction of the British and Americans."[53] One striking development of these years was a thawing in the relationship between the shrine priests and the monks of Mount Hiei. In 1937 the monks celebrated the 1,550th anniversary of Saichō's founding of the Enryakuji temple complex. The senior Tendai prelate, a monk called Umetani, descended the mountain and gave thanks to Ōnamuchi after the festival of that year was over. This was an extraordinary moment, the first time in the 70 years since the Restoration that a Buddhist monk had prayed before the Hie kami. In 1938 a party of monks attended the Sannō festival. They received a ritual purification in the Western Main Shrine and made offerings to Ōnamuchi before paying their respects to each of the Hie kami in turn.[54] These developments did not mean a retreat from the "clarification" with which the modern era had begun, but they did mark the establishment of a new "civility" in shrine-temple relations. It is a civility that endures to the present day, for Tendai monks now participate every year in the Sannō festival in April, and they return to the shrine on May 26 to recite the Lotus sutra before the kami Ōnamuchi.

The challenge of the postwar years

The Allied Occupation (1945–52) effected a transformation on shrines in general and the Hie Shrine in particular hardly less drastic than that in 1868. The Occupation dismantled "state Shinto," by which it meant the imperial myth and all the political and social structures sustaining it. Severing the links between the state and Shinto shrines like Hie was essential to this task, and the 1947 Constitution duly accommodated, as we have seen, the principle of separation of state and religion. Like the vast majority of shrines, Hie sought security amid the new uncertainties by signing up to the National Association of Shrines. It did so under the name of Hiyoshi Taisha, Hiyoshi being an alternative reading of the characters "Hie"; Taisha or "great shrine" in deference to its elite status in imperial Japan. NAS was launched by prewar Shinto intellectuals and bureaucrats, precisely to prevent the demise of shrines without which Shinto had no meaning. Hiyoshi has, however, experienced more problems in its relationship with NAS than many other shrines; and the more local problems it has faced with the Sannō festival have made for a difficult postwar.

It was after the Occupation, from the mid 1950s, that the festival began once more to attract crowds in the tens of thousands. The Ōtsu tourist board improved transportation, and of course cherry blossom viewing played its part. Visitors were clearly not deterred by the abbreviated form that the festival perforce adopted. The transport of the *mikoshi* up and down the mountain, the violent rocking of the *mikoshi* on the night of April 13, and the *mikoshi* procession on April 14 were often sacrificed in the early postwar years. But there was always, after all, the colorful flower procession, and the progress of extravagantly clad Tendai monks to Ōnamuchi's shrine. The problem was a shortage of strong, young men. Many had simply left Sakamoto or had found work in office jobs and were not physically up to the task. The shrine's commissioning of seven new lightweight *mikoshi* was part of the solution. The truck was another. In the absence of bodies able and willing, trucks were commandeered to carry the seven *miko-shi* down through Sakamoto to the Lake Biwa. The situation has also been ameliorated by the full participation of all Sakamoto's communities in all aspects of the postwar festival. Hiyoshi has had to cope with another, entirely different, problem in the post-war period, however. It concerned issues of authority.

The *Sankei* newspaper reported on December 4, 1987 that Hiyoshi Taisha had "filed for divorce" and was planning to desert NAS. As it turned out, NAS flexed its considerable muscle and blocked divorce proceedings. Hiyoshi remains to this day a paid-up member, but the dispute is revealing of the fractious, and far from uniform, world of postwar Shinto. The problem had distant origins in the 1950s with a personality clash between the chief priest, Munemiya, and his assistant, Sugimura; Sugimura eventu-ally yielded to NAS pressure and resigned. When Munemiya himself retired in 1978, Hiyoshi's shrine committee (*yakuin kaigi*) proposed that Sugimura be invited back as his replacement. NAS thought better of it, and appointed a certain Takenami; it then sent in another man by the name of Murata as his number two. These two men detested one another, largely it seems because they had graduated from rival Shinto universities.[55] In 1987 the shrine committee forced both to resign, and NAS agreed Sugimura might now finally return to Hiyoshi, but only as a stop-gap replacement. Sugimura duly arrived in August, livid at the treat-ment Murata had received; bitter too that, notwithstanding the Hiyoshi committee's recommendation, his appointment was stop-gap. After several months of discussions, Sugimura persuaded the committee that Hiyoshi Taisha's future lay outside NAS. In November 1987 he notified NAS of his intention to "file for divorce," and in February the following year he submitted the requisite paperwork to Shiga Prefecture.[56] What blocked the "divorce" was not the prefecture, but NAS's swift dispatch of a replacement for Sugimura, as well as a campaign by Hiyoshi parishioners. It is not clear who was behind the petition that gathered 4,000 names, or what really was at stake. There was mischief-making, though, as petitioners accused Sugimura of destroying hundreds of trees in protected woodland. They also accused him, quite without foundation, of discriminating against Hagiyama villagers. Sugimura was dismissed amid much rancor, but this was not the end of the matter. Seven priests resigned in protest in 1989 at further NAS interference in shrine personnel matters. In the 1990s, tensions of a quite different sort surfaced when a junior priest set upon the chief priest with a metal pipe. At the start of the twenty-first century, harmony has been restored to the shrine and the shrine's relationship to NAS, or so it seems.

What, then, does the future hold for the great Hiyoshi Shrine and its festival? The financial challenge is undoubtedly the greatest, but at present that challenge is being met. The shrine receives government support for the upkeep of a number of its structures owing to their "cultural status"; for the rest it relies on worshipers' donations and income from rites performed. The main sanctuaries of the Western and Eastern Main Shrines are both designated *kokuhō* or "national treasures." There are 17 other wooden structures on the site recognized by the government as "important cultural properties" (*jūyō bunkazai*); in addition, three stone bridges and seven *mikoshi* palanquins are so recognized. The government covers around 60 percent of the costs for repairs for these treasures; Shiga Prefecture and Ōtsu city between them cover another 25 percent, leaving the remainder to be met by the shrine. In the immediate postwar period, the shrine established a society for fundraising and, at the same time, started charging visitors a modest entrance fee, which today stands at 300 yen. According to shrine priests, these initiatives enjoyed only limited success, and it was only the launch of a new campaign in the 1990s that made major repairs viable. The greatest outlay is for rethatching the seven shrines with cypress bark, and the initiative involved visitors "sponsoring" strips of cypress bark at 2,000 yen a time, in return for an honorable mention in the Hiyoshi Taisha newsletter.

Worshipers' contributions are needed also to maintain 400,000 square meters of land, much of it woodland, and to pay the wages of nine shrine priests. Priests themselves play a vital role in generating income, of course, through their performance of specially commissioned rites for a range of "this-worldly benefits." For example, the supplicant requesting prayers and offerings to be made to the kami Ōnamuchi for the bestowal of three such "benefits" – family health, safe birth and exam success, say – will pay 30,000 yen.[57] Fees for Shinto wedding rites start at 50,000 yen while ground-breaking rites and assorted purifications can be as much as 70,000 yen a time. Many of the larger, more famous shrines in Japan earn sufficient income at New Year to survive the year ahead, but Hiyoshi Shrine is not one of these. In 2008, it was visited by 103,000 people over the New Year period, an increase of 7,000 on numbers from the previous year, to be sure, but a better comparison might be with the nearby Taga Shrine. This less famous but more accessible shrine was visited by more than 400,000 in the same period.[58] Finally, it is important to understand that Hiyoshi Shrine receives no financial support at all from NAS; quite the contrary – it is shrines like Hiyoshi that keep NAS afloat. An annual (undisclosed) membership fee is payable to NAS, and the association also requires Hiyoshi to raise further funds by selling amulets from the Ise Shrine. This is a fraught matter to which we shall return in Chapter 6. The financial burden of the Sannō festival does not, incidentally, fall on the shrine itself. It is organized by a special festival committee, and funded by local business and the municipal authorities, although shrine priests do play a part in soliciting festival funds through their shrine worshipers' network, and from businesses near and far. At the start of the twenty-first century, it seems safe to assume that Hiyoshi Taisha, while hardly wealthy, will remain viable, and that the festival which draws thousands to the shrine every year from across central Japan will continue to thrive.

Chapter 4

The History of a Myth
The Sun-Goddess and the Rock-Cave

One of the central episodes in the court histories on the Age of the Gods recounts how the sun-goddess, Amaterasu, was harassed by her brother, Susanowo, to the extent that she retired into a cave, plunging the world into darkness. In *Kojiki* the tale runs as follows:

> When Amaterasu was in the sacred weaving hall weaving divine garments, [Susanowo] made a hole in the roof and threw a heavenly piebald horse that he had flayed backwards into the hall. The heavenly weaving maiden was shaken, pierced her genitals with her weaving shuttle, and died.
>
> Amaterasu was frightened by this sight, opened the Rock-cave of Heaven, and confined herself in it. The whole of the Plain of High Heaven became dark, and all of the Central Land of Reed Plains was dark too. Because of this, eternal night reigned. The voices of the myriad kami filled [the air] like summer flies, and a myriad evils arose.
>
> Therefore, the eight hundred myriad kami gathered on the bank of the Peaceful River of Heaven in a divine gathering. Takami-musubi's son Omoikane was ordered to devise a plan. The long-crying birds of Tokoyo were gathered and ordered to cry. [The kami] collected heavenly rocks from the upper reaches of the Peaceful River of Heaven and iron from the Iron Mountain of Heaven, and sent for the smith Ama-tsu-Mara. They charged Ishikoridome with making a mirror and Tama-no-Ya with making five hundred [strings of] shining curved beads, eight *saka* [c. 96 cm]

in length. They summoned Ame-no-Koyane and Futodama, drew a shoulder bone from a great stag of Mount Ame-no-Kaguyama, gathered heavenly *hahaka* wood from Mount Ame-no-Kaguyama, and made them perform divination [by reading the cracks that appeared in the shoulder bone when it was burnt in the *hahaka* fire]. They dug up a *sakaki* tree with five hundred [branches] on Mount Ame-no-Kaguyama, attached the five hundred [strings of] shining curved beads to its upper branches, hung the mirror of eight *ata* [c. 96 cm] on its middle branches, and let white and blue cloth trail from its lower branches. Futodama held up these goods as splendid offerings, Ame-no-Koyane pronounced splendid words of praise, and Ame-no-Tajikarawo stood hidden next to the cave.

Ame-no-Uzume tied up her sleeves with heavenly *hikage* vines from Mount Ame-no-Kaguyama, wore heavenly *masaki* vines [in her hair], and held heavenly *sasa* leaves in her hands. By the Heavenly Rock-cave they overturned a tub, and she made it thunder by stamping on it. She became kami-possessed, pulled out the nipples of her breasts and pushed her skirtstring down to her genitals. Then the Plain of High Heaven shook, and all the eight hundred myriad kami laughed together.

Amaterasu was startled, and slightly opening the door of the Heavenly Rock-cave she asked from within: "Because I have hidden myself, the Plain of Heaven must be dark, and the Central Land of Reed Plains likewise. Why then is Ame-no-Uzume dancing, and why do all the eight hundred myriad kami laugh?" Ame-no-Uzume replied: "We rejoice, laugh and dance because there is a kami superior to you." While she said this, Ame-no-Koyane and Futodama held up the mirror and showed it to Amaterasu. [Seeing her own reflection in the mirror,] Amaterasu was even more startled. When she leaned out of the cave to look at it, Ame-no-Tajikarawo, who stood hidden, took her arm and drew her out. At the same time, Futodama pulled a *shirikume* rope behind her and said: "You cannot cross this [rope] and go back inside." When Amaterasu appeared, the High Plain of Heaven and the Central Land of Reed Plains became light once more.[1]

This tale is representative of the heady mix of sex and violence that pervades kami myth and ritual. Also, it has a complicated but quite well-understood history, and a rich afterlife in both premodern and modern Japan. An analysis of this tale and its trajectory through history will illustrate many aspects of the formation, usages, and transformations of kami myth.

Origins

Kojiki and *Nihon shoki* tell about ancient gods and heroes in solemn, poetic language. The genre is instantly recognizable from other cultures across the globe, and few have hesitated to call these books works of myth. But what does that mean? What defines tales like the rock-cave legend as myths, and what happens to our reading of them when we approach them from that perspective?

There are countless definitions of myth, ranging from "simple lies" to "psychological prototypes," and many do not apply here. Taking inspiration from Bruce Lincoln (1999), we will focus on one universal feature of myth that is equally characteristic of the Japanese case: myths tell us about the origins of things in a distant past, a time that was in some way more "true" than our own. Myths answer the question of how things came to be the way they are today, and seek to establish once and for all that this is how they should be. As is clear from *Kojiki* and *Nihon shoki*, in which the "Age of the Gods" fades seamlessly into the "Age of Man," this focus on the past makes myths overlap with history; but there is also a difference between them. History is a narrative form that relativizes the present by showing that things were different before. Myths, however, present the order of things as absolute and unchangeable, hallowed by that order's origin in a divine age.

When we approach myth from this perspective, mythology appears as a dynamic process. "Myth" is not a closed corpus of tales from a distant age before history; rather, mythmaking is a continuous practice that occurs at all times. Myths consistently present themselves as tales without an author, thus creating the illusion that they belong to a special dimension, as tales told by a divine voice – or, in a more modern view, by humanity's collective subconscious. This is an effect of the particular rhetoric of myth, a device to establish lasting authority by transcending the historical context in which the myths are produced and reproduced. Rather than slipping into the myths' own rhetoric, however, we will here attempt to read the tale of the rock-cave as an example of what Lincoln calls "ideology in narrative form": as an attempt (or, more accurately, a long series of attempts) at creating authority by means of origination legends.

At first sight, the myth of the heavenly rock-cave looks like a straightforward "nature myth" in the sense that term was employed by Max Müller, the nineteenth-century philologist who argued that all myths are in essence prescientific attempts at explaining natural phenomena. If we take such a perspective, the myth of the rock-cave can be readily understood as an explanation of sun eclipses, or of the sun's decline in autumn and "rebirth" after the winter solstice. Indeed, this is a very widespread mythological theme right across the northern hemisphere, and as we shall see below, such a reading is confirmed by the fact that this myth was closely connected with rituals that were performed on the very day of the winter solstice.[2] There is no doubt that the rock-cave myth can indeed be read as an explanation for the sun's weakening, as a recipe for reviving the sun, and as a guarantee for the success of such a procedure. Yet there is much more to this story than a "primitive" explanation of a natural phenomenon. First of all, such a simple view ignores the myth's political and ideological aspects. Amaterasu is not only the sun-goddess but also the imperial ancestor, and the plot of this story sends the message that, without her, the world will simply stop functioning. It will soon become clear that the myth as it appears in *Kojiki* was a thoroughly historical product, shaped by political and social changes in a very specific context. If we explain the rock-cave tale as an ancient nature myth in a structuralist, static manner, the particular dynamics behind its composition become invisible.

Moreover, it is worth noting that Amaterasu is presented not only as the sun-deity but also as a weaver. This opens up a very different interpretation of the myth's background and meaning. Michael Como has pointed out that there are striking structural resemblances between Chinese legends about the origins of sericulture on the one hand, and the tale of the rock-cave on the other.[3] In Como's reading, the rock-cave tale describes how the weaving maiden Amaterasu died and entered a confined space similar to a cocoon, only to re-emerge in great splendor after a dangerous incubation period. This mirrors the life of the silkworm, known in China as the miraculous "insect of three transformations." In fact, in another context *Nihon shoki* describes how "the way of raising silkworms began" when Amaterasu "put cocoons into her mouth and drew thread from them" (Aston 1972: I, 33). Como shows that immigrant groups of weavers from the continent conducted silkworm cults at shrines dedicated to a sun deity called Amateru or Amaterasu at various places in Japan. This suggests that sericulture and weaving were, at least at an early stage, at the very core of the rock-cave myth.

In the larger narrative of the Age of the Gods in *Kojiki* and *Nihon shoki*, however, this connection with sericulture was no longer functional. Rather, the episode of the rock-cave was carefully dovetailed into another central episode, namely the descent of the heavenly grandson, Ninigi, from the Plain of High Heaven to the Central Land of Reed Plains (that is, Japan). On this journey, Ninigi was accompanied by many of the deities that also figure in the tale of the rock-cave. Ame-no-Koyane, Futodama, Ame-no-Uzume, Ishikoridome, and Tama-no-Ya joined Ninigi as heads of occupational groups (*tomo*), serving him by performing specific tasks that were all related to ritual. In the story of the descent from heaven, they are explicitly identified as ancestors of the main priestly lineages at the court. As Table 3 shows, the priestly tasks that these lineages performed at the court coincided with the roles played by their ancestors in front of the rock-cave. Even Omoikane and Tajikarawo are mentioned among Ninigi's

Table 3 Priestly lineages

Deity	Lineage	Ritual function
Ame-no-Koyane	Nakatomi	Officiating priests (recitations)
Futodama	Inbe	Officiating priests (offerings)
Ame-no-Uzume	Sarume	Dancers
Ishikoridome	Kagamitsukuri	Mirrormakers
Tama-no-Ya	Tama-no-Ya	Beadmakers

entourage, leaving little doubt that the two episodes of the rock-cave and the descent from heaven were designed to correspond. Together, they explain not only how the imperial line was established, but also how the priestly lineages of the court attained their present positions. Like the emperors themselves the court priests claimed heavenly descent, and in the rituals they represented the heavenly gods as their direct descendants. Rituals worked not only because they followed the right procedure, established in heaven, but also because they were performed by the right persons, authorized by their roots in that same heaven. Both episodes, then, can be read as origination legends of the imperial line and its priests. The tale of the rock-cave is not only about the seasonal return of the sun, or even about silk; more importantly, it staged the emperor as Amaterasu's representative on earth.

What does this reveal about the historical context in which this myth was composed? A closer analysis of the sources suggests that Amaterasu's rise to prominence as the main ancestor of the imperial line was a rather late development. Even in court mytho-history, her status is somewhat ambiguous. Here, *Nihon shoki* is an important source because it contains different versions listed below a "main version," thus opening up the possibility of comparison. In some of these other versions of the episodes of the rock-cave and the descent from heaven, Amaterasu is not mentioned by name or else plays a subordinate role. In these variants, the main deity of the rock-cave episode is simply called the "sun deity," and it is not Amaterasu but Takami-musubi (Omoikane's father in the rock-cave myth) who orders the descent from heaven. The sudden rise to prominence of Amaterasu in *Kojiki* is one of the main differences between this text and the slightly later *Nihon shoki*.

This emphasis on Amaterasu is often seen as a direct reflection of the beliefs and preferences of Emperor Tenmu, who ordered the compilation of the *Kojiki*. Tenmu came to power by way of a coup, known as the Jinshin war (672), in which he took over the throne from his late brother by deposing his young nephew. We have already seen that these events had a great impact on the Hie Shrines; the same was true of Amaterasu's shrine at Ise. Ise is located some 100 kilometers east of the Yamato plain, near the shore of Ise Bay, and served both as the closest harbor with access to eastern Japan and as a source of sea products. While Ise had also been a major recipient of Yamato worship even before Tenmu, it experienced a leap in status when Tenmu came to power. Tenmu appears to have attributed his victory in the Jinshin war to Amaterasu's support, and he developed a personal relationship with this deity that found expression both in the court's treatment of Ise itself and in Amaterasu's standing in the *Kojiki*, which was commissioned by Tenmu soon after his victory.

The *Kojiki*'s account of the myth of the rock-cave reflects these circumstances by incorporating a number of Ise elements (Miyake 1984: 74–112). Not only Amaterasu, but also Ame-no-Uzume, Omoikane, and Tajikarawo are deities with roots in Ise. Other elements in the myth can be traced to Ise too. The "long-crying birds of Tokoyo" reflect an Ise rite in which a priest makes a crowing noise "like a rooster" before entering the shrine; and according to the *Nihon shoki*, Amaterasu praised Ise as "a land washed by the waves of Tokoyo."[4] It is striking that while all of these Ise elements are echoed in the "main version" of the *Nihon shoki*, they are absent from the second and third versions recorded there. These are the versions that do not name Amaterasu, which suggests that these elements were added to an older tale in Tenmu's time, when Ise priests gained a foothold at court.

This in turn raises the question what the original context of these elements may have been in Ise. The key to an answer is hidden in Ame-no-Uzume's provocative dance in front of the rock-cave. In the episode of the descent from heaven, Ame-no-Uzume behaves in a very similar way. A version of the tale in *Nihon shoki* relates how one of the gods who had been sent in advance to clear the way for Ninigi's descent turned back and reported:

> "There is a god who dwells at the eightfold crossroads of heaven, whose nose is seven hands long and who is more than seven fathoms tall. Moreover, a light shines from his mouth and his posterior. His eyeballs are like an eight-hand mirror and have a ruddy glow like lampion flowers." […]

[Ninigi] commanded Ame-no-Uzume, saying: "You are superior to others in the power of your looks. You must go and question him." So Ame-no-Uzume forthwith bared her breasts and, pushing down the band of her skirt below her navel, confronted him with a mocking laugh. Then the god of the crossroads asked her: "Ame-no-Uzume! What do you mean by this behavior?"[5]

It turns out that this deity of the crossroads is called Saruta-hiko, and he has come to meet Ninigi and his entourage. After accompanying Ninigi to earth, he settles together with Ame-no-Uzume on "the upper reaches of the river Isuzu" in Ise. The shrine, called Saruta-hiko Jinja, still thrives today and is located a short walk from Amaterasu's Inner Shrine.

In both these myths, Ame-no-Uzume emerges as the deity of a lineage of female priests called the Sarume. The Sarume addressed their worship to the shining, dawn-like Saruta-hiko; or to the "sun-deity"; or to Amaterasu, depending on which version of the myths we prefer. Saruta-hiko appears to be Ame-no-Uzume's closest associate, both in the myths and in the geography of Ise, so perhaps he was the original object of Sarume worship before this lineage was incorporated into Tenmu's sun cult. Our quotation from *Nihon shoki* presents Saruta-hiko as a luminous solar deity, but he also has markedly phallic features. His long nose is one such trait; also, Saruta-hiko has been closely associated with phallic markers (called *dōsojin*) placed at crossroads. In fact, Ame-no-Uzume's sexual dance makes more sense when it is addressed to Saruta-hiko than it does in the rock-cave tale. Like Ame-no-Uzume, Saruta-hiko is a deity of sex and fertility, and his appeasement in midwinter may well have been a local rite to secure renewed fecundity in the coming spring season. The combination of the phallic Saruta-hiko and Ame-no-Uzume's exposure of her breasts and genitals makes for a striking fertility ritual. In the rock-cave myth, the only function of Ame-no-Uzume's sexual titillation is to evoke laughter and thus make Amaterasu curious enough to open the cave door.

With Ise's rise to prominence at Tenmu's court, the Sarume found a place in court ritual. The many Ise elements in the episodes of both the rock-cave and the descent from heaven can be explained as a result of the incorporation of Sarume legends into court myth. This becomes very visible in a court ritual that is closely related to the rock-cave myth, called *chinkonsai* in Sino-Japanese or *mitama-shizume* in Japanese, both meaning the "settling of the spirit."

Chinkonsai was performed every year at the winter solstice, one day before the rite of offering the first fruits (*niiname*, or, in case of a new emperor, *ōname* or *daijōsai*). Occasionally it was also performed at other times, notably when the emperor was ill, to strengthen his spirit. The oldest sources on this ritual date from the ninth century, so it is only partly possible to reconstruct its original form. *Chinkonsai* took place at the worship hall of the Council of Kami Affairs or, from the late Heian period onwards, in a tent pitched at the site of what had been that Council's building. Here, court priestesses called *mikannagi* performed a dance in which an overturned tub was struck with a *sakaki* stick decorated with bells. Music was played on *koto* zithers and flutes, and songs were intoned in praise of various objects held by the dancers to attract the deities (a sword, a bow and arrows, the stick, *kazura* vines). The last two of these songs announce the "revival" (*tama-agari, tama-kaeshi*) of the spirit of a deity called Toyo-hirume, the "Fertile Sun-Goddess." Meanwhile, a court lady would shake a chest containing a set of the emperor's clothes, while the head of the Council of Kami Affairs made knots in short threads of flax kept in another chest. The dancing, shaking, and tying of knots all served as rites of reviving and stabilizing the spirit of both the sun and the emperor, who in this ritual merged into one. The proceedings continued with a number of other dances, including one performed by Sarume maidens. They also included an offering of food to the revived spirit of the sun/emperor, and ended with a communal meal (Matsumae 1974: ch. 3).

It is not difficult to recognize the rock-cave myth in these procedures. By the ninth century the Sarume had receded into the background, but the reference to Ame-no-Uzume's dance is still obvious. The *chinkonsai* combined a number of rites that shared the same aim of strengthening the spirit of the sun/emperor and preventing it from wandering. Matsumae Takeshi, a scholar of Japanese mythology, has proposed that these different rites can be traced to different lineages: the tying of knots to an ancient tradition of the Yamato royal line itself; the shaking and the sword to the Mononobe from the Isonokami Shrine near Miwa; and the striking of the tub to the Sarume from Ise (Matsumae 1974: 137–8). The Sarume rite would have been the most recent of these, added after Ise eclipsed the older Isonokami and Miwa shrines in Tenmu's time. Matsumae's reading suggests that the rock-cave myth and its corresponding ritual, *chinkonsai*, were of special importance to Tenmu because they underscored the unity of the emperor and the sun.

Others, however, have interpreted the *chinkonsai* and its relationship with the rock-cave in a very different manner. Herman Ooms (2008: ch. 7) argues that Tenmu's performance of the *chinkonsai* in 685 was not only the first *recorded* instance of the rite, but its first performance full stop. Ooms maintains that the rite actually performed for Tenmu was very different from the *chinkonsai* as it was recorded in the ninth century. Rather than assuming that Tenmu's rite drew on the myth of Amaterasu's emergence from the rock-cave, Ooms argues that it was a purely Daoist procedure introduced by a Korean priest conversant in Chinese medicine, at a time when Tenmu was dangerously ill.[6] Only in the course of the eighth century, Ooms proposes, when priestly lineages such as the Mononobe and the Sarume were being sidelined at the court by the Nakatomi, did these lineages relate the Daoist rite of *chinkonsai* to the rock-cave myth, in which their divine ancestors played a prominent role, in an attempt to claim ownership over this ritual and thus strengthen their position within the palace.

With the limited sources that are available, it remains impossible to decide whether the *chinkonsai* was a Daoist ritual reinterpreted in terms of the rock-cave myth or an older ritual that is reflected in that myth. Either way, however, the tale of the rock-cave is a perfect illustration of the dynamics of mythmaking in ancient Yamato. Beneath the surface of this apparently simple tale there are many layers of different origins. These layers are traces of power struggles between lineages from various parts of Yamato's inner sphere. At the court, these various elements were woven into a single narrative with one dominant theme (imperial power), updated time and again on the basis of recent political developments. While we tend to think of mythology as a timeless reflection of primeval truths, the Yamato myths derived their significance from their ability to stay in tune with their own time. As soon as they lost their ability to adapt to the circumstances, they also lost much of their authority. Yet there would be other uses for the myth of the rock-cave, and it was not allowed to lie dormant for long.

The Rediscovery of Court Myth

We have seen that the tale of the rock-cave revealed the sacred origins of the court cult of Amaterasu, of its priests, and of the *chinkonsai* ceremony. Of course, that is not all. For example, this myth also relates the divine origin of mirrors as ritual objects. In particular, it introduces one very special mirror: the mirror that was cast by Ishikoridome and that was used to lure Amaterasu out of the cave. This mirror reappears in the tale of the descent from heaven; Amaterasu hands the same mirror to Ninigi with the words: "Have it with you as my spirit, and worship it just as you would worship in my very presence" (Philippi 1969: 140). Through developments that we will not pursue here, this mirror was said to have ended up in Ise already in ancient times. However, in the tenth century the same mirror suddenly appeared in the imperial palace as well, where it came to serve the focus of new imperial rituals (Saitō 1996: ch. 5).

The appearance of Amaterasu in the palace in the tenth century marked the beginning of a renewed interest in kami myth and ritual at the court. By this time, as we have seen in Chapter 2, the *jingi* cult was fading rapidly. The emperor tended to be viewed in Chinese terms, as a Confucian monarch whose rule was in harmony with Yin and Yang and the principles of heaven. The ritual calendar was dominated by Buddhist ceremonies, including ceremonies for the kami. Why, then, this sudden interest in Amaterasu? It was not due to a revival of "Shinto"; rather, it reflected developments in the position of the emperor and his court within the political system.

By this time, the public bureaucracy of the so-called *ritsuryō* legal system first introduced around Tenmu's time had stalled. In practice, the state was now run from the private headquarters of the Fujiwara nobles, competing, later in the eleventh century, with private quarters run by the retired emperor as the head of the imperial house. As the old legal basis of court rule withered away, private rituals addressing the ancestral deities of ruling line-ages gained new importance. Among these were rituals address-ing the ancestor of the imperial line, Amaterasu. When court ladies (*naishi*) discovered Ishikoridome's mirror in a "sacred chest" in a palace storehouse in 938, quite out of the blue, this was most opportune: it once more gave that divine ancestor a concrete pres-ence within the palace. Gradually, this mirror grew into the most sacred imperial treasure kept at the court. Emperor Go-Ichijō (r. 1016–36), for example, "secretly visited the mirror every night."[7]

Still, another century would pass before the court again cast its eyes on the classical works of court myth. Myths cannot make themselves relevant if they are mere tales of a distant past. It is only when they are actively applied in creative processes that they generate interest. In spite of the reappearance of Amaterasu in the palace, *Kojiki* and *Nihon shoki* were not on the reading lists of even the most scholarly nobles in the eleventh century.[8] From the twelfth century onwards, however, the mythical texts quite suddenly resurface in the form of quotations and references – not in works of history or politics, but, perhaps surprisingly, in trea-tises on Japanese poetics. In early medieval Japan, poetry was to become the main arena in which myth found a new function.

Again, this new development was closely related to the politi-cal situation at the time. In the twelfth century court hegemony was undermined by the emergence of warrior groups. Towards the end of that century, central rule disintegrated and the country was ravaged by war. Order could only be restored by incorporat-ing warrior elites into the political system and by recognizing their claims to influence. Thus, the first shogunate was estab-lished in Kamakura (1185), and in the course of the thirteenth century the balance of power shifted away from the court. These developments dealt a decisive blow to the classical *ritsuryō* state and marked the beginning of what is conventionally known as the medieval period. In this new age, the classical drift towards centralization that had produced the myths in the first place was increasingly undercut by political and economic fragmentation. The court had to share its power and its control over economic resources with the new warrior government. Also, increased production and trade, which flourished beyond the reach of the established elites, made it possible for new actors to gain some autonomy. As we have seen in the case of Hie, temples and shrines were among the greatest beneficiaries of this trend.

For the old elites, these changes meant that new forms of authority had to be created and maintained. The ancient myths, which had seemed less important after Buddhism sidelined the *jingi* cult in the ninth century, now regained their attraction as a source of cultural capital for the court. Even more typical of the medieval period, however, was the dispersal of classical court symbolism into the periphery. The ancient imperial myths found new audiences, who used them to add luster and give legitimacy to a wide range of activities. In the process the myths merged with the Buddhist-dominated culture of medieval Japan, and as a result they changed almost beyond recognition.

The Way of Poetry

One important source of cultural capital for court nobles was Japanese poetry. Composing and exchanging poetry was an integral part of cultural life among courtiers, warriors, and clerics, and it was generally regarded as an area in which the court had supreme expertise. Moreover, the composition of *waka* poetry was perhaps the only cultural activity of high prestige that turned people's eyes away from the Asian continent, towards Japan's ancient roots in an age when the land was populated by kami. The first and most renowned of all imperial collections of poetry, the *Kokinshū* (Collection of *waka*, old and new; 905), celebrated Japanese verse as an art that was begun by the kami at the time when heaven and earth were first separated from each other. In *waka* verse, and even in the prose of one of the *Kokinshū* prefaces, a strict distinction was made between Japanese and Chinese vocabulary, and the countless Chinese loanwords that had become part of the language were systematically shunned by poets.[9] Thus, *waka* poetics naturally developed into a nativist discourse that stressed the inherent value of things Japanese and that sought to explain the qualities of Japanese poetry in terms of its divine origins. It was in this context that the ancient records of Japanese mytho-history, which at this time were referred to collectively as *Nihongi*, caught the eye once more.

Towards the end of the thirteenth century, *waka* poetics was institutionalized along the lines of Buddhist Dharma lineages. In the Buddhist world (especially in the more esoteric schools), teachings and ritual procedures were transmitted to novices in the form of initiation ceremonies called *kanjō* ("head-sprinkling rites"); now, similar ceremonies were also designed to transmit poetic expertise in closed lineages. These ceremonies were strikingly religious in character. Ultimately, they were based on the idea that the "way of poetry," like Buddhist practice, is a method to access the enlightened realm of the buddhas. Thus, *waka kanjō* initiations made use of poetic mantras and mandalas, and bestowed upon initiates both secret teachings and initiation documents that gave details of an unbroken transmission with sacred roots (Klein 2002).

Competition between different lineages created a need for new insights into the sacred origins of *waka*. The tale of the rock-cave was one of the myths that was adapted to serve this new purpose. A fascinating example of the rewriting of myth in this new context can be found in a commentary on the *Kokinshū* preface by the poet and commentator Fujiwara-no-Tameaki (1230s–90s), labeled by modern scholars as *Kokin wakashū jo kikigaki sanryūshō* (Lectures on the introduction to the *Kokinshū*, with a summary of three lineages; 1287?):

> When Amaterasu ruled the land, Susanowo, the evil deity Matarajin, and a thousand other evil deities built a stronghold in Udano in Yamato. They set one thousand eight-toothed swords in the ground and gathered an army. In her great compassion, Amaterasu realized that many deities would die if it came to war, and seeing no other solution, she called together the moon-deity, Tajikarawo, Ikinaga-tarachishi and Akatamayuri-hime, as well as the eight hundred

myriad deities, and led them into the heavenly rock-cave on Mount Katsuragi in Yamato. Because of this, the land was plunged into darkness for six years. The moon-deity's son, Onemi, was not included in Amaterasu's following and was left in the dark. He gathered the deities who longed after Amaterasu on Ame-no-Kaguyama. They built a fire and cast an image of Amaterasu. Their first attempt failed; this is the sun-deity of the *naishidokoro* at court [that is, the mirror discovered by the *naishi* court ladies in 938]. [...]

They hung the mirror from a *sakaki* branch and the gods performed songs and dances. This is what we call *saibara* today.[10] Their voices could be heard faintly in the rock-cave. The sun-deity wondered whether there were deities who longed for her and ordered Tajikarawo to open the cave. Then the sun-deity peeked out of the rock-cave. In the bright light emanating from her face, she appeared white, and [the gods] exclaimed: *Ana omo-shiro ya* ("Ah! A white face!"; or, "Ah! How fascinating!"). Since this time, striking things have been called *omo-shiro ya*.

The sun-deity left the rock-cave and appeared on Mount Kaguyama. It was at this time that the land was first opened up and became bright, and this is called the beginning of heaven and earth. Amaterasu noticed a warbler that landed in a plum tree and said:

Aoyagi no ito / uchinobete / uguisu no nuu / chō kasa wa / ume no hanagasa
The hood that the warbler weaves of fresh willow twigs –
it looks like those hoods called plum blossoms[11]

The meaning is that the plum flower that fell on the head of the warbler looked like a hood. This was the first *waka* of thirty-one syllables. (Katagiri 1971–87: vol. 2, 235–6)

Much could be said about the details of this radically reworked version of the rock-cave myth; but space does not permit that here. What strikes one first of all is Tameaki's boldness in rewriting the myth. Tameaki is merciless when it comes to discarding elements of the myth that are irrelevant to his own ends. There is no longer any trace of the deities who lured Amaterasu out of the rock-cave and who later accompanied Ninigi to earth as ancestors of the court's priestly lineages; they did not interest him. Only the general plot of Amaterasu retreating into the cave and emerging again is retained and filled out with a wealth of new details.

In spite of the rewriting, though, there is no doubt that Tameaki's version, too, is an origination myth of great power; perhaps even more so than its classical original. In Tameaki's commentary, the rock-cave figures as the site of the initial "opening" of the world after a standoff between good and evil deities. Further on in the same commentary, the cave even becomes the site of the first act of procreation. We are told that while the gods were locked into the cave, Ikinaga-tarachishi "wed" Akatamayuri-hime there. In Tameaki's account, these two kami, who do not figure in *Kojiki* or *Nihon shoki*, effectively take on the roles performed by Izanagi and Izanami in the classical myths. The main point, however, is that these two cosmic events both culminated in the composition of the first, foundational *waka* poems. Amaterasu was met with the seven-syllable phrase *ana omo-shiro ya*, and she celebrated the "beginning of heaven and earth" by creating the first ever 31-syllable verse. In the subplot of Ikinaga-tarachishi and Akatamayuri-hime we are told that the latter's brother became jealous of her husband and created the second 31-syllable *waka*; fittingly, it spoke of unrequited love.

Major themes in medieval *waka* poetics are echoed in this new rock-cave myth. *Waka* transmissions elaborated on the religious meaning of love and sex as a sacred union of Yin/female and Yang/male, and as the source of all life. They were inspired by markedly Tantric forms of Buddhism and linked the carnal way of sex celebrated in love poetry to Buddhist teachings about the nonduality of desire and enlightenment. This deep insight was then expressed in the form of *waka*, sacred words imbued with the power of the Dharma that corresponded directly to the *dhāraṇī* spells of India. In a sense, it was the *waka* pronounced in the rock-cave that created the world. The new version of the rock-cave myth, then, initiated budding poets into the secret of the cosmogony itself, and taught them that the world arose from *waka*, the sacred words of the kami.

Buddhist Readings and Ritualizations: The Way of the Gods

Once the classical myths had made a comeback in the cultural life of the capital, it did not take long for them to spread to other spheres of intellectual activity. The temple-shrine complexes around Kyoto were among the first to catch on to the new trend. Already in the eleventh century, not long after Amaterasu had reappeared in the palace, scholar-monks who performed Buddhist services for the emperor began to develop ways to incorporate Amaterasu in their teachings. A well-known early example is Seison (1012–74), a Shingon prelate much favored by the court, who launched the idea that the World-Buddha Dainichi (Mahāvairocana) appeared in Japan in the guise of Amaterasu, and that this is why Japan is known as the "original land of Dainichi" (Dainipponkoku).[12] It was only in the thirteenth century, however, that kami myth suddenly became a major theme of Buddhist lore. We have just seen that the "way of poetry" (kadō) developed into a form of Buddhist practice in that century; the notion that there was a distinct "way of the kami" (jindō, Shinto) that could open up the realm of Buddhist enlightenment arose at the same time. In fact, the kadō and jindō discourses developed in tandem and borrowed from each other to such a degree that it is difficult, and perhaps pointless, to distinguish between them.

Several sites emerged as centers where Buddhist texts on the kami were produced. Ise was among the first; another was Hie. As we have already seen, a group of Hie monks called "record-keepers" (kike) specialized in collecting and transmitting knowledge about the kami of Mount Hiei, and they spun a web of associations around these deities that ultimately hinged on the identification of Hie's "Mountain King" (Sannō) with Amaterasu. Naturally, this also drew their interest to the rock-cave myth. In Keiran shūyōshū (1348), the recordkeeper Kōshū recounted this tale in a version much closer to Kojiki and Nihon shoki than Tameaki's, and added an explanation of its Buddhist meaning.

In Kōshū's view, the tale of the rock-cave was a Japanese equivalent of the foundation legend of esoteric Buddhism itself: the myth of the Iron Stupa. This legend tells of a closed stupa in southern India. Eight hundred years after the Buddha's death, the bodhisattva Nāgārjuna gained the mantra of Mahāvairocana in meditation. After reciting it in front of this impregnable stupa for seven days, he finally succeeded in opening its gates. As soon as he had entered the stupa the gates closed, and Nāgārjuna spent many days inside it. Here he received the teachings of the esoteric sutras from the bodhisattva Vajrasattva, who had deposited Mahāvairocana's teachings in this stupa until the time when the world would be ready for them. When Nāgārjuna finally emerged from the stupa it marked the beginning of the transmission of the esoteric sutras in the world.

Drawing on this famous Buddhist legend, Kōshū explained the deeper meaning of the rock-cave myth as follows:

> When we relate this [tale of the rock-cave] to the Dharma, [we see that] Amaterasu is the Dharma-body that is our own nature, or the King of Dharma-nature. Susanowo is ignorance, or Devadatta.[13] The Iron Stupa is the stupa of the Dharma-realm. Retiring into the rock-cave and closing it means that ignorance follows Dharma-nature; opening the stupa means that Dharma-nature follows ignorance. The two kami [Omoikane and Tajikarawo] who open the cave are the two methods of *samādhi* and *prajñā*[14] – think of the sutra that reads: "The power of *samādhi* and *prajñā* is magnificent; with their power the sentient beings can be saved." Lighting a bonfire [in front of the cave][15] is the teaching of the various skilful means. The eight myriad kami [who gathered in front of the cave] are the eight myriad sacred scriptures. Ultimately, the retreat into the rock-cave stands for the ignorance of the sentient beings; the opening of the rock-cave stands for the opening of the gates of the Dharma-realm.[16]

Here, Kōshū reads the rock-cave myth not so much as a tale of ancient origins but rather as a metaphor for the mind of enlightenment itself. We are all like iron stupas or, indeed, rock-caves. We carry the full insight of the Dharma in our minds; it is ours from birth. However, the gates to this insight may be closed. In that case, we can rely on the two methods of *samādhi* (Omoikane) and *prajñā* (Tajikarawo), on the skillful means of the buddhas (the bonfire), and on the countless Buddhist teachings (the eight myriad kami) to open up our minds to the Dharma.

Again, these were not only abstract thoughts; they had to be formed into concrete practices if they were to mean something. Buddhist readings of the myths were employed to develop a new theology of shrines and a new procedure of shrine worship. Medieval lineages specializing in the "way of the kami" created their own *kanjō* initiations, complete with kami mandalas, mantras, and secret transmissions. Such lineages flourished both in the broader capital region and in the Kantō area in the fourteenth and fifteenth centuries, and some, notably the so-called Miwaryū and Goryū lineages, succeeded in spreading even further in the Edo period, attaining a second heyday as late as the nineteenth century.

Among the most common transmissions of these lineages was the "important matter of the torii gate" (*torii-no-daiji*). An example of this transmission is preserved at the temple complex of Daigoji near Kyoto.[17] There, we read that all torii gates represent the entrance to "the palace of the rock-cave." As such, "the precincts of every shrine are [identical with] the Palace of Thusness in the Pure Land of Mahāvairocana [*mitsugon jōdo*]," and the pilgrim who enters a shrine is in effect leaving the karmic realm and entering the absolute domain of the World-Buddha. This knowledge is ritualized in another "important matter" that transmits a secret rite of entering shrines (*shasan-no-daiji*). Before passing the torii, one forms the mudra of "opening the stupa" with one's hands and recites the syllable *a*, representing the female aspect of Mahāvairocana, that is, compassion. Then one proceeds to the kami hall, where one forms the same mudra and recites Mahāvairocana's second syllable *vaṃ*, representing the male aspect (insight). Finally, one visualizes how *a* and *vaṃ* merge in nondual union, and one recites the third syllable *hūṃ* while forming the mudra of the five-pronged vajra. The syllable *a* is the torii; *vaṃ* is the mirror in the shrine; and *hūṃ* is one's own heart/mind.[18]

This simple procedure transforms each shrine into a specimen of Amaterasu's rock-cave. Inside the cave male and female merge, creating the highest form of enlightenment: the physical reality of life. The cave is the shrine, and the shrine is the heart/mind. Hidden in the cave/shrine/heart, according to yet another "important matter,"[19] is the original source of all kami: *raga* (from Skt. *rāga*), "desire," appearing before us in the form of a snake. This is why the snake is the basic guise of all kami. Thus, the ultimate insight of Buddhist shrine worship was that innate desire, represented by the kami as snakes, is the very essence of Mahāvairocana's Dharma-realm.

The Rock-Cave Myth as a Performance, and the Way of Noh

On a rather less metaphysical level, it is obvious at a glance that the rock-cave myth is closely connected with dance. Tameaki noted that the "songs and dances" performed by the gods in front of the rock-cave were the origin of what he called *saibara*, a word believed to mean "songs of packhorse drovers." *Saibara* were Japanese melodies incorporated in ceremonial court music (*gagaku*), a genre that was of largely continental origin. In fact, the *waka* about the warbler that Tameaki put into Amaterasu's mouth was one of the best-known of all *saibara*, sung at numerous occasions at the court.[20] The rock-cave myth, then, also became important as the origination legend of a range of performative traditions, and notably of performances that took place in the context of kami worship. At the peril of straying somewhat from the main focus of this chapter, namely the myth of the rock-cave, we will here allow ourselves a brief excursion into some of these performative traditions. They are relevant to our topic because in many contexts they constituted the main medium that gave expression both to kami worship in general, and to the rock-cave myth more specifically.

To explain the development of such performances dedicated to the kami, it will be useful to return to the appearance of Amaterasu's mirror in the palace in the tenth century. One of the rituals introduced to celebrate this mirror at the court was *mi-kagura*. *Mi-* is an honorary prefix; *kagura* (or *kami-asobi*) refers to the worship of kami by means of songs and dances. The word occurs for the first time in *Kogo shūi* (Gleanings from ancient tales; 807), which notes that performing *kagura* is the hereditary task of the Sarume (*ST* Kogo shūi: 29). Yet *kagura* does not appear to have been a prominent ingredient in court ceremonial at this time. Continental *gagaku*, with its stylized movements, exotic instruments, and extravagant costumes, was much more elegant and better suited for use at court. Ancient *kagura* was not so much an aesthetic performance designed to please an audience as a powerful and unpredictable rite. If the rock-cave myth is anything to go by, *kagura* must have involved sexually charged dancing and spirit possession.[21] In its rawest form, it was more like voodoo than ballet, and as such it was hardly a natural ingredient of formalized court ceremonial.

Yet *kagura*-type songs and dances must have been ubiquitous at ritual sites across Japan. *Kagura* was the very foundation of ancient kami worship, and has survived in many different forms until the present. The rock-cave myth can be read as a reflection of *kagura*'s function as kami worship. The myth conjures up the image of a *kagura* performance in which a priestess dances in front of a sacred place (a "kami seat"[22]) and goes into a trance, allowing a kami to manifest itself by taking possession of her. The kami, one imagines, would then have bestowed blessings on the community, made its will known through an oracle, or simply made itself available to worship as the recipient of offerings and the object of other rites. Priestesses performing possession rites of this kind appear to have been quite common. We have already met the *yorikidono* of Hie; the Sarume maidens, the *mikannagi*, and even the *naishi* at the court must have played similar roles, and shrine maidens called *miko* or *monoimi* served the same purpose at many other places. Even imperial princesses functioned as spirit mediums, at least in name. The court sent unmarried priestesses to the imperial shrines of Ise and Kamo, and although they no longer functioned as actual mediums in historical times, there are indications that they once did. The imperial priestess at Ise, for example, was known by the name of *mitsueshiro*, a "spirit staff" in which the Ise deities would manifest themselves as recipients of imperial worship.[23]

Over time, however, as such rituals became routinized, the aspect of possession was toned down. At Ise the imperial priestess no longer served as a medium in actual practice even in classical times. In the palace, "kami songs" were sung by court nobles as a part of musical performances, most famously on the third day of the *daijōsai* ceremony; but our only detailed source, the eleventh-century court diary *Hokuzanshō*, does not suggest that there was any dancing involved at all (Müller 1971: 115–17). At Kamo, *kagura* was performed by male dancers and musicians, chosen for their technical skill rather than their shamanic properties. These dancers also served at the imperial palace as military guards (*konoe toneri*); the musicians were professionals from the Office of Music (Gagakuryō) at the court.

The history of *kagura* at the court entered a new phase in 1005, as a new ritual in worship of the court's mirror of Amaterasu (Saitō 2002: 231–46). The occasion was a great fire in which the chest containing Amaterasu's mirror was also burnt. Similar fires occurred at regular intervals. The discovery of this mirror in 938 was also occasioned by a fire: the mirror was found unscathed in the ashes, and its new status as an object of special powers was inspired by this miracle. In 1005, however, the mirror was reduced to a few morsels of shining metal. To deal with this calamity it was decided that Amaterasu should be soothed by means of *kagura*, performed by the *naishi* themselves with assistance from the *konoe* guards. At first, then, court *kagura (mi-kagura)* was staged in response to acute crises such as the 1005 fire. Not much later, however, it became a regular ceremony, conducted every year in the twelfth month.

Mi-kagura was quite unlike the rowdy performance described in the rock-cave myth. To be sure, there are similarities: it was performed at night, by the light of a bonfire, in front of a "kami seat." As during *chinkonsai*, songs were sung in praise of a range of objects that would originally have been held by dancers to attract the kami, such as branches and sticks, bows and swords. However, at least by the time the ceremony was codified in court records (in *Gōke shidai* [Protocol according to the Ōe house], c. 1090), none of these songs were accompanied by actual dances. Only two dances were performed, both by the *konoe* guards who also danced *kagura* at the Kamo Shrine. It would appear that these guards with their professional skills in the art of *kagura* replaced the *miko*-like *naishi* as soon as the *mi-kagura* became a regular ceremony. There is no doubt that the *mi-kagura* was a religious occasion; yet the music and the dancing were not meant to induce a trance in a medium, and nothing "spectacular" was expected to happen. The *mi-kagura*, then, almost reminds us of a concert, a recital in front of the gods.

This impression is confirmed by the fact that the *mi-kagura* also featured comical acts (called *sangaku*, "miscellaneous acts," or *sarugaku*, "monkey acts"), and folk songs. Such acts could be quite acrobatic and were mostly performed by a physically fit *konoe* guard. They were a genre of farcical comedy. On one occasion, commemorated in a collection of popular tales, the young emperor asked for a "special" act. The *konoe* guard, who also served as master of ceremonies, asked one of the musicians, a man called Yukitsuna, to come up with something:

> The master of ceremonies came forward and announced Yukitsuna. Pretending to be really cold, Yukitsuna hoisted his skirt up above his knees, showing his bony shins, then in a quavering voice which suggested he was shivering, he shouted: "It's v-v-very l-l-late, I'm f-f-frozen s-s-stiff, I th-th-think I'll w-w-warm m-m-my b-b-balls," and ran ten times round the fire. The whole audience, the emperor along with the rest, exploded with laughter.[24]

This way of making the assembly laugh is not unlike Ame-no-Uzume's act in front of the rock-cave. *Mi-kagura*, then, functioned both as a ritual and as a theatrical performance. As such, it may be compared to the *daijōsai*, which also combined solemn ritual with a more relaxed display of dances and other entertainments from the provinces.

Court occasions such as *daijōsai* and *mi-kagura* were an important stage for the development of all kinds of performative arts. So were temple ceremonies in the capital region. In the summer, the court sponsored the performance of *goryōe*, festivals for the prevention of epidemics, whose modern-day heir is the famous Gion festival. The *goryōe* featured numerous kinds of performances and became an important model for festivals across Japan. One example of this is the appearance of "paddy dancing" (*dengaku*) in the capital (Geinōshi Kenkyūkai 1982: 172–232). *Dengaku* started as a rural accompaniment to the planting of rice in spring, but grew into a popular performance staged both at the court and at court-connected shrines in the tenth and eleventh centuries. *Dengaku* invaded the capital with a vengeance on the occasion of a *goryōe* in 1096, when even court nobles joined the masses of dancers that took over the streets of the city.

We can witness the result of this development at a shrine on the outskirts of Kyoto, now known as Uji Shrine. This shrine had risen to fame as the tutelary shrine of the famous Byōdōin, a large Fujiwara temple built in 1052–3. A courtier described the spring festival of this shrine as follows:

> 1134, fifth month, eighth day. Today is the day of the Uji festival. This year the parade passed by the gate of Lord Ogawa, and I watched it from a pavilion there. There were ten horse races in which the people of Uji competed against the folks of Makishima [...] Wherever the *mikoshi* stopped, it received worship. [The parade included] over thirty *miko* shrine maidens, tens of horsemen in costume, and countless others both in formal attire and in costumes. Some carried *heihaku*,[25] others bows and arrows. The drums and flutes of the *dengaku* performers made an ear-splitting noise, and the *miko* let their garments fly through the air. The roads were crammed with spectators. The parade passed in the hour of the sheep [around 2 p.m.]. At the shrine, there were horse races, offerings were presented, and so forth.[26]

Many of these performers were paid by Fujiwara sponsors as a donation to the shrine. Over time, *dengaku* came to occupy a more and more prominent place within this festival, and numerous *dengaku* groups competed with each other in the shadow of the *mikoshi*. In this way, all kinds of performances became a natural ingredient of shrine festivals. In the process, many festivals were almost overtaken by groups of *dengaku* and *sarugaku* performers.

Another famous stage for various performances was the Kasuga Shrine in Nara. This shrine was closely connected to Kōfukuji, the mighty lineage temple of the Fujiwara. When Kōfukuji developed into a great landowner, a new shrine called Wakamiya was built at Kasuga, and from 1137 onwards Wakamiya became the focus of a new festival: the Wakamiya Onmatsuri. The *mikoshi* of Wakamiya was taken to nearby Kōfukuji holdings and celebrated there by means of an endless variety of performances. Armed monks performed horse races and archery competitions, Kasuga shrine maidens danced *kagura*, Nara musicians played Chinese court dances (*bugaku*), and troupes of actors performed *dengaku* and *sarugaku* acts.

It was in this setting that Japanese theater traditions such as Noh, at the time known as *sarugaku nō*, first took shape. In contrast to most performative traditions, including Noh's main rival *dengaku*, Noh has left a written record that goes back to medieval times. Not only playscripts, but also pedagogical and theoretical treatises dating back to the fifteenth century have survived and are treasured to this day. The appearance of kami and spirits of various kinds and their interaction with human actors (often monks) is a dominant theme in Noh, reminding us of its origins in the context of temple-shrine festivals.

Not surprisingly, Noh plays and commentaries display a profound influence from the transmissions on poetry (*kadō*) and the Buddhist "way of the kami" (*jindō*, Shinto) mentioned above. The earliest Noh author whose works have survived the centuries was Zeami Motokiyo (1363–1443), leader of a professional troupe under the protection of Kōfukuji/Kasuga in Nara. Zeami succeeded in winning the patronage of shogun Ashikaga Yoshimitsu (1358–1408), and developed Noh into its classical form under the profound influence of the various artistic traditions that flourished at the shogunal headquarters in Muromachi near Kyoto. The *kadō* and *jindō* transmissions were an integral part of this setting. It is only natural, then, that the rock-cave myth also found its way into Noh.

In his earliest treatise on Noh, *Fūshi kaden* (Teachings on style and the flower; c. 1400), Zeami stated that *sarugaku nō* originated with Ame-no-Uzume's dance in front of the rock-cave:

> Hearing the voice of Ame-no-Uzume, the sun-goddess opened the rock door slightly. The land became light and the faces of the gods shone white [*omo-shiro*]. It is said that such entertainments marked the beginning of *sarugaku [nō]*.[27]

As A. H. Thornhill III (1993: 68 ff.) has pointed out, Zeami's reference to the rock-cave myth served initially to legitimize his art as a divine practice, but in due course Zeami came back to this tale as a starting point for sophisticated reflection on the nature of theatrical performance. In a later work, Zeami read the rock-cave myth as no less than a sacred revelation on the process of creating fascination on the stage.[28]

This process begins with the darkness (*myō*, "the wondrous") that enveloped the world when Amaterasu retired into the rock-cave. This darkness, Zeami writes, stuns the audience and "cuts off all speech," opening up an awareness beyond discursive thinking. Then the cave is opened and Amaterasu emerges. The return of the sun (termed *hana*, "the flower") induces a spontaneous feeling of surprise and joy in the onlookers. Finally, this joy is expressed in speech: *omo-shiro* ("white faces; fascinating"). Through this expression, the audience is able to experience the state of "no-mind" by sublimating the spontaneous delight of *hana* into true fascination. In this way Zeami presents the rock-cave myth as an account of the ideal response of an audience to a play. This response has three stages, all occurring (in Thornhill's words) "in a single moment of aesthetic experience":

1 *myō*: anticipation, suspension of cognition;
2 *hana*: an emotional response, delight;
3 *omo-shiro*: recognition of one's response, fascination.

By watching *sarugaku nō*, then, the audience in effect experiences ultimate enlightenment in the form of union with the sun-goddess, as the Japanese equivalent of the World-Buddha himself.

This vision of rock-cave enlightenment was also acted out on the stage. The Noh play *Miwa*, which is usually attributed to (the circle of) Zeami, ends with a depiction of the rock-cave myth.[29] The main protagonist (*shite*) of the play is Amaterasu herself, here figuring as the deity of Mount Miwa south of Nara; like Hie, Miwa was identified with Ise and Amaterasu in medieval kami lore. Amaterasu visits the monk Genpin, who lives as a hermit in a hut on Mount Miwa. Every day she brings him water; finally, she asks him for a robe and disappears into thin air. Wondering who his visitor may have been, Genpin searches for her and finds the robe he gave her, spread over the lower branches of a pair of ancient cedar trees. Suddenly, Amaterasu appears and begins to tell the legend of Miwa's origin. Finally, apparently quite out of the blue, she begins to talk about the rock-cave. She shows how she once concealed herself in the rock-cave by hiding her face behind a fan, and then performs the role of Ame-no-Uzume by dancing *kagura* to, by Noh standards, quite energetic musical accompaniment. In the background, the chorus chants:

> When Tenshō Daijin [i.e., Amaterasu] opened the rock-cave slightly, the clouds of eternal darkness were dispersed; the light of sun and moon shone brightly and the white faces of the people became visible once more. This is the tale of the wondrous origin of that call of the gods: *omo-shiro ya. (SNKBT* 57: 131)

In keeping with Noh thought, then, the rock-cave episode culminates in that fascinating word, *omo-shiro*. As we have seen, this phrase was understood to induce enlightenment in both performers and spectators, not as an abstract concept, but as a direct experience of "fascination," rooted in the nondiscursive state of "no-mind." Like the closely related ways of *kadō* and *jindō* Noh was ultimately validated as a Buddhist practice that gave direct access to the insights of the buddhas. In all of these three "ways," the rock-cave myth served as the main image to express this grand idea.

The End of the Medieval World

In medieval Japan the classical myth of the rock-cave was reinvented to fulfill a new role: to give mythological basis to the "ways" of poetry, kami worship, and Noh theater. Earlier, such activities had been rejected as worldly distractions, or as "local" phenomena much inferior to the "universal" Dharma from India; now they were praised as legitimate forms of Buddhist practice in their own right. The rock-cave myth was at the core of a broad discourse on a range of obviously Japanese forms of cultural practice. The myth served as a channel through which the Dharma could be made relevant to Japanese practices. It made it possible to apply the highest goal of Buddhism, universal enlightenment, to apparently worldly, peripheral practices, and to raise their stature to truly cosmic dimensions. In this intellectual environment, the myth flourished as never before.

This environment changed radically in the transition from the medieval to the early modern period, around the sixteenth and seventeenth centuries. We have already seen that the great temple-shrine complexes lost much of their power in the fifteenth century. Instead, power was increasingly concentrated in the hands of the warrior class: the Ashikaga shoguns, competing warlords, and, from 1603 onwards, the Tokugawa shoguns. As a new elite took control over the land, they established a new culture. The warrior leaders imported novel religious and intellectual trends from China, Zen and Song Confucianism foremost among them; at the same time, the old temple-shrine complexes slowly fell behind, losing much of their economic might and struggling to adapt to the new times.

In the late and post-medieval world, established authorities were openly challenged in an atmosphere of critical distance and skepticism. The old myths lost some of their aura, and the secret transmissions that had grown up around them came to be regarded as dubious products of an outdated, or even corrupt, past. Increasingly, new impulses from the continent set the agenda. In China, Buddhism had long since lost the position of intellectual hegemony that it still enjoyed in medieval Japan. Instead, it had become the favorite whipping boy of the now dominant Confucian establishment. In Japan, the final destruction of Buddhist secular power in the unification wars of the sixteenth century set the stage for a similar move away from, or at least towards a relativization of, Buddhism.

As Buddhism was marginalized by Confucianism, a new hermeneutics took over. Secret knowledge handed down in lineage transmissions was no longer regarded as legitimate; instead, knowledge now had to be grounded in an objective analysis of canonized texts.[30] Analyses of this kind tended to confirm secular morality by emphasizing the Confucian virtues that supported the maintenance of a stable social order. Such a reading was by necessity very different from the medieval discourse, which had been more inclined to search for a nondual realm where "desire and enlightenment are one," beyond the superficial morality of the secular world.

Under this new intellectual regime, the myths were no longer seen as revelations about a different dimension. Instead, they retained some of their interest as encoded messages about secular "virtues" and about the distant roots of the social and political stability that depended on those virtues. This opened up the way for two possible readings of the myths: as morality, and as history.[31] The myths were either read as parables or as encoded accounts of real events from the past. Some Confucian scholars, for example Hayashi Razan (1583–1657) and Yamazaki Ansai (1618–82), interpreted the gods as metaphors for the presence of the cosmic principle of the Way in the human mind. Worship of the gods, then, became a practice of moral self-improvement, with the ultimate aim of actualizing the innate virtue of one's own mind. Others again, Arai Hakuseki (1657–1725) and Motoori Norinaga (1730–1801) among them, read the myths as actual history. Arai argued that the transmissions about the gods were the garbled remains of orally transmitted history, revealing the early workings of the Mandate of Heaven in Japan's distant past. Motoori, on the other hand, saw the myths as an accurate account of real events in a divine age, and as a revelation of the will of mighty kami who determine the affairs of the world even to this very day. Moreover, as we have already seen in Chapter 2, scholars like Yamakazi and Motoori used the myths to stress the superiority of Japan over other countries as the land where the gods were born, and as the only nation to be ruled by an unbroken imperial dynasty of divine descent.

In early modern Japan, then, the myths came to be seen as tales of morality, history, and patriotism. While the approaches of thinkers like Razan, Yamakazi, Arai, and Motoori were fundamentally different in many ways, they all shared a deep contempt for the medieval transmissions about the myths, which they regarded as outrageous from both an ethical and a methodological point of view. They also shared the notion that the myths contained a message that should be made known to the people. This was very different from the medieval understanding that the myths are a source of "magical" (*siddhi*-like) power that should only be divulged to initiates.

This new view of the myths inspired a broad movement to bring them to the people. While in medieval times the texts and their secret meanings had been handed down in closed lineages, they were now printed, glossed, commented upon, and sold in bookstores. This made the texts available for all kinds of new purposes. Shrine traditions that were not in accord with the now canonized "national histories," notably *Nihon shoki*, were "corrected" or rewritten to fit in with the authoritative version that was now accessible, at least in principle, to all who could read. Even more strikingly, the myths were incorporated in actual shrine festivals and kami rituals. This process is best illustrated by the development of *kagura* in this period.

Kagura

As we have already seen, different forms of *kagura* dancing had been performed as part of kami rituals for a long time; the rock-cave myth itself suggests that *kagura* had truly ancient roots. In late medieval Japan, two forms of *kagura* appear to have been most widespread. The first focused on the figure of the *miko*, a female (but, after the seventeenth century, more and more often male) medium. In this kind of *kagura* a *miko* went into a trance and became possessed, either by a protective spirit blessing the villagers in an oracle, by a demon who had to be driven out from the human domain to the hills beyond, or by the spirits of the dead who had to be guided to a Buddha-land (Iwata 1994). A second common type were so-called "boiling water" dances (*yudate kagura*), performed around a large cauldron. To the accompaniment of drums and flutes, performers, who as a rule were priests of some kind, danced around the cauldron while holding various objects believed to attract the deities (*torimono*). When the *kagura* reached its climax, they would whip the boiling water out of the cauldron over themselves and the audience, either as an act of purification, as a prayer for blessings, or as a means to induce oracles. The *yudate* was being performed at sites such as Kumano and Ise by the twelfth century at the latest, and spread from there to all corners of the land.

In the early Edo period, however, a new form of *kagura* emerged. Traditional *kagura* was a dramatic way to enact the appearance of the kami, mostly carried out by ritual specialists such as *miko* shamans, priests, Yin-Yang diviners (*onmyōji*), and mountain practitioners (*yamabushi*). It had little or no plot; in essence, it was a ritual procedure in the form of a performance. The new *kagura*, however, was more like a pantomime. It drew on contemporary forms of theater for its effects, and on the myths in *Nihon shoki* and, later, *Kojiki* for its scripts. *Kagura* pieces depicting episodes from the classical texts were first introduced in the festivals of larger shrines by priests and intellectuals of various kinds. From there, they spread widely to become a part of village rituals throughout the country.

The earliest known instance of such a theater-like form of *kagura* dates from the early seventeenth century. The *kagura* troupe of Sada Shrine, in what is today Shimane Prefecture, traces its origin to the priest Miyagawa Hideyuki who traveled to Kyoto in the Keichō years (1596–1615) to study Noh (Ishizuka 2005: 123–70). After returning to Sada, he composed Noh-like pieces depicting various episodes from the kami myths, which he incorporated into the *kagura* repertoire performed at the shrine. At Sada the more traditional "ritual" pieces were performed first, followed by the traditional opening piece of Noh (*Shikisanba*), and then, as a grand finale, the new "kami Noh." In addition to pieces of more local interest, such as a piece on the founding of the Izumo Shrine not far from Sada, the kami Noh also included versions of classical myth, among them a piece called *Iwato*, "The rock-cave."

Sada's *Iwato* begins with the entrance of an unmasked "retainer of Amaterasu" called Sōjin, who in a long chant tells of Amaterasu's reasons for hiding herself in the rock-cave. Then Sōjin summons four deities: the two retainers Wakamiya and Tamahoko, and the more recognizable kami Uzume (that is, Ame-no-Uzume) and Tajikarawo. Wakamiya carries a tent-like appliance onto the stage, which represents the cave; Amaterasu is already hidden inside. Wakamiya performs a sword dance while circling around the cave. Next, Tamahoko appears, places a *tsuzumi* drum in front of the cave and performs a *yudate* dance, pretending the drum is a cauldron. Next is Uzume, who carries a young girl's mask and dances *kagura*. Finally, Tajikarawo appears wearing a demon's mask and holding a long staff. After much ado, he opens the cave. Amaterasu emerges, wearing a girl's mask; Tajikarawo takes her place in the cave. As Wakamiya carries away the cave, Susanowo enters the stage wearing a deity mask and performs a final dance together with Amaterasu.

In the Sada version of *Iwato*, we recognize elements from many different sources. Most of the deity names derive from the *Nihon shoki*; some, however, appear to be local innovations. The story roughly follows the classical plot, but with *kagura* elements such as Wakamiya's sword dance and Tamahoko's *yudate* thrown in. The use of masks and stage props (*tsukurimono*) is derived from Noh; the unmasked "retainers" remind one of the comical *kyōgen* pieces that are customarily mixed in with Noh performances. In its ritual context at Sada, "kami Noh" served as a new kind of entertainment offered to the gods, not unlike *dengaku* and *sarugaku* in earlier times. No doubt the adoption of a Noh-like performance enhanced the status of the shrine and its priests, as well as attracting more people to the festival. *Kagura* was also an attractive way of fundraising. In many places, *kagura* was sponsored by "clubs" called *kagura-kō*. The members of these clubs collected funds that were paid to the shrine for the donation of a *kagura* performance to the deities.

From places like Sada, the new, pantomime-like type of *kagura* spread rapidly across the provinces, especially from the early eighteenth century onwards. As a result, permanent *kagura* stages (*kagura-den*) were built at many shrines. Written sources are few and it is impossible to reconstruct the "original" details of local performances, but even if we limit ourselves to *kagura* as it is performed today, the variety is stunning. What is striking, in all this diversity, is that there is hardly a local tradition that does not feature the rock-cave tale in some form or other.[32] In many places the rock-cave *kagura* entails little more than Ame-no-Uzume's dance, with little or no plot. Tajikarawo is also a popular figure. He usually appears as a demon-like strongman, and his efforts to remove the cave door are often the climax of the piece; Figure 4 shows a modern example of this scene. Sometimes comical interludes are

Figure 4 A 1988 performance of *iwato kagura* at Isozaki Shrine in Shingū (near Fukuoka). Tajikarawo pulls open the rock-cave with the help of a white rope made of cloth. After the performance the rope is cut into small pieces which are distributed to pregnant women as charms for an easy delivery. *Courtesy of Arne Kalland.*

inserted. When Ame-no-Uzume kindles a fire to light up her dancing, she fans it with her skirt, until she suddenly notices that her private parts are getting roasted. When Tajikarawo is showing off his muscles, none of the other gods deigns to take any notice, and he has to be stopped from leaving the scene in a huff of hurt pride.

What is especially striking is that in many places, from Kyūshū to northern Honshū, the rock-cave *kagura* gained special significance as an indispensable part of shrine ritual. At Sada, *Iwato* was but one of 12 episodes on the kami; there is no evidence that it was treated any differently from the others. In contrast, for *kagura* groups in Buzen (northern Kyūshū) the rock-cave was the climax of the entire program. Here, as at most places, *kagura* was performed in the darkest months of winter. The dancing would begin in the evening and continue until dawn. The rock-cave piece was the last on the schedule, timed to coincide with sunrise (Hashimoto Kōsaku 2005: 36 ff.). While most other pieces were regarded as optional, the rock-cave was not, and a *kagura* session could not be brought to an end without the cave being opened. Likewise, at Kasugai in Yamanashi Prefecture the shrine's kami was transferred to the *mikoshi* at the very moment that Amaterasu emerged from the cave on the *kagura* stage. In Fukushima Prefecture to the north of the Kantō plain, a rock-cave model was even a permanent feature of most *kagura* halls. Such a model was attached to the back wall of the stage. A small opening was made in the wall, which revealed a mirror or a candle when Tajikarawo finally tore away the curtain.

In many places, then, the rock-cave myth became a central feature of shrine rituals in the course of the Edo period. In fact, it was at this time that the classical kami myths, and especially the rock-cave tale, became common knowledge among the general populace for the first time. With the diffusion of *kagura* pantomime, the classical court myths finally became a common frame of reference shared by virtually all Japanese. This also explains why depictions of scenes from the myths began to proliferate in various media around this time. Paintings with themes from kami myth were almost nonexistent in the medieval period, but from the eighteenth century onwards it became a popular practice to make donations of votive tablets (*ema*) carrying pictures of such episodes as the rock-cave or Susanowo's slaying of the *orochi* monster.[33] Such tablets were then displayed in a conspicuous place at the shrine, sometimes even in a specially constructed *ema* hall.

By the end of the Edo period, the rock-cave even drew the attention of commercial printmakers, the producers of the cheap and enormously popular *ukiyoe*. These usually confined themselves to subjects from the popular *kabuki* theater or from the geisha quarters in the cities, with occasional excursions into the world of popular religion. Religious *ukiyoe* tended to focus on the most novel and trendy deities of the day, cashing in on popular cults that emerged in response to smallpox epidemics and natural disasters such as earthquakes, or mass-producing colorful prints of lucky deities that could be displayed in shops to put customers in a spending mood. It is striking, then, that in the

Figure 5 Utagawa Kuniyoshi, *Shichifukujin iwato no kurabiraki* (The Seven Gods of Fortune opening the storehouse). Undated. *Private collection, courtesy of Shibuya Kuritsu Shōtō Bijutsukan.*

last decades of the Edo period, the famous *ukiyoe* master Utagawa Kuniyoshi (1798–1861) produced a three-sheet set of prints on the unusual topic of the opening of the rock-cave (Figure 5). In this triptych, we see Ame-no-Uzume dancing around a bonfire while, behind her, a distinctly Chinese-looking Tajikarawo lifts a huge rock, releasing golden rays of light from the cave. When we take a second look, however, we soon notice that something is awry. The orchestra consists of some unusual members. Daikokuten (Skt. Mahākāla), the god of riches and of the kitchen, is beating a *kagura* drum with his magical mallet. Hotei (Ch. Budai), the god of contentment and happiness, plays the flute on his fan, and the god of longevity and wisdom Fukurokuju (Ch. Fulushou) holds the scroll that contains all the knowledge in the world in front of his face to mimic the long nose of Saruta-hiko. Now we also notice that Ame-no-Uzume in fact looks more like Benzaiten (Skt. Sarasvatī), the lute-playing goddess of the arts, and we understand that Tajikarawo is actually Bishamonten (Skt. Vaiśravaṇa), the Indian god of war and dispeller of demons. In short, the classical deities of the rock-cave myth are replaced by the popular Seven Gods of Fortune. Finally, when we take a closer look at the cave itself, we realize that the light emerging from it is emitted not by the sun-goddess, but by a huge pile of money chests. The sacred room opened by the gods of fortune is not Amaterasu's rock-cave at all; it is a bank vault.

Comical prints of this type show that the rock-cave had now become a truly current image, familiar to all owing to the ever more popular *kagura* pantomimes.

The Rock-Cave Myth after Meiji

Joking aside, it is clear that many took *kagura* very seriously as a medium for teaching the populace about the ancient history of the nation. This became especially urgent in the mid-nineteenth century, when Western nations forced Japan to open itself to the world. As kami myth became a matter of national interest, it came to be seen as imperative to spread correct knowledge about Japan's divine past to the people.

The effects of this can be observed in the modern history of *kagura*. In the late nineteenth and early twentieth centuries, *kagura* performances were both rewritten and restaged on a grand scale. In Iwami (today the western half of Shimane Prefecture), the *kokugaku* activist Fujii Muneo (1823–1906) rewrote *kagura* playbooks throughout his district. He corrected plots against the *Kojiki* and inserted monologues and dialogues full of ancient phrases. Similar adaptations to new orthodoxies took place in all corners of the land. On the tiny island of Iki west of Fukuoka, for example, the local *kagura* was revised in 1845 to bring it into accord with the *Kojiki* account. Even so, further rewritings were deemed necessary in 1871, 1886, and 1918 (Ishizuka 2005: 146).

In Buzen, *kagura* pantomimes were actively promoted by shrine priests from the latter half of the nineteenth century onwards. By the mid twentieth century, *kagura* groups had been formed at more than 90 places throughout the province, all drawing on the older *kagura* traditions of a mere six sites in the area. In the Edo period, *kagura* had mainly been conducted by priests or by professional troupes, but in 1882 the Meiji state forbade shrine priests from engaging in "religious activities," which included *kagura*.

This inspired many priests to teach groups of amateurs to perform the new plays (Hashimoto Kōsaku 2005: 22 ff.). At least in Buzen, *kagura* served as a vital medium for the propagation of Shinto. In this process, it was natural to revise the plays so as to bring out their Shinto message more clearly. *Kagura* teachers sought to maintain a subtle balance between preserving local traditions, on the one hand, and correcting "deviations" from the classics on the other. It is not surprising, then, that after the war, the Occupation forces targeted *kagura* as a possible medium of nationalist propaganda. This caused some *kagura* troupes to make another round of revisions, this time to make sure that their repertoire would pass Allied censorship.

These events reflect the changing status of Shinto in post-Meiji Japan. This new status is perhaps expressed most eloquently in the accounts of kami myth in history textbooks approved by the state for use in schools. In the early twentieth century kami myth was groomed to serve a new purpose: building the modern Japanese nation-state. To preserve independence and withstand the pressure put on Japan by the imperialist powers, it was seen as vital that the population was imbued with a strong sense of national identity and patriotism. As compulsory education became established, official textbooks served as a major channel through which this message was spread.

The first state-approved history textbook for primary education appeared in 1903. Tellingly, its first pages are dedicated to Amaterasu:

> Amaterasu Ōmikami is the ancestor of our Emperor. Her merits are extremely high and can be compared to the sun in the sky, shining down upon the world. This great deity gave the land to her grandson Ninigi-no-Mikoto, saying: "The imperial lineage will prosper as long as heaven and earth exist." It was at this time that the foundation was laid for our everlasting Great Japanese Empire. (*NKT* 19: 441)

The text continues by explaining that Amaterasu bestowed upon Ninigi three regalia, among which the mirror preserved in Ise is the most august. After Ninigi, the tale jumps to Emperor Jinmu, who established the empire "more than 2,500 years ago"; according to the new Japanese era introduced in 1872, 1903 was the year 2563. The text then moves on to Yamato-takeru, who pacified the Japanese islands through his military exploits, and to Jingū Kōgō, who forced the kings of Korea to "submit to our land."

In this textbook, the myths are treated as a prologue to history. While the effect is to mystify the origins of the imperial dynasty, the myths are rationalized as much as possible. The sun-goddess is a human ancestor of great merit rather than a deity, and she is associated with the sun merely as a metaphor. Thus, kami worship becomes ancestor worship, a simple expression of gratitude to the founders of the Japanese nation. This approach was in tune with the redefinition of Shinto earlier in the Meiji period: as a nonreligious body of patriotic ritual, in which human ancestors and "Great Men" are honored in a "secular" manner, rather than prayed to as gods in a "religious" way.

In subsequent textbooks, the section on Amaterasu was gradually expanded. In the edition of 1920, the tale of the rock-cave was included for the first time (*NKT* 19: 622). The function of the episode in this text was simply to explain the origin of the three regalia, and it was presented as mere background knowledge. No references were made to the rock-cave in the corresponding textbooks on ethics (*shūshin*). In effect, the whole episode was reduced to a tale about the origin of Amaterasu's mirror. This came in handy because it gave teachers an opening to explain the connection between the imperial house and Ise.

In contrast, the first official history textbook that appeared after the war, *Kuni-no-ayumi* (The nation's journey; 1946) does not mention the myths at all. In all postwar textbooks, history begins with the Stone Age, not with the establishment of the imperial dynasty (*NKT* 20: 388). Under the new regime, all references to kami myth were prohibited as nationalist propaganda. In fact, all education about religious matters was banned from public schools. At the same time, *kagura* began to fade from the direct environment of the large majority of Japanese, bracketed out of mainstream culture as instances of idiosyncratic, fossilized "folklore." These developments in effect marked the end of the "modern" phase of the myths' history.

Of course, the disappearance of the kami myths from the public stage has also opened up new possibilities. For the first time, the myths can be studied and analyzed in an academic manner, without any ideological bias. This has resulted in an extensive scientific literature on which much of this chapter is based. Even more importantly, the fading of the myths from collective memory has also made it possible for them to be rediscovered afresh. Today there are perhaps some signs that the myths of the past may be entering a new, "postmodern" phase. As the rationalistic interpretations of Meiji retreat into the past, the myths appear to a new generation as exotic tales full of wonder, triggering the fantasy of many. Yet it is hard to see how these tales will once more function as myths in the sense articulated by Bruce Lincoln: as "ideologies in narrative form" that fix the present by referring to ancient divine origins. Today, they are merely ancient tales, fascinating in their dazzling otherness, but rarely perceived to be "true" as carriers of sacred authority.

Chapter 5

The *Daijōsai*
A "Shinto" Rite of Imperial Accession

The present emperor Akihito took his first steps towards enthronement on the day his father died, January 7, 1989. In a rite known as *senso* (literally "stepping into the imperial office"), he now acquired two of the three imperial regalia, the sword and jewel (*kenji*).[1] On November 12, 1990, after a full year and more of mourning, he underwent the second enthronement rite, *sokui*, a public proclamation of his accession. Dignitaries from 158 nations attended the event, and some 100,000 people lined the parade route in Tokyo. In a public statement on that day, the emperor pledged henceforth to "observe the Constitution of Japan and discharge my duties as symbol of the state and the unity of the people." Ten days later he underwent the third and final stage of the enthronement process. This was the *daijōsai*, or "Rite of Great Tasting." It took place in a complex of wooden buildings, known as the Daijōkyū, or Shrine of Great Tasting, temporarily erected in the grounds of the Imperial Palace in Tokyo. The shrine comprised three main structures: the Kairyū Hall, and the Yuki and Suki Pavilions. On the night of November 22 the emperor, enveloped in the garment known as *ame-no-hagoromo* ("the heavenly robe of feathers"), purified himself in the hot waters of the Kairyū Hall before proceeding to the Yuki Pavilion. He took chopsticks in his hands and offered rice and other fruits of the land and sea to the sun-goddess before partaking of them himself. He then repeated the procedure at the Suki Pavilion. He emerged at dawn the next day, his transformation from crown prince into emperor now complete.

Rites of a mystical variety that transform mere mortals into sovereigns are of especial interest in this secular age. But Akihito's *daijōsai* rite was, for other reasons, too, an event of interest. In 1946 his father, Hirohito, had renounced all claims that he was a living kami. And yet here was his son communing with the sun-goddess, intimating at least that he partook of those qualities that made his father a kami. Again, Akihito's *daijōsai* was the trigger for much speculation about the symbolism of the rite. Why did the two pavilions contain a bed, a pillow, and a shroud? Elsewhere, questions were raised about the state's involvement. This *daijōsai* was funded by the Imperial Household, but this was, nonetheless, taxpayers' money. Was there not a special irony at this time in the emperor declaring his commitment to the Constitution, with its provision for the separation of state and religion?

Questions of constitutionality and contested meaning occupy the first section of this chapter, but the remainder adopts a more historical approach, the better to identify how and why the *daijōsai* and its meanings shifted between different historical periods. The second section argues that the *daijōsai* gave essential meaning to the emperor-centered nation-state in the nineteenth and early twentieth centuries. As such, it was the defining rite of modern state-sponsored Shinto. The focus of the third section shifts to a much earlier period of Japanese history when the notion of Shinto had yet to arise. What can we know of the early *daijōsai* rite and its beginnings? How did the *daijōsai* transform over time, and what do those transformations tell us about the Japanese emperor and the Japanese state?

Ritual Controversy

Lawsuits

Under the postwar Constitution, the emperor is, as Akihito him-self declared, "symbol of the state and the unity of the people." He makes no claims to divinity, but the dramatic appearance in the *daijōsai* of the sun-goddess accords that rite a distinctly religious dimension, unlike the more secular *senso* and *sokui* enthronement rites that precede it. Given the Constitution's provisions in Article 20 for the separation of state and religion, there was an inevitability about the filing of lawsuits by citizens' groups.[2] These lawsuits serve to highlight the extent to which the *daijōsai*, for the first time in its long history, became an issue of contention between the state and its citizens. It can also be observed how, in the course of these legal processes, the *daijōsai* underwent a subtle but significant realignment.

It was the Kagoshima prefectural governor's use of public moneys to attend the *daijōsai* in November 1990 that prompted legal action. His attendance, or so it was alleged by a group of Kagoshima citizens, breached not only Article 20 but also Article 99, which obligates public officials to uphold the Constitution. The plaintiffs sought compensation from the government. The Kagoshima district court judge acknowledged the Shinto religious dimension to the *daijōsai* but still absolved the governor of guilt in October 1992 (Momochi 1995). He did so by applying what is known as the "object and effect standard" (*mokuteki kōka kijun*). The judge ruled that the governor's "object" in attending the *daijōsai* was not religiously significant; what motivated him was a desire to celebrate the emperor's enthronement. Nor might his attendance be said to have had the "effect" of supporting one religion or oppressing another. This "object and effect" precedent was earlier established in a landmark ruling in the Supreme Court in 1977. Then, the case in question involved the mayor of Tsu City in Mie Prefecture, who used public funds to pay a Shinto priest to perform a ground-breaking rite for a municipal sports facility. He was sued for breach of the Constitution. But the judge was not persuaded that either the "object" or the "effect" of his actions amounted to state support for, or state oppression of, any religion; he thus deemed the mayor's actions constitutional. This standard has since been applied to many cases relating to Article 20, most notably those concerning official patronage of Yasukuni, the Tokyo shrine to the war dead.[3]

It was also applied to a suit filed by citizens in Ōita. The case in question arose out of that prefecture's special role in the *daijōsai*. The districts in which rice would be cultivated for use in the rite were determined by divination, and court diviners alighted on

Ōita in the southwest and Akita in the northeast as suitable. Ōita rice would be used in the Suki Pavilion; Akita rice in the Yuki Pavilion. The Ōita governor attended the ritual harvesting and bowed his head towards an altar set up on the site. An Ōita citizens' group sued him for "participating in, and performing acts of worship at, a Shinto rite which imparts sacred status to the emperor. The governor's participation and worship had the object of supporting Shinto (state Shinto as a religion) with the emperor as its head" (Momochi 1995: 5). In June 2004 Justice Maruyama granted the religious nature of the *daijōsai* and associated rites, but applied the same object-effect standard to reach a "not guilty" verdict. In his final ruling, however, he made several observations. The *daijōsai* shared nothing substantial with Shinto rites performed at shrines, he opined; the *daijōsai* was not intended to disseminate a particular religious faith, nor were its premises those of now defunct state Shinto. As for the governor, his actions were "a social performance, celebrating the new emperor's accession to the throne," and so were "not obviously motivated by religious faith."[4]

What distinguished the third suit, filed by Osaka citizens in 1992, was that it sought a ruling on the constitutionality or otherwise of the *daijōsai* itself. The government funded that event indirectly through the Imperial Household; the event was religious and it therefore breached Article 20. This was the gist of the Osaka plaintiffs' case. They sought compensation for the mental anguish caused. The plaintiffs gave the judge few difficulties. Where they demanded that the state desist from funding the *daijōsai*, the judge ruled there could be no "post factum desisting." The plaintiffs insisted that their "basic rights as taxpayers" had been breached but, observed the judge, such rights were not constitutionally recognized in Japan. He also ruled that the plaintiffs may have found the *daijōsai* "unsavory," but this hardly amounted to "mental anguish." An appeal court judge in 1995 dismissed an appeal, but then summed up with some personal observations. "[The *daijōsai*] is quite evidently a Shinto rite," and it was "not possible to reject out of hand" the view that the *daijōsai* breached Article 20 of the Constitution "to the extent that it aided ... state Shinto" (Momochi 1995: 9). For this judge at least, the object-effect standard did not absolve the accused. With the notable exception of this last case, the application of the object-effect standard has functioned to allow state representatives to attend Shinto rites. It is interesting to observe that one effect of its application to the *daijōsai* has been to nudge it out of the difficult realm of religion into that of "custom" or "social performance." It does so subtly, and by implication. The Kagoshima governor, it was ruled, was celebrating the emperor's accession to the throne, so the *daijōsai* becomes by implication a simple celebration. The Ōita judge determined the governor's actions to be "a social performance," implying that the Constitution had no business interfering with those.

The emperor, his bed, and a shroud

The legal controversy over the *daijōsai* was preceded by much contestation over meaning, which focused on the material symbols within the pavilions. This contestation had its origins in a particular reading of the *daijōsai* by the great anthropologist Orikuchi Shinobu, whom we encountered in Chapter 1. The reading in question concerns Orikuchi's essay *Daijōsai no hongi* (The true meaning of the *daijōsai*). It first appeared in 1928, prompted by the *daijōsai* of Emperor Hirohito, but only became widely known after the war when it acquired the status of orthodoxy. So influential, and controversial, did it become that in 1990 the Imperial Household Agency took the extraordinary step of publicly refuting it.[5] So, what was the burden of Orikuchi's *daijōsai* theory, and wherein lay the controversy? Orikuchi focused on the shroud that lay on the bed in each pavilion. He saw this as the vital link between the *daijōsai* and the mythical account of the founding of the imperial line. After all, the *Nihon shoki* account of the descent to earth of the sun-goddess's grandson Ninigi also features a shroud, referred to as *matoko ofusuma* ("the shroud of the true bed"). The kami Takami-musubi wrapped the shroud around Ninigi, before dispatching him to rule the realm of Japan. It could hardly be a coincidence that a shroud featured both in the ritual and in the mythical narrative. Or could it?

Orikuchi surmised that, as the shroud had enveloped Ninigi, so in origin it enveloped the emperor. The emperor lay on the bed, wrapped in the shroud waiting for the sun-goddess to descend from heaven, join him in the chamber, and then enter his body. Orikuchi here adduced evidence that the emperor's body was regarded in ancient times as a "vessel" that might be entered by "the imperial spirit" (*tennō rei*). As Ninigi in the myth cast the shroud aside to become Japan's ruler, so too did Hirohito, transformed and empowered by the sun-goddess, cast the shroud aside to emerge as Japan's new emperor. Orikuchi was the first ever to explore the meaning of emperor, bed, and shroud in the *daijōsai*; but others followed in his wake. After the war, the priest and Shinto scholar Mayumi Tsunetada accepted Orikuchi's theory uncritically (Mayumi 1989: 154–6). Mainstream scholars soon took it in intriguing directions. Saigō Nobutsuna, for example, read the emperor-wrapping shroud as a metaphor for the womb, and the *daijōsai* as a rite of rebirth. The emperor incubates in the shroud before he casts it aside to emerge as an incarnation of the divine child Ninigi, ready to assume rule over the realm (Saigō 1973: 145–8). Okada Seishi has made explicit the sexual implications of the bed. He points to evidence that each of the *daijōsai* pavilions was originally furnished with two beds. The new emperor, he surmised, lay in one bed, the empress in the other. After Amaterasu entered his body, some form of conjugal rite would commence (Okada Seishi 1989: 5–6). The British folklorist Carmen Blacker, prompted by Saigō's observation that ancient Japanese rulers were the "principal dreamers" in the land, proposed that *daijōsai* chamber, bed, and shroud served such dream-prompting purposes in ancient times. Could the emperor have lain on the bed, "incubated" in the shroud, slept, "and experienced a dream in which the apparition of an ancestor conferred blessings and advice on the coming reign" (Blacker 1990: 194)?

The shroud is, indeed, a striking symbol common to the *daijōsai* ritual and the Ninigi myth, but ritual and myth do not obviously share anything else in common. Above all, the *daijōsai* is a ritual of feasting, and yet feasting appears nowhere in the Ninigi myth, or indeed in Orikuchi's theory (Okada Seishi 1989: 14). As we shall see, recent scholarship interestingly finds more persuasive correspondences between the Ninigi myth and the *sokui* enthronement rite that precedes the *daijōsai*. Then there is the question of historical sources. Orikuchi applied much-needed imagination to the *daijōsai*; the absence of sources made his approach highly desirable. That absence was never total, however, and the sources that do exist lend Orikuchi no obvious support. Okada Shōji has been Orikuchi's most relentless postwar critic. Okada examines an array of medieval *daijōsai* commentaries by courtiers who witnessed the *daijōsai* from the most privileged perspective, and yet none hints that the emperor ever approached the bed, let alone lay prone upon it wrapped in the shroud. Nor do any of these commentators suggest a structural link between the rite and the Ninigi myth. What they all emphasize, rather, is the shared tasting of rice by the emperor and the sun-goddess (Okada Shōji 1990: 29–30, 84–92). Okada concludes that the bed, the pillow, and the shroud were never there for the emperor to occupy; their purpose was to welcome the weary sun-goddess. His stern verdict: "The *daijōsai* involves emperor ... welcoming sun-goddess [into the two *daijō* pavilions]. At the ritual's heart are [the emperor's] offerings to the kami and a shared tasting of rice. The emperor invites the sun-goddess onto the bed where she spends the night. The bed is a kami seat, not to be approached even by the emperor ..." (Okada 1990: 116–17).

It was indeed Okada Shōji's work that prompted the Imperial Household Agency to issue that 1990 statement denying the Orikuchi thesis. There was "nothing mystical" about the *daijōsai* rite, insisted an Agency spokesman (whose comment that the emperor is "always accompanied by a maiden" hardly made for greater clarification). Medieval sources make it clear that the emperor's role is to offer thanks to the sun-goddess for the harvest; there is no suggestion that he acquires any sacred attributes through the rite. At no time, insisted the spokesman, did the emperor "so much as touch the kami bed, or in any way become one with the sun-goddess."[6] Of course, neither the statement nor, indeed, Okada's research demonstrates that bed and shroud were never deployed in the manner suggested by Orikuchi. This was, nonetheless, a valuable statement. It explained what Akihito would and would not do in the 1990 *daijōsai*, and there is little reason to doubt it. But it is also intriguing. For it denies that the emperor acquires any divine attributes in the *daijōsai*, and it insists, notwithstanding the sun-goddess's presence, that the rite does not partake of the mystical at all.[7] The government, of course, had a keen eye on the Constitution; it could not allow the interpretation that the emperor becomes a kami like his father. There was a real danger, too, that once acknowledged as mystical, the rite might slip into the awkward realm of the religious.

A comparative perspective has been distinctly lacking from *daijōsai* studies thus far.[8] It would reveal that all rites of accession have a transforming effect. They transform a man or woman into a sovereign, and are inherently, therefore, mystical, magical dramas. As Hocart pointed out long ago, the consumption of food is one of ritual's universal techniques for effecting such a transformation (Hocart 1927: 70–98). In a comparative context, it makes excellent sense to see the *daijōsai* as a sacred, mystical event, and the emperor's consumption of rice as a transforming moment. The ritual transforms the man by locating him for the first time in the cosmic order. The *daijōsai* grants the emperor access to the sun-goddess, as intimate as it is privileged; it confirms him as her descendant, and her as his ancestress. Notwithstanding the Agency's insistence to the contrary, the *daijōsai* rite clearly invests the new emperor with a sacred, numinous quality. Thus invested, he emerges from the Suki Pavilion as a ruler straddling both earthly and cosmic realms. He is a man *and* he is a kami. This leads to an essential point about the *daijōsai* and, indeed, all ritual performances. The *daijōsai*, whatever readings may be yielded by its different symbols, is an exercise in power, and its function is to produce and reproduce a particular, emperor-centered order.

The Daijōsai *and the Modern Nation-State*

The Meiji model

> When the celestial grandson, Ninigi no Mikoto, descended upon earth, his celestial grandparent, Amaterasu, spake saying "I give the country of Toyoashiwara [Reed-plain-fair-rice-ear] to my child

to rule over," and she gave him some of the [rice] ears which grew in her sacred garden. The celestial grandson descended from heaven to the palace of Takachiho in Hiuga, first planted the seed of paddy, and ate the new rice. This was the origin of Daijo [*sic*]. [...] The celebration of the Daijo in the commencement of each reign is a ceremony which symbolises the fact that a new sovereign rules over this country, and that he received investiture from the celestial grandparent. It is therefore the gravest affair, which concerns the State. On the day of the Hare of the present month [eleventh month, fourth year of Meiji (1871)], His Majesty sacrifices to the gods of heaven and earth and on the day of the Dragon, seated on his throne, he partakes of a banquet of the new rice and bestows [rice and rice wine] on his officers and ministers.

Thus reads a contemporary translation of one section of the Meiji government's official notice of the 1871 *daijōsai* (Satow 1871). The rite marked the accession to the throne by Japan's first modern emperor. It sealed his relationship, and that of his successors, with the sun-goddess and was thus was a vital moment in the modern articulation of the myth of the emperor's descent from that goddess. The myth resonated across modern Japan at higher or lower pitch depending on circumstances, but it was never challenged. Government bureaucrats, intellectuals, religious leaders, and, within a generation or two, the common Japanese man and woman invested in this modern Japanese myth enacted by the emperor in the *daijōsai*. They did so for easily discernible reasons. The myth drew on the most ancient written sources to make sense of the revolutionary event that was the 1868 Restoration. The myth served to inspire and to justify the dramatic change that followed the Restoration, from the *daimyos*' surrender of their domains to the emperor in 1869 to the promulgation of the Meiji Constitution in 1889 (Breen 2007a). Above all, the myth endured as a marker of difference. It set modern Japan and its modern emperor apart from the international community of nation-states and sovereigns, and thus gave it meaning.

The Meiji *daijōsai* was the most dramatic claim for the emperor's divine descent made by the new regime. It was more besides. It cast the emperor as a filial sovereign since he offers rice to his divine ancestor as a way of recompensing her blessings. The Meiji *daijōsai* was framed as an event of international significance, too. A week before the *daijōsai*, the Foreign Ministry dispatched invitations to the diplomatic community to attend the post-*daijōsai* feast on the eighteenth day of the eleventh month. The British declined the invitation, but the French, Dutch, American, Spanish, and Italian ministers were all present. It was an extraordinary event, the significance of which was articulated in the toast proposed by Foreign Minister Soejima Taneomi:

> This is a great rite performed once in each imperial reign ... Ever since their birth several thousand years ago, our people have been ruled by a sovereign. To this day the line of sovereigns remains without change. Such examples are surely rare in foreign countries ... The radical reforms which began four years ago are now complete, thus enabling this *daijōsai* to take place.

Soejima, who referred here to the abolition of the feudal domains and the end of the early modern, warrior-centered social order, then reflected finally on the event's international significance: "Authority is restored today to the one sovereign of the land. Surely, this will be the guarantor of the happiness of our people and of foreign peoples too.... Let us drink a toast to the sovereigns, the presidents and the peoples of your countries and ours!" (Takeda 1996: 299). Soejima issues here an international declaration of the birth of modern Japan, no less.

There was a real sense in which the new nation of Japan was being born in the Meiji *daijōsai*. Prime Minister Sanjō Sanetomi followed the emperor into the Yuki and Suki Pavilions and read out a *norito* prayer precisely to stress that this was a state event, not a private court affair; all ministers of the emperor's government were in attendance (Takeda 1996: 287). The event cast the men and women of towns and villages across the land as his loyal subjects. This was achieved by exhortations to celebrate and opportunities to participate. The official government notice on the *daijōsai* cited above concluded: "All the people of the realm are to rest from work [on the 17th] and worship at their local shrines, where they shall wonder at the virtues of the sun-goddess and celebrate the abundant happiness that is [her gift]." There is certainly evidence of festivities in the capital of Tokyo, with lantern processions and dancing in the streets on the 18th and 19th, the two days set aside for the *daijōsai* feasting (Takeda 1996: 295). But the extent to which such activity was replicated further afield is far from clear. In Shiga Prefecture, for example, officials lined up at the governor's office on the 18th to receive gifts of imperial rice. *Daijōsai* rice was also sent to the chief priest of Hie and other major shrines. On the 17th, Hie Shrine priests had held a celebratory rite, as per government instructions, but prefectural records reveal nothing of popular participation. Prefectural and local officials, as well as Hie priests, presumably did what they could to muster support; these were, after all, national holidays. For the rest, it was the imperial subjects of Koma District of Yamanashi Prefecture and Nagasa District of Awa Province who were most closely involved. Tortoiseshell divination in the imperial court had identified these districts, to the east and west of Tokyo, as auspicious for the production of rice to be used in the Yuki and Suki Pavilions.

Taishō and empire

Emperor Meiji reigned for 45 years, and by the time of his death in July 1912 he had presided over Japan's extraordinary transformation into Asia's first modern empire. His son, Emperor Taishō, received the regalia on the day of his father's death and then performed the *sokui* and *daijōsai* rites in November 1915. The *daijōsai*, originally planned for November 1914, was postponed for a full year owing to the death of the empress dowager. In its *mise-en-scène*, Emperor Taishō's enthronement reflected the dramatic experiences of the Meiji years, but it was specifically determined by new legislation on the succession (*tōgyokurei*), promulgated in 1909. A new feature was the collapse of the *sokui* and *daijōsai* rites into a single November enthronement sequence. Another was the scripting of a role for the empress, although her pregnancy actually prevented her from taking part. Most striking of all was the spatial redefining of the rite. Taishō's enthronement took place not in Tokyo but in Kyoto, in fulfillment, it was asserted, of the late Emperor Meiji's wishes. The new emperor traveled by steam train from the modern to the ancient capital, and underwent the *sokui* rite in the Shishinden Hall of the Kyoto palace. The *daijōsai* then took place in the *daijō* complex erected in the Shishinden garden. The emperor finally proceeded by train and carriage to the Ise Shrines, to Emperor Jinmu's mausoleum in Nara, and to the Kyoto mausoleums of emperors Kōmei, Ninkō, and Kōkaku before returning to Tokyo via Kyoto. The purpose of his extended pilgrimage was filial: to report his succession to his ancestors.

The state's capacity to coordinate and to communicate was vastly greater in 1915 than in it had been in 1871, even if society was unrecognizably more complex. Japan's experiences of war, victory, and empire and the popular pride in the imperial institution to which these experiences gave rise made for greater receptivity, too. The government and the national press worked in tandem to ensure the Taishō enthronement engaged every corner of the empire. In April 1915 Prime Minister Ōkuma Shigenobu convened the year's first conference of prefectural governors, and the enthronement topped the agenda. This was, he insisted, "an unrivaled occasion for the people to turn their thoughts to [Emperor Jinmu's] founding of Japan and the true meaning of the Japanese polity [*kokutai-no-hongi*]." Ōkuma asked the governors to spare no efforts "to ensure the people manifest devout sincerity."[9] The Education Ministry meanwhile produced an accessible guide to the enthronement, styled *Tairei yōshi*, which it distributed to all schools in the land, with orders for teachers to give "continuous instruction" on the subject prior to November.[10] *Tairei yōshi* stressed the link between the sovereign, transformed by the enthronement, and his subjects:

> Our nation is ruled by a line of emperors unbroken for ages eternal. Our polity is thus without comparison anywhere in the world. Generation after generation of emperors have nurtured their subjects according to the wishes of Amaterasu and Jinmu. Imperial subjects have responded since time immemorial by serving the imperial family with loyalty and piety. Thus are the customs of this land rendered resplendent. (Tokoro 1993: 114)

Clearly, Japan's entire future depended on lessons being learned from the Taishō enthronement.

The *Yomiuri* newspaper signposted the *sokui* and *daijōsai* rites in a major feature as early as January 1915. The emperor "will take his seat on the heavenly throne" in a state rite that is "noble and solemn without compare at any time or in any place." The *Yomiuri* granted that the *sokui* betrayed Chinese influences until these were purged in 1868, but the *daijōsai* was different. It had its origins in the heavenly grandson's descent to earth, and had been performed ever since the time of Jinmu. "It is from start to finish an unadulterated rite, unsurpassed in its solemnity and sacredness." As the enthronement approached, the press carried striking visual images of the throne and the *daijō* complex, with detailed schedules of all events. Every aspect of the *sokui* and *daijōsai* rites was explained and explored, but never criticized. On the day of the *daijōsai*, the *Yomiuri* reminded its readers, for example, that the sun-goddess is the ancestor of all. "That Amaterasu is the sun personified and that we are all descended from the sun is a perfectly valid interpretation in the light of science today."[11] The press was especially interested in provincial engagement with the enthronement, and reported, even as it stimulated, prefectural plans for celebration from Hokkaido to Okinawa.

A most striking feature was the government's engagement of schools. In Shiga Prefecture, for example, every school appeared to be involved in some way.[12] On November 10, 1915, pupils from across the prefecture gathered in schoolyards and at precisely 3.30 p.m. Led by headmasters and local officials, they raised three shouts of *banzai* ("long live the emperor"). This was the very moment at which Prime Minister Ōkuma, standing before the newly enthroned emperor in the Kyoto palace, shouted *banzai* three times. In the evening, Ōtsu City pupils paraded to the prefectural office with lanterns. "There was a sea of fire, and all were intoxicated with the joy of celebration." Now again, "the earth trembled with shouts of 'long live the emperor'." Elsewhere in the prefecture, Hikone Middle School, Hachi High School, and Mizoguchi Agricultural School organized their own flag and lantern processions. Hikone Girls' High School hosted a four-day athletics meeting. On November 14, the day of the *daijōsai*, Zeze Middle School processed to Takebe Shrine to pray for the emperor, and let off 21 blasts of the canon. Nagahama Agricultural School opened its celebratory athletics competition on this day, organized a lantern procession in the evening, and published a special issue of the school journal. Earlier, on November 7, the emperor had passed through Ōtsu on his way to Kyoto, and all Shiga officials and army reserves, as well as pupils and teachers, were instructed to gather at designated points along the route. Shiga teachers and pupils were among the tens of thousands who headed for Kyoto to welcome the emperor on that day. They were certainly represented in the huge crowd that gathered outside the palace in the afternoon of November 10, and perhaps they were in the procession of some 70,000 that wended its way through the streets of Kyoto from the inn of one foreign ambassador to another. British Ambassador Green opened his bedroom window, acknowledged the crowd, and, to their delight, clapped his hands.

The government was keen to engage every imperial subject in this event, and to this end deployed several strategies. November 10, 14, and 16 (the latter the day of the enthronement feast), were declared national holidays. The 3.30 *banzai* on the 10th was replicated the length and breadth of Japan. On that day, the emperor published a list of subjects to receive honors, and granted an amnesty to convicted criminals in Japan's prisons. On November 14 major shrines across the land were visited by imperial emissaries and held solemn rites. Shrines and public buildings were everywhere festooned with flags and drapes. Many festivities focused on the enthronement, but one innovation in particular engaged people far and wide with the *daijōsai*: prefectures were encouraged to send samples of local produce to be displayed for the emperor's pleasure outside the Yuki and Suki Pavilions. Shiga Prefecture, for example, provided two baskets of azuki beans, 20 turnips, and 200 carp from Lake Biwa. Also on display was produce from Japan's colonial possessions. From Korea there was dried abalone, cabbages, pears, and apples; from Taiwan, dried bonito, citrus buntan, and bananas; from Canton, dried bream, pears, and apples; and from Karafuto (Sakhalin), dried cod, seaweed, and potatoes (*Ontaireiki*, 272).

The enthronement days were also attended by diplomats from across the globe: Britain, Japan's partner in the Anglo-Japanese alliance, and Russia, Japan's recently defeated enemy, sent ambassadors, as did China, the US, Italy, France, Portugal, Belgium, Spain, the Netherlands, Switzerland, Denmark, Norway, Chile, Argentina, Brazil, and Thailand. It was this international dimension to the Taishō enthronement that inspired an emotional Prime Minister Ōkuma to issue an extraordinary statement on November 10. "That Germany alone amongst the great powers of the world is not present is a matter of regret," he began. He referred here, of course, to the fact that Japan was at war with Germany. He continued:

> Not since Genghis Khan conquered India and Central Asia ... and ascended to the throne, summoning ambassadors from across the globe into his presence, has such an event taken place in Asia. We cannot help but be overcome by the glory of our nation. The wondrous sight of His Majesty seated upon the throne issuing a rescript to his people moved all foreign emissaries to a sense of devotion.

This observation prompted another: "To see foreign emissaries obviously struck in this spiritual way made me realize that this was precisely how a religion comes into being: it arises when a sentiment of awe such as this fills the air" (*Ontaireiki* 1915: 245).

The Taishō emperor returned to Tokyo on November 27, empowered both by his ritual experience and by the Meiji Constitution of 1889. For he now took his place in "a line of emperors unbroken for ages eternal," and was therefore "sacred and inviolable" (Articles 1 and 3). He was head of the empire in whom sovereignty resided, and he was supreme commander of the army and navy (Articles 4 and 11).[13] It was entirely fitting, therefore, that the enthronement sequence came to a formal conclusion on December 2 with the emperor's review of some 33,000 troops in the Aoyama Parade Ground in the heart of Tokyo.[14]

Shōwa perspectives

Despite the public joy that accompanied his enthronement, Emperor Taishō never settled into his role as sovereign. A dynamic figure as crown prince, he resented the deprivation of freedom that accompanied his succession. He had been prone to illness as a child, and collapsed from strain even before the enthronement. Soon he neglected both his ritual and his more political duties, and absented himself too from military reviews. By 1919 it was clear he was suffering from some mental affliction and was effectively "retired"; his son was appointed regent and assumed imperial duties. The Taishō emperor never recovered his health and died in 1926 after a reign of just 14 years. The enthronement rites of his son took place in November 1928, and they were modeled very closely on those of Taishō. The only difference that merits recording here is that new technology, in the form of the radio, meant that the capacity of those in authority to communicate prior to the event was greater still than in 1915.[15] Silence was the chosen strategy for the day itself: all the radio broadcasting companies that had so enthusiastically advertised the *daijōsai*, this "ancient, mystical rite" of "unparalleled solemnity," agreed to commemorate it by shutting down from the night of the 14th to dawn on the 15th.[16]

It was, of course, this Shōwa enthronement that inspired the reflections, discussed above, of Orikuchi Shinobu. Orikuchi first articulated his theory of bed and shroud in September 1928, at a meeting of the Shinano Educational Society. The theory was certainly not dismissed by the Shinto establishment at the time. The great Shinto scholar Miyachi Naokazu (1886–1949) gave Orikuchi's theory his seal of approval in the 1930s (Okada Shōji 1990: 44). The Shinto scholar Ono Sokyō, best known today for his postwar classic *Shinto: The kami way* (1962), accepted it wholeheartedly. For Ono, it was the *daijōsai* that transformed the man into a living god, and for this his bodily contact with the sun-goddess in the bed in the *daijōsai* rite was critical. What is of particular interest is that Orikuchi's theory drew inspiration from Hoshino Teruoki, an Imperial Household official, who was appointed Taireishi, or Enthronement Commissioner, in 1928. In brief, Hoshino was single-handedly responsible for the conduct of the Shōwa emperor's rites of enthronement. His view was that "the bed in which the kami resides was, in ages past, the emperor's bed. Or rather, it was the bed of the emperor as kami" (Miyachi 1991: 25). It is of further interest that Hoshino made this statement not merely in private conversation to Orikuchi, but publicly too in the government gazette known as *Kanpō*. He did so immediately before the Shōwa emperor's enthronement on November 7, 1928. Hoshino's views offer the most striking contrast to those of the Imperial Household Agency in 1990.

As the authoritative prewar voice on the enthronement, Hoshino merits some attention. For Hoshino, the physical throne or *takamikura*, the centerpiece of the *sokui* rite, was none other than the shrine of the sun-goddess. By taking his seat on it, the emperor became a sovereign and much more besides. It was his enthronement that inspired the instinctive appreciation common to all Japanese of "our emperor as a kami, a living kami, a kami incarnate, the great kami Amaterasu in human form" (Hoshino 1991: 33). It is thus as kami, "a partner of the kami" (*kami-no-aibō*), that the emperor enters the presence of the sun-goddess in the Yuki and Suki Pavilions erected for the *daijōsai*. "In the *daijōsai*, His Majesty receives the new rice from the heavenly rice field, in which the spirit of the heavenly ancestress is deeply, deeply ingrained … It is at the very moment when he physically receives the spirit of the heavenly ancestress that his life as a kami may properly be said to begin" (Hoshino 1991: 37). This was the officially sanctioned interpretation of the *daijōsai* rite in 1928.

But what can Hoshino's view – or, indeed, that of Orikuchi – tell us about the "original meaning" of the *daijōsai*? What is now knowable about its origins and early development? What, in brief, was the *daijōsai*, before it became the defining rite of modern state-sponsored Shinto?

The Daijōsai *and Enthronement Rites in Premodern Japan*

Origins

The first thing to be said is that the *daijōsai* is a rite of great antiquity, but it is not the primordial and "unadulterated" rite claimed by some nineteenth- and twentieth-century nationalist commentators. It is quite clearly a late addition to the sequence of early Japanese enthronement rites. Moreover, as far as we can tell, its core meaning had nothing in origin to do with rice or, indeed, with the sun-goddess. With regard to the question of its dating, the *Nihon shoki* (720) refers to rites of enthronement for all the 41 emperors whose reigns it records, but these were clearly not *daijōsai*; rather, they were rites of regalia transfer later known as *senso*, and/or rites of enthronement (*sokui*). These were of very great vintage and usually took place in the new year before the planting of rice. To the autumn *daijōsai* there is but one clear reference in the whole *Nihon shoki*. This occurs in the fifth year of the reign of Empress Jitō (r. 690–7), the last sovereign to feature in the *Nihon shoki*. The *daijōsai* cannot therefore pre-date Jitō's reign. Mizubayashi Takeshi (2001: 329–30) argues persuasively that it should be dated even later, to the reign of Jitō's successor, Monmu (r. 697–707).

The earlier rites, namely transfer and enthronement, are recorded clearly for the first time in the reign of Ingyō in the fifth century, but detail is lacking until Jitō (Okada Seishi 1989: 11). We know, for example, that prior to the reign of Jitō a sovereign would abdicate and personally hand over the regalia to his or her successor. In Jitō's time, however, the Inbe ritualists assumed for the first time a key role in regalia transfer. This seems to reflect a new understanding of the regalia as sacred objects that the sun-goddess had bestowed on her grandson, Ninigi (Mizubayashi 2001: 319). Jitō's reign coincides after all with the early formulation of the mythical narratives, which were later incorporated into the *Kojiki* of 712. Okada has also demonstrated that the enthronement of the future sovereign reveals important correspondences with those narratives. The future sovereign's approach to the throne, surrounded by maidens bearing cloud-like screens to obscure his view, re-enacts Ninigi making his way through eight-layered clouds to alight on the Takachiho peak. The emperor's dramatic emergence from behind the curtains enwrapping his canopied throne is a dramatization of Ninigi casting aside his coverlet after alighting on the Takachiho peak. Again, the Ōtomo warriors, who in the mythical narrative constitute the vanguard of Ninigi's descent, stand guard by the emperor in the enthronement rites of the mid seventh century. These and other commonalities between enthronement rite and myth are, indeed, far more numerous and persuasive than any between myth and *daijōsai* (Okada Seishi 1989: 29–33). At the very same time, however – that is, in the second half of the seventh century – the enthronement rite began to acquire an outer layer identifying it with practices in the mighty Tang dynasty. Already during the reign of Tenji (r. 668–71), for example, Japanese sovereigns began to wear Tang Chinese crowns, ornaments, and court garb. They now added to the regalia of mirror, sword, and jewel the Chinese symbols of legitimate succession: a sword and a gold plaque, known together as *tachi kei*. Incense was burned to notify the gods in heaven of the momentous event of succession, and shouts of *banzai* greeted Tenji's accession; both features are Chinese in origin (Okada Seishi 1989: 31).

So much for regalia transfer and enthronement in the latter half of the seventh century, around the time of Jitō. What then of the quite distinct and obviously newer *daijōsai*? The latest research by Mizubayashi Takeshi, provocative and persuasive in equal measure, demonstrates that, in origin, *daijōsai* had nothing to do with the sun-goddess; neither can it have been a harvest rite. He makes the obvious point that the lunar eleventh month in which the *daijōsai* took place is far too late for harvest celebrations. Moreover, the court already had a harvest rite involving the presentation of the first fruits to Amaterasu in Ise in the lunar ninth month; this was the so-called *kanname* rite. The intimate connection between sun-goddess, rice, and *daijōsai* was a subsequent refinement. It appeared perhaps in the late eighth or early ninth century, but it can only be verified in the tenth-century *Engi shiki*.

The *Kojiki*, drawing as it does on earlier seventh-century texts, must hold the clue to the original meaning of the *daijōsai*. A rite of such importance could not be unrelated to the state-founding myths. In the *Kojiki*, there is one episode that features the son of heaven and a palace building containing bedding, and which involves feasting. The episode occurs in chapter 43, and its main character is Sora-tsu-hiko or Ama-tsu-hiko (son of heaven), the third son born to Ninigi and Princess Konohana-no-sakuya-hime. In this episode, Sora-tsu-hiko, a man of great beauty, is sent to the palace of the sea kami. When he arrives, he encounters the kami's daughter, the beautiful Princess Toyotama-hime. When she reports to her father the presence of a fine-looking man waiting nearby, her father invites him into the sea palace. To welcome this handsome imperial visitor, the sea kami spreads out eight-layered sealskin mats within a palace hall. On top of them he places eight-layered silks, and then he has Sora-tsu-hiko take a seat upon them. The sea kami "set out hundreds of tables laden with gifts, prepared a feast for him and gave him his daughter Princess Toyotama-hime as his wife" (Philippi 1969: 150–2).[17]

The striking similarity between this narrative and the symbols of the *daijōsai* drama is apparent at a glance: the emperor, the palace building, the eight-layered mats, and the feasting are all present. There is no other narrative in the *Kojiki* that contains all these elements, and Mizubayashi argues persuasively that the *daijōsai* was in origin a dramatization of this story (Mizubayashi 2001: 208–11). The *daijōsai* is of course a complex rite replete with meanings, not exhausted by this tale. For example, the earliest historical references to the *daijōsai* feature the presentation of offerings from two provinces either side of the capital, which between them represent the emperor's realm. These are the Yuki and Suki districts, whose governors and people bring offerings to the palace. In other words, the *daijōsai* was not uniquely about the sea; it was about the land as well. As we have seen, this was not a rice harvest ritual, nor is there any evidence that the produce brought to the capital was in origin first fruits. Mizubayashi sees here an enactment of the mythical narrative describing the ceding of the realm to the descendants of the sun-goddess by the kami Ōkuninushi. Whether or not this is the case, it is clear that the Yuki and Suki offerings symbolize the realm being gifted to the sovereign. At its most fundamental level, then, the original *daijōsai* dramatized the new emperor's claims both to the oceans (*unabara*) and to rice-abundant land (*ashihara*). In the *senso*, and *sokui* rites of regalia transfer and enthronement, his inheritance of heaven was already clear. Only now in receipt of the earthly realm in its entirety does he merit the title of *tennō*, or divine sovereign (Mizubayashi 2001: 224–30).

One particularly striking feature of the *Kojiki* sea-kami narrative is the marriage: the son of heaven weds the sea kami's daughter. In its original form, the *daijōsai* drama, too, must have involved a marriage. The beds in the *daijōsai* pavilions – there were originally two in each – evidence this fact. Mizubayashi argues that the marriage was intended to bind the emperor to the sea and land through his marriage to marine and earthly maidens. The earliest detailed accounts of the Yuki and Suki sequences of the *daijōsai* ascribe a prominent role to virgins, known as *sakatsuko* (a word written with characters meaning "rice-brewing maidens"). These maidens were selected from the districts that were divined as Yuki and Suki, the former of which were all located by the sea. These Yuki and Suki maidens were brought to the capital. That they assumed a critical role in the *daijōsai* rite is evident in the fact that they alone were carried on palanquins to the Yuki and Suki Pavilions at the start of each sequence; they then accompanied the emperor into the pavilions. It is entirely reasonable to suppose that the emperor "wed" these maidens from the sea and the land. Through his weddings, the emperor acquired the magical means to rule the entirety of his realm (Mizubayashi 2001: 256–9).

If Mizubayashi is correct – and the rigor with which he makes his case, as well as his judicious use of circumstantial evidence, leaves little room for doubt that he is – then it is clear that the *daijōsai* in its earliest manifestation was an altogether different rite from that which it later became. It was certainly intimately related to the mythical narratives later incorporated into the *Kojiki* – the sea kami story and perhaps Ōkuninushi's ceding of the realm; and these mythical narratives and the *daijōsai* itself were, of course, all designed to legitimate imperial power. But it was not a harvest rite, nor was it directly related to the imperial line's descent from the sun-goddess; still less does it have any structural or other connection with the myth of Ninigi's descent. At the end of the eighth or beginning of the ninth century, however, the meanings of the *daijōsai* appear to have shifted, and the ritual symbolism was revised accordingly. The understanding of a marriage between the emperor and a maiden as a symbolic claim on the realm was lost, although regional offerings and the Yuki and Suki Pavilions survived. The bed – where there had been two beds, there was now only one – came to be interpreted in a new way, too: it was there in preparation for the arrival of the sun-goddess. She would rest her weary self, having traveled from heaven to earth for the ritual encounter with her descendant the emperor. The idea that the emperor was being served with a feast now yielded to the interpretation that that feast was an offering from the emperor to the sun-goddess to welcome and revitalize her. It is this revised rite whose features can be confirmed in the tenth-century *Engi shiki* codes (Mizubayashi 2001: 392).

The new sophisticated *senso, sokui,* and *daijōsai* rites were developed by Emperor Tenmu and deployed from the reigns of Jitō through Monmu as a key part of a new strategy of consolidating domestic power after the Jinshin rebellion that had brought Tenmu to power. They were also a response to seismic change on the continent. In the 660s, the Korean kingdom of Silla, with Tang military assistance, destroyed the neighboring states of Paekche and Koguryŏ in quick succession. Paekche royalty fled to Japan seeking support, and the Japanese duly dispatched troops to the peninsula, only to be crushed in a major battle in 663. The specter now arose of a joint Tang and Silla invasion of Japan, and this added huge impetus to the centralization of power in seventh-century Japan. In fact, Silla soon changed tack and sought subtly to dispel Tang influence from the Korean peninsula, a strategy that for Japan meant the specter of invasion yielding to a new scenario, as Tang and Paekche dispatched goodwill envoys seeking alliances. If Japan were to respond to Chinese and Korean expectations, and of course guarantee its independence in East Asia, its sovereigns had to comport themselves in a recognizably "civilized" manner, as determined by Tang China. The Chinese exterior to the *sokui* rite served as a public expression of the new civilized Japan. Simultaneously, though, from Tenmu's reign there was a powerful pull in the direction of difference. The ritual dramatization of key passage in the imperial myths, from the transfer of regalia through the enthronement to the new invention of the *daijōsai* itself, all seem to proclaim this. Indeed, the new enthronement in its totality imparts vital meaning to the title of *tennō* (literally "heavenly sovereign") which Tenmu, Jitō, and their successors now assumed, and also to *Nihon,* or "the sun's origin," the new international referent for the Japanese realm.

The demise of the *daijōsai*

Certainly by the time of the *Engi shiki* in the tenth century, perhaps as early as the late eighth or early ninth centuries, the *daijōsai* had acquired a form that endured into the modern era. We need to be extremely wary, however, of over-stressing continuity. The *daijōsai* did not establish itself now as the sole or even necessarily the most important signifier of Japanese emperorship. For one thing, we shall find a powerful Buddhist influence at work; for another, the *daijōsai* was for many generations not performed at all. A no less important point concerns meanings rather than form: the meanings attributed to the *daijōsai* by the modern state were themselves modern ideas. There is no evidence, as we shall see, that the Meiji reading of the *daijōsai* had any currency before Meiji.

Here an appreciation of Buddhism's ever-increasing influence on the court and Japanese society as a whole is called for. Emperor Shōmu (r. 724–49) saw no inherent contradiction in, say, communing with the kami in his enthronement rites only then to declare himself "slave of the Buddha" and to embark on a massive state-wide program of Buddhist temple construction. Indeed, as we saw in Chapter 2, Tenmu, the very architect of the new enthronement sequence, repeatedly did obeisance at Buddhist temples, demanding that Buddhist sanctuaries be placed in every household of the realm. For Tenmu, Shōmu, and their successors, identity with the kami, on the one hand, and devotion to the Buddha on the other were in no way contradictory. Others in the imperial court took a different view, and then took action. In the year 871 the court published the *Jōgan shiki*, a code of procedures compiled with the apparent intention of preserving the integrity of the myth of the emperor's descent from the sun-goddess. This code imposed a ban on the performance of Buddhist rites at court for the duration of the *daijōsai*. This suggests that the shift in the *daijōsai*'s meaning discussed above had already taken place: the *daijōsai* was now associated with the sun-goddess. The same code similarly protected the many other *jingi* rites at court from Buddhist encroachment.

It was Shōmu who had initiated the practice of emperors taking the tonsure upon retirement and devoting their remaining years to the Dharma. For centuries, though, there remained an unwritten law that incumbent sovereigns, however devout, would not take Buddhist orders (Kamikawa 1990: 245). Never again would they submit themselves to the greater authority of a specific prelate or lineage, as had happened in the eighth century when Empress Shōtoku (r. 764–70) fell for the monk Dōkyō.[18] As a result, Japanese emperorship was immune to further Buddhist encroachments at least until the end of the thirteenth century.

In 1288, however, Emperor Fushimi (r.1287–98) underwent an enthronement rite entirely without precedent. As he ascended the throne on the fifteenth day of the third month in that year, Fushimi fashioned his hands in the shape of the wisdom fist mudra and recited the *dharaṇī* spell of Ḍākinī. The wisdom fist mudra was that formed by Mahāvairocana (Dainichi); the *dharaṇī* of Ḍākinī invoked a Tantric demon deity representing the fierce powers of Mahāvairocana's twin aspects of wisdom and compassion. Fushimi had been initiated in these techniques two days earlier by his regent Nijō Morotada (Kamikawa 1990: 251–2, 262; Teeuwen 2006). This marks a striking development in the theory and practice of Japanese emperorship. After all, by forming a mudra with their hands and *dharaṇī* spells with their lips, Japanese emperors were now achieving a mystical identity with Mahāvairocana.

What made sense of this *sokui kanjō*, as the rite was known, was a hundred and more years of theorizing by monks about the relationship between buddhas and kami, focusing especially on great kami like Amaterasu. In 1203 the Tendai monk Jien (1155–1225) had a dream revelation concerning the imperial regalia of sword, jewel, and mirror. In his dream, the jewel turned into a sheath that encased the sword (Abé 1999: 363). Jien fashioned a sophisticated Buddhist interpretation of his vision, which he duly reported to the emperor. The union of sword and jewel mirrored that of emperor and empress. The emperor-as-sword is the Buddha Ekākṣara-uṣṇīsacakra: the form in which the sun-buddha Mahāvairocana manifests itself as a *cakravartin* or sage king. The empress-as-jewel is Buddhalocana, the eye and the mother of all buddhas. As sword and jewel unite, so do the laws of buddhas and kings. Together, they give birth to the third divine treasure, the mirror of Amaterasu kept in the Naishidokoro elsewhere in the palace, which represents both the son of heaven produced by the imperial union and the manifestation of Mahāvairocana in the land of Japan. "That is why," Jien wrote in his report, "the ruler of our world, when he ascends to the *takamikura* enthronement dais, forms with his hands Ekākṣara-uṣṇīsacakra's mudra of the wisdom fist" (Abé 1999: 364).

Here Jien seems to imply that such ritual acts were already part of imperial enthronements in his day, but this was probably not yet the case (Kamikawa 1990: 249–51). The centrality of Ḍākinī in recorded performances of *sokui kanjō* is not reflected in Jien's dream report, suggesting that there was a gap between his vision of a Buddhist enthronement rite and its actual implementation. More important, however, is the point that it was already natural for Jien, and other theorists besides, that emperors would make manifest in their enthronements what was now a generally accepted thesis: the sun-goddess was the sun-buddha, and Japanese emperors, directly descended from the former, were naturally the embodiment of the latter. That identity was properly made manifest when the man became emperor.

The new enthronement that accommodated the *sokui kanjō* became *de rigueur* for Japanese emperors from the time of Go-Komatsu (r. 1382–1412), about a century after Fushimi, and was consistently performed as part of the *sokui* rite until the enthronement of Emperor Kōmei in 1846. The *sokui kanjō* did not, however, displace the *daijōsai*. Indeed, the latter remained of sufficient importance to merit an attempt at reinterpretation by Yoshida Kanetomo in the fifteenth century.[19] In his *Yuiitsu Shintō myōhō yōshū*, Kanetomo referred to the Yuki and Suki Pavilions as representing the two worlds of one-and-only Shinto. Those two worlds, he explained, were identical to the Outer and Inner Shrines of Ise, and by the same token they constituted the Diamond and Womb mandalas, "the original form of the Yin and Yang of heaven and earth." Such was Kanetomo's reading of the cosmic significance of the 1460s *daijōsai* performed by Go-Tsuchimikado (r. 1464–1500): it was the ultimate manifestation of cosmic truth. Go-Tsuchimikado's successor Go-Kashiwara (r. 1500–26) had the distinction of being the first adult sovereign for 800 years not to undergo the *daijōsai*; thereafter it was abandoned altogether. Japan was after all in the throes of the Ōnin wars, which prompted a century of civil conflict. Indeed, so turbulent were the times that fully 22 years were to pass between Go-Kashiwara's receipt of the regalia in 1500 and the performance of his enthronement. It was not for another hundred years that the first condition for the *daijōsai*'s reinstatement – order in the realm – was met.

The *daijōsai* and its early modern revival

Long before Tokugawa Ieyasu established the Tokugawa military regime in 1603, Japanese emperors had relinquished their claim to rule Japan. Indeed, for the last 500 years they had authorized military lords to rule in their name. This at least was the theory. In fact, of course, a succession of military dynasties, the Minamoto (twelfth to fourteenth centuries), the Ashikaga (fourteenth to sixteenth centuries), and now the Tokugawa (seventeenth to nineteenth centuries) seized power by main force and demanded that emperors authorize their rule. Emperors were inevitably often contemptuous of the military, or at least of their mores. In turn, different shoguns had different degrees of respect for the incumbents of the imperial line, but there were none who did not covet the shogunal office. Indeed, several Tokugawa shoguns held the court and its traditions in high esteem. Tsunayoshi and Yoshimune, the fifth and eighth shoguns respectively, were two of them. It was Tsunayoshi (r.1680–1709) who sanctioned the revival of the *daijōsai* in 1687; after another hiatus, Yoshimune (r. 1716–45) reinstated it for all subsequent emperors in 1738.

The Tokugawa demanded that emperors devote themselves to learning, and several took this as a cue to investigate traditions of court ritual. Go-Mizunoo (r. 1611–29) led the way, and his son Reigen (r. 1663–87) took decisive action, petitioning the Tokugawa to reinstate numerous defunct rites. Reigen argued, for example, that the *daijōsai* was once an integral part of enthronement rites, and it was, moreover, a rite "entirely unique to Japan." His petition bore fruit. After several months of negotiation, shogun Tsunayoshi allowed Reigen's son Higashiyama (r. 1687–1709) to undergo the first *daijōsai* for 221 years, even though it was an abbreviated affair. Tsunayoshi had a clear understanding of ritual performance as a correct technique for ordering the realm. He knew shogunal authority could no longer depend on displays of military might, for the realm was now at peace. By restoring the *daijōsai* and dispatching to the court gift-bearing emissaries, Tsunayoshi and his successors declared to the realm their abiding concern for ritual order, even as they cast themselves as paragons of loyalty to the court. Their purpose was, of course, always to enhance shogunal power.

And yet Higashiyama's son Nakamikado (r. 1710–35) was deprived of a *daijōsai*. The explanation, it seems, has to do with the intervention of Arai Hakuseki (1657–1725). Arai was Confucian adviser to the sixth shogun Ienobu, and he had a quite different approach to shoring up shogunal authority. His self-appointed mission was to transfer sovereignty from the imperial house to the Tokugawa military government, rendering the court redundant (Nakai 1988: 311–16). For Arai, nothing embodied imperial sovereignty more than the *daijōsai*, and it seems highly likely that he blocked Nakamikado's *daijōsai* the better to argue that Ienobu was the man now sanctioned by heaven to rule the realm. Had Arai's influence endured, the *daijōsai* might have disappeared forever, but he was ousted in 1716 when Yoshimune came to power. Yoshimune had a keen interest in the court and its rites, and he ensured the resumption of the *daijōsai*. Divination of the Yuki and Suki districts was reintroduced, which confirmed Shiga and Kuwata as suitable for the production of rice; there was also a performance of Shiga and Kuwata songs, but the sources do not reveal their content, who recited them, or where or exactly when. Nonetheless, the *daijōsai* rites were now re-established, and they have remained an essential part of imperial enthronements ever since.

The modern *daijōsai* discourse was still, however, nowhere to be seen in Yoshimune's time. That discourse comprises two ideas: (1) that the rite has its origins in Amaterasu's dispatch of her grandson to earth, bearing the gift of rice; and (2) that the rite is of a national, state-determined character that serves to draw transcendental emperor and human subjects together (Maeda Tsutomu 2006: 254–5). These elements emerged for the first time in the writings of nativist scholars in the late eighteenth and early nineteenth centuries. The key players we have encountered already in Chapter 2: Motoori Norinaga, Aizawa Seishisai, and Hirata Atsutane. Motoori, for example, regarded the emperor's feasting as the pivotal ritual moment. For him, the *daijōsai* was not a "Chinese-style rite" in which the emperor worshiped the sun-goddess as his ancestor. Hirata Atsutane for his part argued that the origin of the *daijōsai* was to be found in Ninigi's planting of rice in the imperial rice field. His disciple, Suzuki Shigetane (1812–63), then proposed that the function of the *daijōsai* rite, through the emperor's feasting on rice, was to effect his transformation into a living kami (Maeda 2006: 262–5). None of these ideas had been articulated before.

Aizawa Seishisai exerted a still more decisive influence on the modern understanding of the *daijōsai*. His theorizing was prompted by a most profound sense of crisis. Japan, Aizawa believed, was trapped between the Russians and the British and was powerless to resist. It was not the foreigners' weaponry so much as their religion that filled him with dread (Wakabayashi 1986: 86–90). Japan's only hope was to deploy the emperor. His performances of state ritual alone would be sufficient to stir dispositions of awe and loyalty throughout society. Only then would Japan be ready to take on the threat from without. No rite could be more efficacious in this regard than the *daijōsai*. Aizawa writes of its transforming effect:

> When the Emperor, Amaterasu's own flesh and blood, solemnly performs this *daijōsai* rite in Her honour, Her own countenance presents itself to all who gaze on His Majesty. The court nobles looking on, both high and low, imagine themselves to be in Amaterasu's presence. The feeling of communion arises naturally among them and cannot be suppressed, for they too are descendants of the gods. (Wakabayashi 1986: 157–8)

Aizawa invested the *daijōsai* with a core Confucian meaning, and saw the divine emperor's offering of rice to Amaterasu as the ultimate act of filial piety. Filial piety was synonymous with loyalty, and there existed no better technique for its dissemination than ritual performance. Rituals were a means of political rule, and political rule was identical to ethical inculcation. Thus explains Aizawa in his *Shinron* (New theses) of 1825. He imputed to the *daijōsai* the power to transform not just the political elite but the whole of society. In his *Sōen wagen* of 1836, he explained that this transformation depended on the *daijōsai* being revived in its former magnificence.[20] People from all provinces must again bring the fruits of the land to Kyoto and offer them to the emperor, who will place them before his ancestor, the sun-goddess. "In ancient times, the emperor thus took upon his own sacred body the sincerity with which his subjects sought to recompense heaven. He conveyed this to the kami. The people knew this, they rejoiced and were filled with heavenly blessings" (Arakawa 1989: 361). Aizawa was aware of the incendiary potential of his views and never published *Shinron*, although it circulated widely amongst activists in the 1850s and 1860s. *Sōen wagen*, however, he did have printed in Mito, and it was distributed among samurai in that domain in 1848. This was a year in which an American vessel was shipwrecked in Japan's northernmost island, a French vessel dropped anchor off the Ryukyu Islands, and a Dutch vessel arrived in Nagasaki with news that British gunboats had set sail to punish China. Here was evidence that the fears Seishisai had articulated in the 1820s were coming true.

With the very important exception that Aizawa envisaged some future for the Tokugawa, it is possible to see in his writings an inspiration for the nation-stirring *daijōsai* performed by Japan's modern emperors Meiji, Taishō, and Shōwa. The writings of Motoori, Hirata, and Suzuki offered vital inspiration, too, for they stressed the *daijōsai* as a dramatization of the emperor's descent from the sun-goddess.

Conclusion

The *daijōsai* is, as we have seen, a rite of great vintage. Its origins can be traced back in some form or other to the seventh century. However, the particularistic *daijōsai* was pre-dated in Japan by the universal rites of regalia transfer and ascent of the throne. The *daijōsai* in its earliest form had a close connection with imperial myth, but not the Ninigi myth, which in the modern period has given the rite its core meaning. In origin, rather, the *daijōsai* dramatized the emperor's acquisition of the realm. The emperor was, of course, understood to be descended from the sun-goddess, and this fact was dramatized not in the *daijōsai*, but in the rites of regalia transfer (*senso*) and enthronement (*sokui*). Even when the meaning of the *daijōsai* shifted in the late eighth or early ninth centuries, the rite can hardly be said to have defined the imperial institution. After all, there was the accretion of Buddhist enthronement rites and, of course, the hiatus that straddled the sixteenth and seventeenth centuries. Emperors were not regarded as less imperial for not performing the *daijōsai*.[21] It was the early modern nativists through their reflections on the kami, the imperial institution, and Japan in its relationship to China and the West who finally, in the nineteenth century, injected the modern meanings into this ancient imperial rite. Those meanings have endured to this day, and present a particular challenge as Japan in the twenty-first century debates its Constitution.

In 2005 the Constitution Revision Committee (Kenpō chōsa iinkai) invited submissions on the subject of the *daijōsai* and the Constitution. At bottom the question that occupied the committee was whether future Japanese emperors might perform the rite without infringing the Constitution and, if not, what needed to be changed. The committee received three submissions. Ishige Naomichi, an esteemed anthropologist who specializes in food culture, rambled before the committee before concluding the *daijōsai* shared much in common with a coming of age ceremony.[22] Two other expert witnesses, representing institutions with a vested interest, emphasized the constitutional challenges for the future and offered contrasting solutions. One was Nozaka Yasushi, a professor at Gakushūin University, the Peers school where imperial princes and princesses are always educated. He concluded that since the *daijōsai* rites are religious, they must in future be conducted not as state events but as private court rites.[23] The other witness was Professor Sakamoto Koremaru of Kokugakuin University, which is one of two Shinto universities in Japan responsible for training shrine priests amongst other things. For Sakamoto, the only solution to the problem was to revise the Constitution to accommodate the performance of the *daijōsai* as a state event. After all, he insisted, the purpose of the *daijōsai* was none other than to unify the state, the imperial court, and the people.[24] It seems that the approach of the incumbent Liberal Democratic Party is very close to that of Sakamoto. Evidence is in the LDP proposals for revising the Constitution in 2005. The new Article 20 forbids "state involvement in religious education and religious practice," but it does so *only when* such practice "extends beyond the realm of social ritual and customary practices".[25] The LDP understand the *daijōsai* as one of those "customary practices." Whether or not this new Article 20 ever becomes law, there can be no doubt that the next emperor will perform the *daijōsai*.

Chapter 6

Issues in Contemporary Shinto

We began this book with a critical survey of Shinto in modern Japan. We identified Shinto's modern invention in the nineteenth century, and then explored the dynamics of its subsequent accommodation to postwar democracy. In the nineteenth century, the modern nation-state had a vital role to play in shaping and defining Shinto. From the second half of the twentieth century, following Japan's defeat in the war, the Allied Occupation, and the promulgation of the Japanese Constitution, the key player has been the National Association of Shrines. Here, we return to NAS to examine its operations and agendas. What matters to NAS in the twenty-first century? What challenges does it face, and how does it meet them? What lies beyond NAS parameters?

NAS: Operations and Agendas

The single most important point to make about NAS is that it continues to idealize Shinto in its prewar, state-sponsored guise. Its agenda is very much that of the prewar years, when Shinto was defined as a "nonreligion" distinct from, and most definitely superior to, all religions. This point about continuity stands, despite the fact that NAS now speaks openly, for example in its weekly newspaper *Jinja shinpō*, about Shinto as a religion (*shūkyō*) and about Shinto faith (*shinkō*). NAS participates, moreover, in the Nihon Shūkyō Renmei, the Japanese Association of Religious

Organizations, along with Christian, Buddhist, and so-called "sect Shinto" groups. It transpires, however, that NAS has little of substance to say on theological matters and, indeed, on many of the issues that preoccupy other religious groups in that organization. The Ise Shrines and the sun-goddess are what give meaning to NAS and all of its undertakings. In 1956 NAS created a document called *Keishin seikatsu no kōryō*, a shrine priests' "Agenda for a life of kami worship." It may serve as a pointer to the priorities for NAS and its priests. The Agenda comprises three duties, binding upon all NAS shrine priests and priestesses. They must:

1   give thanks for kami blessings, and "with bright and pure sincerity" perform rites;
2   serve the kami and so "give form to society";
3   in accord with the emperor's wishes, pray to the kami for Japan's flourishing and world peace.

Their task, in other words, is ritual performance and prayer, and NAS determines the rites to be performed and prayers to be intoned. The NAS category of "Great Rites" (*taisai*) includes, alongside individual shrines' annual festivals, the imperial *kinen-sai* and *niiname-sai*.[1] The next category of "Median Rites" (*chūsai*) is exclusively prewar. These rites include New Year, alongside *genshi-sai, kigen-sai, kanname-sai, Meiji-sai*, and *tenchō-sai*.[2] In 2006 NAS further enriched the ritual list with Emperor Hirohito's anniversary (*Shōwa-sai*), and equinox rites to celebrate the imperial ancestors.[3] Shrine priests are required, moreover, to recite daily the *Ōharae-no-kotoba*, a prayer of purification otherwise known as the *Nakatomi ōharae*.[4]

Since its creation in 1946, NAS has campaigned to replicate the imperial "form" of prewar society, so far as the Constitution allows. It has helped secure the resurrection of State Foundation Day (*kenkoku kinen no hi*) as a national holiday, the nationalization of the flag and anthem, and the legalization of imperial reign names (Hardacre 1989). At the start of the twenty-first century, NAS's consuming passions remain emperor and imperial institution, the Ise Shrines, revising the Constitution, the Yasukuni Shrine, and ethical education. Articles on these issues dominate

Jinja shinpō. A typical headline in September 2008 ran: "Let us make our own Constitution!" Beneath was a report on a Shinto youth group event convened to "clarify the Shinto spirit" that must inform any constitutional revision. For participants, this meant defining the emperor as head of state, underscoring his vital ritual function, and stressing the eternal nature of the imperial line.[5] Other articles on the same front page introduced a new drama-documentary showing in the Yasukuni Shrine cinema, and reported on the 2,400th anniversary rites for the (mythical) Emperor Kōshō at the Imperial Palace and at his Nara mausoleum. October 2008 issues of *Jinja shinpō* recorded the emperor's annual dispatch of emissaries to the Yasukuni Shrine for its autumn festival, and to Ise for the *kanname-sai*. There was much coverage, too, of preparations to mark the imminent twentieth anniversary of Emperor Akihito's enthronement.[6] In November, the discovery of very rare kami statues in an architectural dig in Shiga Prefecture, the crown prince's visit to the Ise Shrines, and a controversial web-based critique of Yasukuni Shrine all featured.[7]

NAS now entrusts much of its political lobbying to a pressure group called Shintō Seiji Renmei.[8] The Shinseiren, in its common abbreviation, has branch offices in every prefecture, but is especially active in the Diet. Of some 700 members in the Japanese Diet, 157 are presently signed up to its debating club (*Kokkai giin kondankai*), and are thus committed to the Shinseiren's five-point agenda. Members campaign, that is, for a society that "treasures the imperial institution"; a new Constitution "of which Japan can be proud"; the performance of national rites at Yasukuni; an education system to "nurture children's hearts" and instill optimism for Japan's future; and the founding of "an ethical nation that will be the envy of the world."[9] The Shinseiren president at the time of writing is Mori Yoshirō (b. 1937). As prime minister in 2000, Mori created a storm with a presentation he made at the debating club. "This land of Japan," he declared, is the land of the kami [*kami-no-kuni*], with the imperial institution at its core. This is what we want all Japanese to take fully on board; it is towards this end that we [Diet members of this discussion club] have been striving."[10] For the liberal media, Mori's speech was nothing less than a prime-ministerial assault on the constitutional principles of popular sovereignty and the separation of state and religion. Mori was relentlessly attacked; he retreated and apologized, but the speech created such a furor that eventually he had to resign. In a June 2008 editorial, *Jinja shinpō* urged the Shinseiren to broaden its targets now to address three more challenges facing twenty-first-century Japan: the right of foreigners to vote, the granting to foreigners of Japanese nationality, and women's legal right to use their maiden name after marriage.[11]

NAS idealizes the prewar principle that shrines are ultimately of imperial Japan, not of the local community, still less of their priests. This is apparent in the imperial rites and prayers demanded of NAS priests, and the special position occupied by the Ise Shrines, regarding which some comment is called for. From the outset, NAS understood its own role to be that of supporting Ise, "the holiest of holies" (*honsō*), but not of course interfering in its operations (Okada Yoneo 1987: 840–1). NAS has as its president (*sōsai*) Ikeda Atsuko, who is sister of the present emperor and *saishu* or "chief ritualist" at the Ise Shrines. The NAS chief executive (*tōri*) is Kuni Kuniaki, the emperor's cousin and erstwhile Ise chief priest. The presidential position is honorary, but the chief executive is the ultimate authority in NAS. The incumbent exercises his powers within NAS and through the network of prefectural Jinjachō or Shrine Offices. To him are devolved, for example, the powers to appoint, dismiss, promote, demote, and suspend shrine priests. The chief executive acts in matters of this nature on the advice of individual shrine committees (*yakuin kaigi*) which, presided over by a shrine's chief priest, run local shrine affairs on a day-to-day basis. The NAS chief executive is not, however, bound by shrine committee recommendations. It goes without saying that his executive powers do not extend to the Ise Shrines, and the Ise chief priest and the Ise *saishu* are to this day both imperial appointments.

NAS does not stipend priests or otherwise support local shrines; it demands, rather, a contribution from them. Statistics are not available, but a fixed sum is payable depending on the number and rank of shrine priests. Priests survive, and sometimes thrive, off shrine income, which is derived typically from worshipers' offerings and the sale of amulets at New Year and other major festivals. Fortune-telling, and payments for prayers recited and other rites performed to order also generate vital income. These latter may include weddings and sometimes funerals, car purifications, and *kagura* dances performed by *miko* shrine maidens. Some shrines also draw an income from shrine land, especially when it is concreted over and redeployed as a car park. There are fabulously wealthy shrines like the Meiji Jingū in Tokyo, but many others border on destitution. All shrines attached to NAS are required to submit annual financial reports, and the disposal of any shrine land or property requires NAS approval. In a legal sense, all shrines under the NAS umbrella are equal, but Ise remains – as before the war – a category apart. Indeed, state-determined categories of shrines from prewar times resonate in the NAS to this day. During the Occupation, NAS designated over 350 shrines as *beppyō jinja* or "special category shrines." Today their number includes all those shrines dedicated to the local war dead, the so-called *gokoku jinja*, which are mostly early twentieth-century creations. The old *ichi-no-miya* shrines, the 22 shrines (*nijūnisha*), and the Meiji-period category of prefectural shrines (*kensha*) feature on the list, as do many of the *kanpei* and *kokuhei* shrines.[12] Hiyoshi Taisha is, of course, included in their number. Sixteen important shrines are further designated *chokusaisha*, which means they receive the emperor's gift-bearing emissaries on the occasion of their annual festivals. The most famous of these is Yasukuni Shrine, which presents something of an anomaly since, as we shall see, it does not in fact belong to NAS.

For NAS, shrines serve the vital function of binding Japanese people to the sun-goddess, the imperial myth and the imperial institution. Nonetheless, communities' attachment to local shrines does not point to a shared ideological agenda. A 2007 NAS survey found the top three occasions for popular engagement with shrines were:

1 New Year (62 percent);
2 children's rites of passage, such as the first shrine visit of the newborn and visits of children aged 7, 5, and 3 (53 percent);
3 prayers for family well-being (37 percent).

No respondents cited imperial, patriotic themes as a reason for visiting their local shrine, a fact that brings into relief an important slippage between the NAS understanding and that of the common man or woman. The same survey revealed in fact that 35 percent of Japanese had no knowledge at all of their local shrine; the figure rose to 40 percent in urban areas.[13] But NAS has a strategy to tackle this apparently bleak situation. The strategy involves deploying Jingū *taima* or Ise amulets. Ise amulets are sacred objects in which the sun-goddess resides, and they bear the legend Tenshō Kōtaijingū (Imperial Great Shrine of Amaterasu). Amulets, which come in different sizes and prices (between 2,000 and 500 yen), are ritually prepared in Ise, and there handed over to the executive director of NAS, who takes responsibility for their distribution.[14] NAS forwards them to prefectural Shrine Offices, which then offload them to shrine priests who are tasked with selling them on to parishioners and others besides. In 1987 NAS began a campaign to get Ise amulets into 10 million homes, one-fifth of the total. An initial surge was followed by a 10-year decline, but sales have started to rise again so that, as of March 2008, the target seems tantalizingly close. For 2008, NAS reported increases in Tokyo and its environs and also in Fukuoka, which more than compensated for sluggish sales elsewhere. As a result, the total of Ise amulets sold in 2008 rose to 8,990,000.[15] These figures, if they are to be trusted, reflect some imaginative promotion.

Shrine Offices across Japan found that people would not buy Ise amulets if they had no kami altar (*kamidana*), so they began to distribute free altar kits, along with instructions on how to worship the amulet. Statistics also suggested that only 18 percent of those who bought Ise amulets did so at their local shrine. It was essential, therefore, to take amulets to the people. A 2006 survey revealed that nearly 50 percent of those who bought amulets did so from local volunteers knocking on doors. Whether sales will continue to rise is difficult to predict. Some 14.6 percent of people who now own an Ise amulet purchased it on a visit to the Ise Shrines, and these visits are likely to increase over the next few years as advertising for the ritual rebuilding of the Ise Shrines (an event which takes place every 20 years and is next due in 2013) intensifies.[16] On the other hand, there is evidence of resistance to this practice among shrine priests. The reasons are probably economical. Priests can make some profit out of Ise amulets, if they sell them. Amulets that remain unsold constitute a loss, however; and priests are under intense pressure to purchase a fixed quota each year, regardless of whether they have sold the previous year's batch. The extent of priestly resistance is impossible to quantify, but it was sufficient to prompt a passionate defense of the amulet strategy in *Jinja shinpō* in the summer of 2008. Kuroiwa Akihiko, former head of the NAS section for promoting Ise veneration, argued that amulets link people to Ise and so counter the malign influences of postwar democracy, namely the loss of "national sentiment" and of "the spirit of devotion and sacrifice." Amulets venerated daily on the household altar instill a sense of awe and respect, and so effect a "return to origins" (*genten kaiki*). Finally, Kuroiwa argued, amulet profits make a vital contribution to the upkeep of the Ise Shrines. This is, indeed, an important point since at least half of Ise's annual income is said to derive now from amulet sales. Kuroiwa concluded with a plea and a promise: if priests spare no efforts in amulet sales, "the sacred land of Japan will one day rise again."[17]

NAS is, like all large organizations, riddled with tensions and contradictions, and it confronts many problems. It has found itself embroiled in several bitter disputes with its own shrine priests in recent years. The disputes merit some discussion because they expose fault-lines in early twenty-first-century Shinto. The most newsworthy concerns Meiji Jingū, the Tokyo shrine which venerates the spirit of the great Meiji emperor and his empress, Shōkō. Meiji Jingū is the wealthiest shrine in the land, and owns vast tracts of prime real estate in the center of Tokyo. The NAS headquarters are, as a matter of fact, built on Meiji Jingū land. The shrine employs around 200 people to cater for the huge numbers of pilgrims from across Japan. In the first three days of January 2009, Meiji Jingū was visited by well over 3 million people, a number far in excess of any other religious site patronized at New Year. Meiji Jingū's success may have contributed to its problems, which erupted in spring of 2004. The occasion was the visit to Meiji Jingū of Emperor Akihito and the empress to mark the ninetieth anniversary of Empress Shōkō's death. Meiji Jingū dispatched formal announcements of the event to the high and mighty, which is where its problems began. The shrine omitted to vet the wording on the announcements which, to the deep embarrassment of all concerned, referred to their imperial guests as "highnesses" (*denka*) rather than "majesties" (*heika*). Chief Priest Toyama Katsushi immediately sent an emissary to the Palace seeking imperial pardon for his oversight, which was granted. NAS, though, demanded that Toyama resign. NAS may have been content perhaps with an offer of resignation, but it was not forthcoming. The relations between Meiji Jingū and NAS had been sour for some time, and NAS bureaucrats hoped to seize the opportunity to remove a man for whom they had little affection or respect. Meiji Jingū, meanwhile, was indignant that NAS was using the emperor and empress as pawns in a power game. Matters got worse.

Prominent Shinto figures spoke to popular weeklies like *Shūkan shinchō*, condemning Toyama. Yuzawa Tadashi, erstwhile chief priest of Yasukuni Shrine, said it was time for Toyama to "acknowledge the shock his actions had inflicted on Meiji Jingū worshipers and on all connected with shrines across Japan, and resign with grace."[18] Right-wing newspapers like the *Kokumin shinbun* accused Toyama of forgetting the 1871 definition of shrines as "sites for the performance of state rites."[19] Ultra-right-wing organizations deployed military-style trucks to circle Meiji Jingū, loudspeakers blaring, accusing Toyama of lese-majesty, and demanding he should go. When an activist stole into the grounds of his private residence, Toyama wisely hired bodyguards. There is no evidence of NAS involvement in these intimidatory tactics, but it chose not to condemn them. When NAS continued to insist on Toyama's resignation, Toyama decided to pull Meiji Jingū out of the organization; his decision was approved by the shrine committee in May 2004.[20] At the time of writing, Meiji Jingū remains outside NAS, and it is clear it can survive perfectly well without NAS. Its belonging, or otherwise, is of no consequence, moreover, to the millions who visit every year, nor indeed to the emperor or empress. It remains to be seen, however, how NAS itself will survive without Meiji Jingū support, financial and moral. After all,

Meiji Jingū is precisely the sort of shrine, imperial through and through, which NAS idealizes.

Meiji Jingū was not the first, nor will it be the last, shrine to leave NAS. The great Nikkō Tōshōgū Shrine pulled out in 1985 over a dispute with NAS concerning shrine personnel.[21] Disputes of this order also blighted Hiyoshi Taisha in the 1980s, as we saw in Chapter 3. Other major shrines have teetered on the brink of leaving: Upper Kamo Shrine in Kyoto, Kasuga Taisha in Nara, and Keta Taisha in Niigata are among them. The Keta Taisha dispute remains unresolved, and is especially bitter. Keta Taisha is a shrine of great vintage that, in premodern times, enjoyed *ichi-no-miya* status; the modern state granted it the rank of *kokuhei taisha* (national shrine of senior rank). In 1982 NAS appointed Mitsui Hideo as chief priest on condition, it seems, that he retire in 1997 at age 65. When 1997 came and Mitsui did not go, tensions surfaced, and NAS began to apply pressure. It was around this time that Keta Taisha enjoyed a surge in popularity. More pilgrims than ever, a large proportion of whom were young girls, converged on the shrine. It transpires they were responding to Mitsui's webpage, which proclaimed the ability of the Keta kami, Ōkuninushi, to help girls find lovers and husbands.[22] This heretofore latent power of the kami has proved far more beneficial to the shrine's coffers than, say, its annual cormorant festival. NAS was not impressed, however, and accused Mitsui of demeaning the shrine. When pressure on him increased, Mitsui decided in 2006 to pull Keta Taisha out of NAS. NAS responded by sacking him and appointing a replacement. As a result, the shrine is in a liminal state. The new appointee has filed against Mitsui for refusing him access to the Shrine Office; Mitsui meanwhile has filed against NAS for unlawful dismissal.[23] At issue here, and in most NAS disputes, is the question of belonging. Do shrines belong to NAS or, indeed, to Shinto? Or again, do shrines belong to the priest, and/or the local community?

NAS has recently been involved in another major dispute, although of a quite different order, with a shrine and its priest in Yamaguchi Prefecture. The shrine is the Shidai Shō Hachiman, its chief priest, Hayashi Haruhiko. In the 1990s Chūgoku Denryoku, the Central Japan Energy Agency, finalized plans to build a nuclear power facility in the Kaminoseki region of Yamaguchi, where the Hachiman Shrine is located. Chūden, as the energy agency is commonly known, needed 100,000 square meters of shrine land to accommodate all of the structures on the site, and offered Shidai Shō Hachiman the sum of 152 million yen. Hayashi refused to sell. He opposed nuclear power on the grounds of its capacity to destroy the environment and human life; it was his responsibility, he maintained, to protect sacred shrine land. This case has attracted a huge amount of interest from environmental groups, including Greenpeace Japan, not least because Japan's safety record with nuclear facilities has been poor. Indeed, Hayashi's case was immeasurably strengthened by nuclear incidents in Tōkaimura in 1999, and Bihama in 2000 and again in 2004. Hayashi knew, however, that a majority of Shidai Shō Hachiman's shrine committee favored selling up, and so he refused to convene it. Committee members were infuriated and approached NAS, and – to cut a long story short – NAS dismissed Hayashi. In his stead, it appointed a new chief priest, who duly approved the sale. The shrine, with NAS approval, signed an agreement with Chūden in October 2004.[24]

It is not possible to dissect NAS motives here with any accuracy, but its position seems difficult to reconcile with the idea, certainly current amongst many non-Japanese, that Shinto and nature enjoy a unique intimacy. This idea is to be found in many English-language publications on Shinto by both Japanese and non-Japanese writers. This intimacy is proclaimed, moreover, on the English-language pages of NAS's website, which feature much discussion of the Shinto spirit of "reverence and appreciation to [sic] nature." It is curious, however, that no references to Shinto and nature are accessible through NAS's Japanese language webpages.[25] The suggestion is perhaps that, when not appealing to a Western audience, NAS's real concerns are not nature-oriented after all. In light of the preceding discussion of NAS's obsession with prewar, emperor-oriented ethics and rites, this need hardly be a cause for surprise. For the same ideological reasons, NAS has also failed to engage with ethical issues such as brain death and organ transplants or the soaring suicide rate, which have taxed other religious groups in Japan for decades.[26]

A *Jinja shinpō* editorial on shrine forests in August 2008 points to the difficulties. The editorial, the first ever in *Jinja shinpō* on the environment, insisted it was time to reappraise our understanding of nature but, it stresses, "not as a contemporary, technical problem." Shrine forests are sacred places where kami and humankind mingle; to learn from such forests is to nurture a heart that is grateful to nature, and predisposed to feelings of awe and compassion. At this point, the editorial changes tack to insist that the real value of shrine forests lies in their ability to generate, in children especially, love of local community and so patriotic love of Japan. Shrine forests are nothing less, the reader learns, than the key to restoring an ethical core to the nation's education system, emasculated by 60 years of malign Western influence.[27]

This ideological reduction of environmental themes is equally evident in a series of pieces in *Jinja shinpō* in August 2008, which reported on an otherwise epochal conference, convened by shrine priests in northeastern Japan to debate the environment. One conference speaker proclaimed Shinto as "a faith unsurpassed in the world" for its record on protecting nature, but offered no evidence of that record.[28] Another articulated a keen awareness of the threat Japan's environment confronts, but offered, by way of solution, only the suggestion that priests seek inspiration from the emperor.[29] A third piece by Kurosu Tsuge, a shrine priest from Aomori, struck a discordant note. He lamented the failure of priests, the prefectural Shrine Offices, and NAS to take constructive action. Shrine Offices should instruct priests and support them; NAS itself should seize the opportunity afforded by the rebuilding of the Ise Shrines in 2013 to stir awareness of environmental problems amongst shrine priests everywhere.[30]

Notwithstanding NAS's lack of interest in the environment, there are two twenty-first-century developments of note that have at least nominal NAS support. The first is the activities of the Shintō Bunkakai or Shinto Culture Society, and the second the creation of the Shasō Gakkai or Shrine Forest Society. The Shintō Bunkakai was founded in 1948 and, until very recently its publishing and research activities shadowed closely the NAS agenda. In 1999, however, it launched a series of annual conferences on "nature and Shinto culture." The ocean, mountains, rivers, wind, and trees are among themes so far covered, and experts from far and wide have been summoned to speak at NAS headquarters.[31] The Shintō Bunkakai marked its sixtieth anniversary with another new initiative: a symposium on life ethics (*seimei rinri*), which sought to define a Shinto position on the thorny issue of organ transplants and brain death.[32] The Shasō Gakkai, for its part, is noteworthy as the first ever environmental society inspired by Shrine priests; it was set up in 2002 to raise awareness of the threat faced by shrine forests and groves. The society has as nominal "advisors" senior NAS figures and the presidents of the two Shinto universities, but it is run by a board of trustees that includes experts in environmental science from all the top Japanese universities, as well as senior shrine priests like Sonoda Minoru.[33] The Shasō Gakkai convenes regular conferences that adopt a critical, multi-disciplinary approach to environmental issues. It carries out quantitative surveys of shrine and temple forests across Japan, and runs a training program for "*shasō* instructors," to whom the upkeep of local shrine and temple forests and groves will be entrusted. The annual bulletin, called *Shasōgaku kenkyū*, carries articles by environmental experts as well as shrine priests and, on the whole, avoids the reductive approach that typifies environmental pieces in *Jinja shinpō*.[34]

The Shasō Gakkai represents a serious attempt to give substance to the idea which, until recently, was fantasy more than it was ever fact: that Shinto is a religion of nature, and that Japan's nature is somehow, of itself, Shinto. As we have seen, the Shinto establishment has demonstrated no genuine interest in nature or the environment; and nature has had nothing obvious to do with the Shinto establishment at all. The activities of the Shintō Bunkakai and the Shasō Gakkai may be poised to change that; after all, shrine forests place Shinto priests in a unique position to speak up and take action on the environment. There will always be a fundamental tension, however, between NAS ideals and the environment. We are still a very long way from Shinto acquiring a national, let alone international, voice on the environment.

NAS and Beyond

What, then, are the possibilities for Shinto beyond the parameters of the NAS? There are several, and the most important of them need to be addressed here. First of all, there are self-consciously Shinto religious organizations that maintain more or less cordial relations with NAS, but keep their distance, much in the way that "sect Shinto" was at one remove from nonreligious shrine Shinto in the prewar period. Then there is the nationwide cult of Inari, centered on the Fushimi Inari Shrine in Kyoto, along with the thousands of Inari Shrines allied to it. Finally, there is the case of Yasukuni Shrine in Tokyo, dedicated to the war dead. Here we deal with each of these extra-NAS Shinto phenomena in turn.

Shinto sects

The religions that constitute *kyōha* or "sect" Shinto today are "Shinto" in the sense that they so define themselves. They inherit this definition from the Meiji state in the nineteenth century. What gave meaning to that definition was that each of them was structured around worship of one kami or another. These religious movements were quite distinct, however, from conventional shrine practice. Each was a new creation, formed in the turbulent decades of the nineteenth century as the early modern order gave way to the modern. Each had a religious founder possessed of a new, kami-inspired vision. The founders construed more or less distinctive theologies, which usually addressed issues unanswered by shrine practice: redemption, death, and the afterlife. Typically, for example, these new Shinto religions performed funeral rites, and responded readily, too, to worshipers' basic needs for fortune-telling, healing, and exorcisms. They were all active in proselytization, drawing in adherents from far and wide. In the last decades of the nineteenth century, several began missions overseas as well (Inoue Nobutaka et al. 2003: 190–1). The religions founded by Kawate Bunjirō, Nakayama Miki, and Kurozumi Munetada, whom we encountered in Chapter 2, were themselves early examples of state-recognized

Shinto religions. In Meiji they acquired the names by which they are known today: Konkōkyō, Tenrikyō, and Kurozumikyō respectively. In each case, the *kyō* suffix means teachings or "religion."

In prewar Japan, there were 13 state-recognized Shinto sects; they formed themselves into the Sect Shinto League (Kyōha Shintō Rengōkai), which is still active today. Like NAS, the league is a member of the aforementioned Japanese Association of Religious Organizations. Today, there are 12 Shinto sects in the league, but the composition is rather different. Significant moves in the postwar period have been the recruitment of Ōmotokyō, much persecuted in wartime Japan, and the departure of Tenrikyō. Of all these different Shinto groups, Tenrikyō along with Konkōkyō were always the egregious presence. They were the exception to the rule that Shinto groups were shaped by belief, however refined and reconstrued, in the kami who dominated the *Nihon shoki* and the *Kojiki* myth histories. To take a few examples of such groups, Ontakekyō worships the three kami Kuni-no-Tokotachi, Ōnamuchi, and Sukunahikona. The pantheons of both Shinshūkyō and Shintō Taikyō are centered on the three creator kami, Ame-no-Minakanushi, Kami-Musubi, and Takami-musubi. Shinrikyō, for its part, worships "all eighteen *kami* cited in the *Kojiki* from Ame-no-Minakanushi to Amaterasu."[35] The contrast between these groups and Tenrikyō and Konkōkyō is striking. The Tenri founder, Nakayama Miki, discovered, and then became, an entirely new kami; Kawate Bunjirō, the founder of Konkōkyō, had a profound insight that revealed to him an entirely new dimension of a popular kami, which he duly became. These kami, with their popular origins, were the antithesis of the state-approved kami of the *Nihon shoki* and *Kojiki*. That Tenrikyō should have left the Sect Shinto League in 1970 is, therefore, not surprising; that Konkōkyō should remain is. In recent years, however, Konkōkyō has suffered recurring crises of identity. In the 1990s, it changed its ritual garb, and restructured its rites so that they were less obviously "Shinto." At the time of writing, Konkōkyō is planning a series of seminars to put an end, once and for all, to the debate about whether it is or is not Shinto.

Fushimi Inari

The Fushimi Inari Shrine in Kyoto, and the 3,000 or so shrines attached to it, worship Inari, the rice god.[36] In the immediate postwar period the shrine declined to accept the NAS understanding that the sun-goddess of the Ise Shrines was still the greatest kami. One consequence of this independence is that Fushimi Inari organizes its own priest-training programs and issues its own priest licenses. This is all despite Fushimi Inari having enjoyed a privileged relationship with the ancient state as one of the 22 shrines, and in spite of its recognition by the modern nation-state as a *kanpei taisha* or "great state-funded shrine."

Fushimi Inari today celebrates three kami with distinctly imperial connections, it is true. The first of them is Uka-no-Mitama, who puts in the briefest of appearances in the *Kojiki* (Philippi 1969: 92). This kami is identified with Inari, a kami whose name means "rice-bearer." The second is Ame-no-Uzume, the female kami who exposed herself to entice the sun-goddess out from the heavenly cave; and the third is Saruta-hiko who acted as guide for Ninigi when he descended to earth. Nonetheless, imperial themes are not celebrated at Fushimi Inari at all, and the shrine's annual ritual program is in its entirety quite distinct from that imposed by NAS on its shrines.[37] The Inari Great Rite is held on the first day of the horse in February, a date that marks both the legendary founding of the shrine and the start of rice-planting. All other rites are related to the rice harvest and/or to the flourishing of commerce. Highlights include the commerce rite (*sangyōsai*) in April, and the Inari rite, which straddles April and May. Then there are celebrations of rice-planting in June, rice-plucking in October, and rice-harvesting in November; they are known as the *taue, nukiho,* and *niiname* rites respectively. Unlike NAS shrines, Fushimi Inari does not interpret the *niiname* rite in imperial terms.

Inari Shrines are visually distinguished from those now attached to NAS, moreover, by the watchful presence of white foxes, Inari's messengers. Many Inari Shrines are still to be found in the compounds of Buddhist temples. The early Meiji "clarification" of Buddhism and Shinto left a good number of Inari Shrines untouched, and the intimacy between the Inari cult and Buddhism finds a striking manifestation today in the May 3 Inari festival. The kami, borne in five *mikoshi*, enter the compound of the great Tōji Temple in Kyoto, to be feted there with offerings by temple monks. This ritual act reflects Inari's origin as the protector kami of that temple.[38] It should be pointed out that differences in kami understanding do not imply that relations between Fushimi Inari and NAS are anything other than cordial. The Japanese webpages of NAS, indeed, begin with images of guardian foxes. Fushimi Inari priests are involved with NAS dignitaries in the aforementioned Shasō Gakkai, as well. But Fushimi Inari in Kyoto heads a nationwide network of shrines, and feels no need for the security of any of Japan's multi-denominational religious organizations. At present, the cult of Inari at Fushimi is vibrant. In the three days of New Year in 2009, the shrine was visited by 2.7 million pilgrims. This made it the fourth most popular New Year site in the land.

Yasukuni and its problems

At New Year 2009, a quarter of a million Japanese visited Yasukuni, the Tokyo shrine for Japan's war dead. This was but one-tenth of the number who headed for Fushimi Inari, but still a sizable number of pilgrims given the shrine's association with the war and the war dead. New Year prayers at Yasukuni are offered for "the peace of the state and the peace of the people," and Yasukuni's efforts to appeal to new generations of Japanese, who have no experience of war and no family connections to the war dead, are clearly enjoying some success. The postwar invention of the *mitama* rite, the Yasukuni version of the summer all souls (*obon*) festival, attracts huge crowds. In 2008 it was participated in by some 300,000 visitors. Yasukuni is also today one of the capital's most popular spots for cherry blossom viewing. Evidently, then, generations of the war-bereaved are being replaced by a new clientele at Yasukuni, many of whom appear oblivious to the controversy that surrounds the shrine. But this is a controversy which no discussion of Shinto in the twenty-first century can bypass, and its key features will be explored here.

It should perhaps be pointed out first of all that Yasukuni is independent from NAS, but this independence is entirely strategic. Successive postwar governments have sought to nationalize Yasukuni, and so bring it in line with sites commemorating the war dead in Western democracies. This process will be considerably less complicated with Yasukuni disentangled from NAS.

Yasukuni is – or at least it has become – quite unlike many of the sites for the war dead in Western democracies. A reflection on difference offers a way in to the heart of the Yasukuni problem.[39] The most immediate of many differences arises from the fact that, in Japan, it is a religious organization in the form of a Shinto shrine which claims the nation's war dead; Yasukuni enshrines the war dead as Shinto kami. In recognition of their special status, priests frequently refer to these kami as *eirei*, or "glorious spirits," though this is not in origin a Shinto term. Yasukuni priests propitiate the war dead in Shinto rites with Shinto prayers and Shinto offerings. All sites to the war dead are by their nature sacred, of course, but the Cenotaph and Arlington, say, make a pretence, at least, of not claiming the dead for a particular religious affiliation. The religious, Shinto identity of Yasukuni is close to the heart of the Yasukuni controversy.

It might well be argued that it is the obligation of the prime minister of a democracy to pay respect to the men and women who died for their country. At Yasukuni, this cannot happen, however, without prime ministers laying themselves open to the charge of breaching Article 20 of the Constitution, which provides for the separation of state and religion. This, of course, explains the intense interest of the liberal media in Japan and beyond as to whether Koizumi Jun'ichirō, for example, went to Yasukuni as a private citizen or in his official capacity as prime minister. The one is acceptable, the other not. Apologists respond, reasonably enough perhaps, citing the "object and effect standard" ruling that was established in 1977.[40] The prime minister's object is to mourn the dead, not to spread Shinto; the spread of Shinto can hardly be seen as an effect of his patronage either.[41] Nonetheless, the constitutional dimension is still far from clear. In September 2005 the Osaka High Court ruled that Koizumi Jun'ichirō's Yasukuni patronage was, indeed, unconstitutional.

Undeterred and with obvious impunity Koizumi returned to Yasukuni in 2006. Certainly, anomalies abound in the application of the law. Every New Year, the prime minister and his cabinet pay what can only be described as official visits to the Ise Shrines, for example; and, as apologists are wont to point out, prime ministers and cabinet ministers patronize Buddhist temples and Christian churches without a ripple of controversy. Asō Tarō, the prime minister in 2008–9, believes the Yasukuni controversy will be solved only when the shrine divests itself of religious symbolism, forgoes its legal status as a religious juridical person, and is nationalized. The state could not enforce such a change on Yasukuni without breaching Article 20, of course, but if Yasukuni priests could be persuaded to take the initiative, constitutional questions would evaporate. Such, at least, is the view Asō articulated in 2006.[42]

There is, however, much more to the Yasukuni problem than the Constitution. In 1978, Yasukuni enshrined 14 men who had been condemned to death as Class A war criminals by the International Military Tribunal for the Far East (IMTFE). "Class A" identified them as guilty of waging "aggressive" or unprovoked war, and prominent amongst these men were former prime minister Tōjō Hideki and General Matsui Iwane, commander of the men responsible for the Nanjing massacre in 1937. The enshrinement was justified by the state's view that Japan's war with the West ended with the 1951 San Francisco Peace Treaty. These men are, in other words, regular "war dead." There are important questions to be asked about the legitimacy of the IMTFE and its judgments,[43] but the fact remains that when postwar prime ministers visit Yasukuni, they *appear* to condone the acts of Class A war criminals. Yasukuni's enshrinement of the Class A war criminals has, for good reason, been at the heart of Chinese objections to Yasukuni (Wang 2008). Chinese pressure, in turn, has periodically prompted proposals in Japan to relocate the Class A war criminal kami to some other site. This dimension of the Yasukuni problem is more intriguing at the start of the twenty-first century for two reasons. First, there is persuasive evidence that Emperor Hirohito (r. 1926–89) opposed the war criminals' enshrinement. The precise nature of his objections remains unclear, but he never returned to Yasukuni after their enshrinement. Second, it is now apparent that leading figures in the postwar Shinto establishment were also opposed. Neither Tsukuba Fujimaro, Yasukuni's chief priest until 1977, nor Ashizu Uzuhiko, the leading Shinto spokesman in the postwar period, favored enshrining war criminals. The pressure to enshrine, it now transpires, was generated by government and its backers (Breen 2008b: 2–11).

Many of the most vociferous critics, including Chinese observers, say that once the war criminal problem is solved, they will voice no further objections to prime-ministerial patronage. This position fails, however, to take account of other distinguishing features of Yasukuni. The first concerns Yasukuni as a mnemonic site. All sites to the war dead are sites of memory, but Yasukuni's ritual performances play with the memory of the past in a way that less encumbered sites, like the Cenotaph and Arlington, cannot do. This, too, is a consequence of the specifically Shinto nature of the site. In its earlier history, Yasukuni priests performed Shinto rituals that enshrined the war dead as kami; today, however, the vast majority of rituals serve to propitiate the kami. The point is that all the war dead, without discrimination, are so enshrined and so propitiated. The Yasukuni pantheon of kami or "glorious spirits" comprises not only those who exhibited extraordinary courage, but also the commanders who botched one campaign after another and the hundreds of thousands who died of starvation, not to mention the war criminals. The consequence is that Yasukuni rites consign much of war's reality to oblivion and leave no scope to reflect on its brutality and cruelty. They dramatize it uniquely as a noble undertaking of heroes and heroic action. The apotheosis and glorification of the war dead, understandable in wartime perhaps, serves after war's end to bury the trauma of suffering, both inflicted and endured, and to absolve the state of its responsibilities (Breen 2008c).

There is a final point to make about difference and the Shinto dimension to Yasukuni. Yasukuni is as close to the heart of twenty-first-century Shinto as it was throughout the nineteenth and twentieth centuries because, more than any other shrine except Ise, it articulates imperial values. Yasukuni is an intensely imperial site. Every spring and autumn it is visited by imperial emissaries who make offerings to the war dead on the emperor's behalf; it is frequently patronized by imperial princes; visually, it is bedecked with the Imperial Family's 16-petal chrysanthemum. But, above all, Yasukuni is imperial in the sense that it celebrates the fact that the "glorious spirits" died for the emperor. It venerates them as paragons of those ethical values that the Shinto establishment sees as twenty-first-century Japan's salvation. It should be stressed that this is a reading of Yasukuni that the shrine and its supporters themselves endorse. For leading apologists like Kobori Keiichirō, Yasukuni is about nothing so much as the regeneration of postwar society. Kobori laments that today's youth have no sense of gratitude for having been born Japanese. If only they could witness the prime minister and the emperor worshiping the heroic war dead at Yasukuni, their attitude, he is persuaded, would be transformed (Breen 2008c: 158–60). This, of course, is why Yasukuni is a magnet for ultra-right-wing groups. They understand Yasukuni for what it is: the ultimate expression of imperial values. It is in this ethical realm that the most striking difference between Yasukuni and democratic sites for the war dead is to be found: Yasukuni's imperial, ethical obsessions leave no room for unencumbered acts of mourning and reflection.

Shinto and Shrines in the Periphery

It is easy, perhaps too easy, to discuss and critique the priorities and preoccupations of NAS. After all, they are very clear and reiterated time and again in its weekly newspaper, *Jinja shinpō*, and through organizations like the Shinseiren. It is, however, far more difficult to get a sense of Shinto life on the Japanese periphery, and of local priorities. Such information is not easily accessible primarily because NAS's attention is forever focused on the political center. It is striking, for example, that NAS has sponsored no opinion surveys on local priests' attitudes towards the NAS or the prefectural Shrine Offices; it has funded no research, either, into the financial and other problems facing local shrines, such as succession and recruitment to the priesthood. We need to know far more about these peripheral issues than we do at present. Anecdote is no real substitute for hard data, but it must suffice here.

When the great Nikkō Shrine left NAS in 1985, an independent survey was carried out of shrine priests' opinions of NAS and its performance, and it uncovered widespread dissatisfaction. The clear consensus was that NAS had no interest in smaller, struggling shrines or their communities and the problems they faced; it offered them no help, financial or otherwise (Breen 2007c). It is not obvious that NAS has changed its priorities since the mid-1980s, and it seems unlikely that satisfaction levels can have improved. The latest Ise amulet campaign has stirred much additional discontent, but again there is little possibility for quantification. One shrine priest in Okayama relates that the greatest problems he faces are selling Ise amulets and raising cash for the 2013 rebuilding of Ise, at a time when his own shrine is in desperate need of repair work. It is unclear how many smaller shrines have been moved to leave NAS or what their fate will be. Outside NAS, there are no doubt fewer pressures and greater freedoms, but there are practical problems too. With the exception of Fushimi Inari, only NAS can issue priests' licenses, so there arises a serious problem for the next generation of priests. Succession itself is a problem affecting smaller shrines everywhere. In Japan at present there are some 20,000 priests and 1,900 priestesses to cater for 80,000 (NAS) shrines. Larger shrines often have multiple priests, which means that many smaller shrines are without a resident priest at all. Rural priests are thus frequently responsible for many different shrines and their parishes. The journalist Yamamura Akiyoshi found one priest single-handedly responsible for 60 shrines (Yamamura 2009). In a 2007 survey, carried out by researchers at Kokugakuin University, 26 percent of shrine priests declared they had no successors (Kobayashi 2008: 79). The problem of priest numbers, which is hardly unique to Shinto, looks set to deteriorate for the foreseeable future. Many priests cannot survive, moreover, on shrine income and have to seek employment elsewhere. Yamamura, who interviewed shrine priests across Japan, has concluded with a grim assessment: shrine Shinto is in crisis (Yamamura 2009).

In a recent interview, Sonoda Minoru, chief priest of the Chichibu Shrine in Saitama, reflected on some of the challenges facing local shrines and their priests. These challenges are by no means all "Shinto" in origin. Sonoda confesses to feeling a deep sense of crisis about the community at large, prompted by the soaring divorce rate and the disintegration of the family. Priests, their shrines, and especially their festivals have a vital role to play, he proposes, in regenerating a sense of community. Shrine festivals are, after all, a unique opportunity for all people, old and young, to come together in a way that twenty-first-century society does not otherwise facilitate. Festivals and community-focused shrine rites, in brief, can teach sociability and communal values and serve to reconstruct disintegrating communities. In Sonoda's view, shrines have never mattered more to the local community. Sonoda occupies the most senior priestly rank, and his views carry considerable weight.[44] The problem for local shrines, however, is that their role in supporting and revitalizing the local community receives no financial or other aid from NAS. It is this fact that, above all others, raises questions about the future of NAS as it has functioned since 1946.

One intriguing phenomenon that emerged in 2008, finally, merits brief mention here, and that is a new Enryakuji-sponsored initiative designed, as the *Kyōto shinbun* puts it, "to revive faith in the combination of kami and buddhas" (*shinbutsu shūgō no shinkō no fukkō*).[45] The initiative has led to the creation of a new Shinto-Buddhist organization called Shinbutsu Reijōkai (Association of Combined Shinto-Buddhist Sacred Sites). The association has the support of some of the most important NAS shrines, including Hiyoshi Taisha, Yoshida, Iwashimizu, the Upper and Lower Kamo Shrines, Matsunoo, and Kasuga; even the Ise Shrines are involved. At present, "involvement" amounts to little more than inclusion in a published compendium of Shinto–Buddhist pilgrimage sites, but the association offers the tantalizing specter of a distant future in which shrines will once more engage dynamically with Buddhist temples.[46]

Conclusion

This book was designed as an experiment aimed at producing an alternative reading of Shinto history. We began by setting aside the abstract notion of Shinto, typically construed to mean "Japan's original Way" or "Japan's indigenous religion." This was not because we understand Shinto to be of little historical importance; far from it. Rather, we see the need to draw a historical distinction between the concept of Shinto on the one hand, and the social reality of kami, shrines, rites, and myths on the other. In our understanding, they are not coterminous: kami, shrines, rites, and myths have their own more or less discrete histories, while the concept of Shinto too has its own history no less deserving of close scrutiny. Much of this book has been engaged with exploring the dynamic processes by which kami, shrines, rites, and myths became Shinto. We have proposed that "Shintoization," a word as useful as it is ungainly, must be a matter of keen interest in any critical study of Shinto.

Two questions emerge from this approach: What has Shinto meant as a concept at different stages of history? How and when has this concept affected shrines, myths and rites? In this conclusion we will draw on our investigations of the development of a particular shrine, myth, and ritual to address these questions in turn.

Shinto as we understand it today took on clear contours in the revolutionary fervor of 1868, when shrines were systematically wrenched from Buddhism and converted into sites of national, imperial ritual. This was a transforming moment, and Meiji Shinto is therefore nothing if not an invented tradition. Yet Meiji Shinto was only the latest – albeit the most definitive – in a series of Shinto incarnations that, with hindsight, can be traced back through history. An earlier critical moment occurred in the fifteenth century with the appearance of Yoshida Kanetomo. He was the late medieval visionary who invented "one-and-only Shinto" as an independent religion, quite distinct from and superior to Buddhism. Before Kanetomo's time, Shinto had no currency in a sense at all recognizable today.

Kanetomo's medieval construct of Shinto laid the foundation on which Meiji Shinto was built; yet it was quite unlike modern Shinto in important ways. Yoshida rites were closely patterned on Buddhist ceremonial and had a distinctive focus on the creator kami Kuni-no-Tokotachi. In contrast, Meiji Shinto was modeled on the *jingi* cult of the classical court and centered on the ancestral deity of the imperial line, Amaterasu. At least in its earliest form, Yoshida theology was deeply informed by esoteric Buddhism, with many Daoist elements mixed in to signal difference; in contrast, Meiji Shinto was passionately antisyncretic and Confucian in spirit. Yoshida Shinto was organizationally distinct, too. It was overseen by a single court family and jealously guarded in the form of secret transmissions. Meiji Shinto, on the other hand, sought to broadcast its transparent and public message as widely as possible. Finally, although the so-called Shrine Clauses of 1665 allowed Yoshida Shinto to bring thousands of shrines and priests under its wing in the course of the Edo period, it never accommodated the greatest shrines in the land within its ranks. The Shrines of Ise, the Izumo Shrine, and even most of the other court-sponsored shrines of late classical times (such as the 22 shrines and the *ichi-no-miya* shrines) all lay beyond its administrative reach. Where Yoshida Shinto affected mainly minor shrines, the opposite was true of Meiji Shinto. Even if the origins of Shinto as an independent religious organization began with Yoshida Kanetomo in the medieval period, it was only with the Meiji revolution of 1868 that Shinto assumed a guise recognizable today.

But even Yoshida Kanetomo's endeavor, for all its historical importance, drew on earlier forms of what we might call "pre-Shinto."

His notion of an autonomous Shinto was directly inspired by medieval Buddhist lineages that specialized in matters of the kami (*shintō-ryū*). These lineages first formulated the idea that the kami (or *shintō*) constituted the primordial essence of the buddhas and their Dharma, as well as the idea that there was a primeval kami "Way" from which even the Ways of Buddhism and Confucianism ultimately derived. Kanetomo's stroke of genius was to revive the *jingi* cult of the classical court by resurrecting the Council of Kami Affairs, while infusing it with new ideas that had been pioneered by the Buddhist *shintō-ryū*.

That *jingi* cult was, of course, another distant ancestor of Shinto. This cult, which was at its height in the eighth and ninth centuries, for the first time defined kami and shrines as a category of their own and designated their worship as a special responsibility of the emperor. The texts prepared as part of the *jingi* cult are the closest we come to a Shinto canon, and without them the twin inventions of Shinto, first by the Yoshida and then by the Meiji reformers, would not have been possible. After all, these inventions were based on the fundamental idea of this cult, namely that imperial power is kami power – an idea that can be traced back even further into ancient history.

Of course, Yoshida and Meiji Shinto have not been the only two attempts to fill the concept of Shinto with meaning. As we saw in Chapter 1, others have defined Shinto as folklore, or, in the case of the Shinto sects, as a universal teaching revealed to the world by a Japanese kami. In Chapter 6 we encountered an even more modern idea, that of Shinto as nature worship and as a Japanese ecological tradition. Clearly, "Shinto" is sufficiently vague as a term and loosely organized as an institution to invite any number of interpretations and reinterpretations. Of course, it is not up to us to determine what it means. The aim of the historical method that we have followed in this book is not to identify the unchanging core of Shinto, but to explore how the concept of Shinto has shifted over time, and how and when (indeed, whether) it has impacted on shrines, myths, and rituals in their past and present manifestations.

With that, let us turn to the findings of our investigations. By what processes and at what points in time might we say that the

Hie Shrine, the rock-cave myth, and the *daijōsai* ritual became Shinto, and what did the impact of Shinto, when it first arrived, entail?

The Hie Shrine has existed in the same location for as long as the sources allow us to ascertain. Yet, in its classical, medieval, and even early modern guises, it was hardly recognizable as a "Shinto" site in either a Yoshida or a Meiji sense of the word. Ancient Hie was run by priests of continental origin and qualifications, who must have employed non-indigenous techniques to control a deity they perceived as a threat rather than a benign force. Their rites were fitted into a Buddhist framework almost as soon as they appeared on the stage of history, and remained so throughout the medieval and early modern periods. It was in that last period that "Shinto" first impacted on Hie. The Shrine Clauses of 1665 inspired Hie's priests to imagine a role for themselves outside of Buddhism. They soon learned that this was not to be, as they were forced back into the fold by the shogunal regime. The priests' ill-advised rebellion against the mighty Buddhist establishment prevented Hie from pursuing autonomy from the Enryakuji temple complex that controlled it. Other shrines were luckier; the Izumo and Kasuga shrines, for example, had already severed their links with the temples of Engakuji and Kōfukuji by the 1660s.

Rising pressure, stored up over centuries, finally exploded in 1868 when the Meiji government ordered shrines to strip away all vestiges of Buddhism from their precincts. At Hie this triggered such an orgy of destruction that it was frowned upon even by the central government. After this epochal event, the history of Hie was formed by the shifting fortunes of Shinto itself. The year 1868 was the point at which Hie became a site of Shinto. This was achieved only through a radical rebranding, which involved the reimagining of its kami, the renaming of its shrines, and the reinvention of its main ritual event, the Sannō festival. Looking back on Hie's history, then, we find that there was a clear enough point at which shrine and Shinto converged. There was an initial stirring in the seventeenth century, but an epochal change in the nineteenth. It is equally clear, moreover, that Shinto was relevant only to a small portion of Hie's story. Landmarks in Hie's history were its incorporation in the Enryakuji temple complex around the year 800; its development into a great holder of estates from around 1100 onwards; its destruction by Oda Nobunaga in 1571; its marginalization in the 1630s; and its incorporation into Shinto in 1868. Only the last of these defining moments was directly related to the formation of Shinto.

The history of the rock-cave myth is just as ancient as that of Hie: it too is first presented to us in Japan's oldest extant works, the *Kojiki* (712) and the *Nihon shoki* (720). Here, it was closely interwoven with another myth, that of the descent of the heavenly grandson to the Japanese islands to assume the task of extending celestial government to the realm of earthly chaos. The myth was an original creation of the Yamato court, inspired in equal measure by ideas from the Asian continent (including the notion that there are heavenly and earthly deities) and by indigenous traditions of kami worship. Soon, however, the myth's appeal waned. It was rediscovered only in the eleventh century, when the court lost its classical power and turned its eyes to the past in order to strengthen its claims to legitimacy and authority. This time, however, the myth was read as a Buddhist simile and served to give Buddhist value to Japanese phenomena and practices: to the emperor as a manifestation of the World-Buddha, to the Japanese islands as that Buddha's original domain, to Japanese poetry as True Words invested with the Buddha's ultimate truth, and to kami ritual as a short-cut to the transformative powers of the Dharma.

In the seventeenth and eighteenth centuries, the myth entered popular practice in the form of *iwato kagura*, pantomimes performed at shrine festivals throughout the land. As a result this court myth for the first time became common knowledge among most Japanese. At the same time, the myth was purged of its Buddhist references and framed in a different discourse: that of Confucian-type ancestor worship. In the nineteenth century, *kagura* was actively used to involve the populace in a national ancestor cult of the sun-goddess Amaterasu, led by her descendant, the emperor. The same message can also be traced in history textbooks used in Japanese primary schools between, roughly, 1900 and 1945. It was only during this last stage that the rock-cave myth came to coincide with Shinto in the narrow sense in which that concept was understood at the time. After all, the myth had already shed its function of legitimating imperial kami power in classical times, and had since served to mystify the origins of a wide range of other cultural practices, ranging from poetry, dance, and theater to the Buddhist worship of kami and much else besides.

What, then, of the *daijōsai* ritual, which became in a sense the defining rite of modern Shinto? After all, the *daijōsai* dramatizes all the core meanings of modern Shinto: that the emperor is descended of the sun-goddess and is thus himself a living kami; that he is the paragon of filial virtue since, in the rite, he recompenses his ancestress with the first fruits; and, finally, that the Japanese nation, bound to the emperor as his subjects, is a unique nation, superior to all others on account of its imperial line. We found that this interpretation of the *daijōsai* by no means articulated that rite's original form. It was not before the nineteenth century that the emperor's mystical feasting with the sun-goddess at the start of each reign yielded these multiple layers of meaning. Nativists of the nineteenth century such as Hirata Atsutane and Aizawa Seishisai were the men responsible. The *daijōsai*, which to these men was of such vital, national importance, had not always been so regarded. There had been, moreover, a hiatus of more than two centuries (1466–1687) in which it was not performed at all. This appears in sharp contrast to the transfer of imperial regalia and the *sokui*, the older of the enthronement rites, which were never abandoned; they remained essential to imperial succession. For hundreds of years of the medieval and early modern periods, moreover, the *daijōsai* took its place alongside a Buddhist rite of enthronement, in which the emperor formed a mudra with his hands and intoned a mantra as he ascended the throne.

If the *daijōsai* was thus not always the defining rite it became in the modern period, there is no denying that it always served to articulate imperial power in its earthly and cosmic dimensions. And yet, in origin, the *daijōsai* said nothing at all about the sun-goddess or her gift of rice. Rather, it re-enacted the tale, later incorporated into the *Kojiki*, of the marriage of the son of heaven to the daughter of the sea kami, so that the *daijōsai* on one level symbolized the emperor's control over the oceans. The point is that, even as the *daijōsai* maintained the closest connection to the imperial family throughout its long history, its meanings and its contexts shifted over time. As with the Hie Shrine and the rock-cave myth, so with the *daijōsai* rite: it was the modern state that fixed its meanings and so defined it as Shinto through and through.

If we look back on these findings, it is clear that many of the building blocks from which Shinto has been constructed and reconstructed over time were already in evidence at the earliest known stage of history. Yet their unambiguous identification as components of something called Shinto was a recent phenomenon. Moreover, it has become evident that some conceptualizations of Shinto have had a great impact on shrines, myths, and rituals, while others proved much less influential than traditional accounts might lead us to expect. The ancient *jingi* cult produced the classical versions of the rock-cave myth and the *daijōsai* rite, but its hold on the signification of both proved tenuous: both soon veered off in unexpected directions. The Hie Shrines benefited from this cult, but were only marginally affected by it; at least, the emphasis that the Shinto establishment has given to the shrines' position within this court cult is clearly out of balance with its historical importance. The invention of Shinto by the Yoshida, on the other hand, triggered dramatic events at Hie by inspiring the shrine priests to dream of a non-Buddhist future. Yet its impact cannot be compared in any way with the revolution caused by Meiji Shinto. Our findings further suggest that the modern vision of Shinto as an ecological tradition or a form of nature worship has no roots in history, and has yet to establish itself as a factor of significant change. Finally, the notions that Japanese folklore is Shinto and that Shinto is a revelatory religion are also both recent and remain peripheral to shrine life, although they are very much alive in more limited circles.

An even more important conclusion to be drawn from this history is that the shrines, myths, and even rituals that we have examined do not need Shinto. Their signification was monopolized by Shinto, first tentatively by the Yoshida and, later, with great force by the Meiji government; but in the end, Shinto has always derived its meaning from shrines, not the other way around. Shrines have used their myths and rituals to promote the notion of Shinto, but their existence does not depend on that concept, however it is defined. Shrine priests can either discard or radically reinvent Shinto at any time, as they have done repeatedly in the past, and their survival does not depend on the continued appeal of historical understandings of Shinto.

Shinto is not a "tradition" of the kind that has been likened to a great river, flowing of its own accord through the plains of history while nurturing Japan's culture and giving meaning to its past, present, and future. There is nothing either natural or inevitable about the spates of invention that have resulted in Shinto as we know it today. Our account of Shinto's history differs fundamentally from the Shinto establishment's emic understanding that kami shrines, myths, and rituals are, of their very essence, aspects of Shinto, and have always been so. We stress, rather, the agency of individual actors at every turn. Shinto, in our view, appears not as the unchanging core of Japan's national essence, but rather as the unpredictable outcome of an erratic history. By implication, that means that its future, too, is wide open to the unforeseeable forces of historical change and the actions of individuals responding to them.

Notes

Chapter 1 An Alternative Approach to the History of Shinto

1 Shrines can, however, receive public subsidies for the maintenance of buildings and objects that are recognized as cultural properties (*bunka-zai*) or national treasures (*kokuhō*), or for the staging of events that have been designated as intangible cultural properties (*mukei bunkazai*).

2 This and other statistics on popular shrine practice mentioned below derive from a poll conducted by the National Association of Shrines: Kyōgaku Kenkyūjo Chōsashitsu 1997: 52. This is an internal document, designed to gain genuine insight into people's interaction with shrines; it shows no signs of a pro-Shinto bias.

3 Orikuchi announced his position in articles such as "Shintō shūkyōka no igi" (The importance of making Shinto a religion) and "Minzokukyō kara jinruikyō e" (From an ethnic religion into a religion for mankind). Both can be found in Orikuchi's collected works, *Orikuchi Shinobu zenshū*, vol. 20.

4 Ashizu describes the reasons for his opposition to Yanagita and Orikuchi in Ashizu 1986.

5 For overviews in English see Breen 2000, Hardacre 1989, Nitta 2000, and Sakamoto 2000. Case studies of individual shrines can be found in Grapard 1984, Inoue Takami 2003, Sekimori 2005, and Thal 2005. For selected original documents, see Yasumaru and Miyachi 1988: 423 ff.

6 With the possible exception of Empress Jitō, who visited Ise province (and possibly the Ise Shrines) in 692.

7 In fact, the Council had already been demoted to the status of a "Ministry" (Jingishō) in 1871.

8   For an illustrated overview, see Plutschow 1996.

9   For an introduction to Yanagita's thought, see Hashimoto 1998 and Harootunian 1998.

10 "Shintō shiken" (My views on Shinto), reproduced in Yanagita's collected works, *Teihon Yanagita Kunio shū*, 10: 432–3.

11 *Kokutai*, often translated as "national polity," was the stick with which dissidents were beaten into submission, especially after 1933. It defined Japan as a divine family state, ruled by an imperial lineage unbroken since the days of the sun-goddess Amaterasu, and it stressed that within this state all Japanese are unconditionally, naturally, and gratefully loyal to their national "father," the emperor.

12 For an introduction to Ise's history, though primarily focusing on the development of Ise thought, see Teeuwen 1996.

Chapter 2   Kami Shrines, Myths, and Rituals in Premodern Times

1   The most likely meaning of *yato-no-kami* (or *yatsu-no-kami*) is "valley deities."

2   *Muraji* was a lineage title awarded to close retainers of the Yamato court.

3   For English translations of these texts, see Philippi 1969 and Aston 1972.

4   For two accounts stressing such differences, see Kōnoshi 2000 and Ooms 2008, ch. 2.

5   See Mizubayashi 2002. Where *Kojiki* writes the frequent name elements *hiko* and *hime* with the characters 日子 and 日女 (meaning "son of the sun" and "daughter of the sun"), *Nihon shoki* prefers 彦 and 姫 ("prince" and "princess"). Even in the name of Takami-musubi himself, *Nihon shoki* writes the final syllable with the character 霊 "spirit," while *Kojiki* uses the character 日 "sun."

6   These edicts are recorded in the official court history *Shoku Nihongi*, which covers the years 697–791.

7   Bentley 2006 presents a very different view on this text, which is critically examined in Teeuwen 2007b.

8   For an English translation of *Engi shiki*, see Bock 1970 and 1972; for a discussion of the selection of shrines listed in this document, see Grapard 2002.

9 *Yamashiro-no-kuni fudoki* (Gazetteer of Yamashiro province), *NKBT* 2: 416; see Como 2009: ch. 5.

10 The source is *Ise-no-kuni Kuwana-gun Tado jingūji garan engi narabi ni shizaichō* (List of the buildings and property of the Tado shrine-temple in Kuwana district, Ise province). For a general introduction to the interaction between Buddhism and shrines, see Teeuwen and Rambelli 2003, "Introduction."

11 On the Saijōsho design, see Fukuyama 1985 and Grapard 1992a.

12 Of several extant versions, those bearing the name of Kanetomo's thirteenth- and fourteenth-century ancestors Kanenao, Kanenatsu, and Kaneatsu are now recognized as Kanetomo's fabrications; they are thus treated here as revealing of his thought. There are two excellent studies in English of Kanetomo's other basic Shinto text, *Yuiitsu Shintō myōbō yōshō* (Grapard 1992b; Scheid 2000).

13 This is the number of kami enshrined in the 2,861 shrines listed in *Engi shiki*.

14 On the *jūhachi Shintō* rites, see Scheid 2000.

15 Bonshun was not only a Yoshida priest but a Tendai monk, a fact that further attests to Yoshida Shinto's essentially combinatory character.

16 This was a phenomenon quite distinct from the case of, say, Sugawara-no-Michizane (849–903), who was apotheosized only when his resentful spirit manifested itself in acts of destruction.

17 For the seventeenth-century resurrection of court rites, see Chapter 5 below. On Yoshida-Shirakawa rivalry in the Kantō area, see Hardacre 2002: 103–4.

18 This oracle was contained in the *Yamato-hime-no-mikoto seiki*, a thirteenth-century text of Watarai Shinto (see Teeuwen 1996: 99–119).

19 On Emperor Reigen, see Chapter 5 below.

20 Sanetsura's influence at court was such that he personally took charge of reforming the *daijōsai* in 1748. On the *daijōsai*, see Chapter 5 below.

21 On Ise pilgrimage, see Davis 1992; on Ōyama, see Ambros 2008; and on Konpira, see Thal 2005.

22 The *Kojiki-den* was published over a period of 30 years between 1790 and 1822.

23 I have adapted the translation of *Naobi-no-mitama* by Nishimura (in Motoori 1991).

24 The classic study of Atsutane's theological debt to the writings of Jesuit thinkers is Muraoka 1920.

25 See Chapter 3 for a study of these edicts in action.

26 On the involvement of Ōkuni Takamasa and Fukuba Bisei in early Meiji religious policies, see Takeda 1996 and Breen 2000.

Chapter 3 The History of a Shrine: Hie

1 Here, I follow Nishimiya Kazutami 1979. The peg or pole (*kui*) could be a pillar on the mountain into which the deity was invited to descend, or a phallic symbol.

2 This tale can be found in *Yamashiro-no-kuni fudoki* (Gazetteer of Yamashiro province; eighth century), *NKBT* 2: 414–15, and in a Hata genealogy recorded in *Honchō gatsuryō* (Protocol of the court arranged by month; 930–46?). The kami of Ubuya Shrine at Hie is today identified with this same kami, Kamo Wake-ikazuchi, but this is a Meiji-period innovation. (On this point, see Chapter 3 below.) The late medieval *Gonjinshō* (Extracts on the august deities), for example, identifies the Ōji Shrine with the famous Ōji ("princes") of Kumano (*ST* Hie: 106).

3 This is explored in Uwai 1988, ch. 3.

4 Okada Seishi 1987: 43–68 refers to two poems in *Man'yōshū* (Collection of ten thousand leaves), vol. 1, attributed to Nukata-no-Ōkimi and Ito-no-Ōkimi.

5 In 859 Great Hie was raised to senior second rank and Lesser Hie to junior fifth rank, higher grade; in 880 Great Hie was granted the highest possible senior first rank, and Lesser Hie junior fourth rank, higher grade. In *Engi shiki* (927), Hie is listed as only one "deity seat," excluding the deities of Lesser Hie from the list of officially sponsored shrines.

6 For *hafuri*, "priests," see Chapter 2; *be* was an ancient appellation for occupational groups controlled directly or indirectly by the court.

7 *Shinshō kyakuchoku fushō* (New extracts from decrees and edicts; tenth century), entry Daidō 1 (806).

8 Note, however, that there is no way to ascertain exactly when these associations became established.

9 *Hie Sannō rishōki* (Record of the benefits of Hie's Mountain King), *ST* Hie: 572. Quoted in Kuroda 1999: 16.

10 Kuroda 1999: 2–20; Sagai 1992, ch. 6.

11 Kuroda 1999: 181. For more on *kagura*, see Chapter 4.

12 Jūzenji (today known as Juge Shrine) is one of the shrines of the eastern compound. Daigyōji Shrine no longer exists.

13 *Shōyūki* (Records of the Minister of the Right of the Ononomiya lineage), entry Chōwa 1 (1012)/6/4. On the *ro-no-miko*, see Satō 1984: 46–59.

14 *Rō-no-miko ki* (Record of the *rō-no-miko*), in *ST* Tendai Shintō ge, 619–22.

15 Faure argues that Jien "had interiorized the secret tradition of medieval Tendai" that "salvation through sex with a *chigo* (medium-child) was in accord with the will of … Sannō Gongen" (Faure 1998: 257).

16 *Hyakurenshō* (A mirror polished hundredfold), entry Hōan 4 (1123)/7/18.

17 On mandalas of other shrines (Kasuga and Kumano), see Ten Grotenhuis 1999.

18 Coincidence makes Kōshū a namesake (although the characters differ) of the founder of the Marōdo Shrine mentioned above.

19 1 *koku* is equivalent to 180 liters of rice, enough to sustain one person for one year.

20 On Tenkai and his involvement in the construction of Tokugawa ideology, see Chapter 2 above and Ooms 1985.

21 On this process, see Chapter 2.

22 On Bonshun and the dispute over Ieyasu's will, see Chapter 2.

23 The *Yoshida sōsho* contains, for example, a transcription of a Fushimi Inari text by the Hie priest Juge Shigeyasu. I owe this observation to Hatakama Kazuhiro.

24 On Yoshida Shinto rites, see Scheid 2000.

25 The source for this rite is *Jōkyō yonen Sannō sengū ki* (Record of the Sannō Shrine rebuilding rite in the fourth year of Jōkyō; 1687). I owe my knowledge of it to Sagai Tatsuru.

26 The ritual calendar operating at the seven Hie Shrines was entirely separate from that of the Hie Tōshōgū. Shrine priests served at the Tōshōgū, but the site was cultivated primarily by Tendai monks.

27 For examples of these screens, see Sanekata 2000.

28 Akisato later reproduced this Hie text and these illustrations without change in his 1830s *Ōmi meisho zue*.

29 For a further discussion of festive displays, see Chapter 4.

30 On the Sakamoto *kunin*, see Takashima 1978 and Yoshida 1995.

31 *Hie sairei kozu* (Ancient map of the Sannō festival). Author unknown. I am very grateful to Yamaguchi Yukitsugu for introducing me to this scroll.

32 *Hie sairei tenkō byōbu* (Panels depicting the Hie festival). Author unknown. Yamaguchi Yukitsugu introduced me to this scroll.

33 On the Sannō-*kō*, see Wada 2006.

34 *Jōi on inori no ki* (A record of prayers for foreign expulsion). I am very grateful to Sagai Tatsuru for introducing me to this source in the Eizan bunko archives.

35 Hie Jinja, comp., *Issha kindai hennen ryakuki* (A shrine's brief modern chronology).

36 As pointed out in Chapter 1, Empress Jitō did venture to Ise in 692, but it is now thought that her purpose was to survey the site on which the Ise shrines would be constructed (Tamura 1996: 181–5).

37 Hie Jinja, comp., *Issha kindai hennen ryakuki*.

38 Hie Jinja, comp., *Issha kindai hennen ryakuki*.

39 Juge Shigekuni, *Saijin oyobi kanjō nenki* (On the Hie kami and the dating of their enshrinement), unpaginated MS (Historical Archives, Prefectural Office, Prefecture). Ōtsu Prefecture became Shiga Prefecture in 1871.

40 See, for example, *Mainichi shinbun*, 19.12.1936.

41 See Chapter 2 above for these new religions.

42 Yamamoto 2002: 31–2. As it turned out this French "missionary" was in fact the great French traveler and connoisseur Emile Guimet (1836–1916).

43 This applied only to shrines which, like Hie, were underwritten by government in any way at all. From the early 1870s, only some 139 major shrines out of a national network numbering well over 100,000 were so funded. Ise and Yasukuni, the new shrine for the war dead, were treated as special cases and never wanted for funds.

44 On the rock-cave myth, see Chapter 4.

45 *Yomiuri shinbun*, 18.4.1879.

46 *Chūgai denpō*, 1.4.1887.

47 Documents relating to Hagiyama's involvement in the Meiji Sannō matsuri have been collated in *Hagiyama mura monjo, Eitai kirokuchō no kenkyū* (Hagiyama village documents: a study of the *Eitai kiroku-chō*). This collection is privately printed by Shiga-ken Dōwa Mondai Kenkyūjo. The citation here is from *Hagiyama mura monjo*, 32.

48 *Hagiyama mura monjo*, 30–2.

49 *Asahi shinbun (Kyōto furoku)*, 16.4.1906.

50 *Asahi shinbun (Kyōto furoku)*, 10.11.1928.

51 *Hie koshiki saiki*, 1943, MS (Hiyoshi Taisha).

52 *Ōsaka Asahi (Shigaban)*, 17.4.1942.

53 *Ōsaka Asahi (Shigaban)*, 18.4.1943.

54 *Ōsaka Asahi (Shigaban)*, 13.4.1938.

55 The two (rival) universities that train men and women for the Shinto priesthood are Kokugakuin in Tokyo and Kōgakkan in Ise.

Shrines have a tendency to recruit from either one of these two universities, rather than mixing candidates from both.

56 *Sankei shinbun*, 26.11.1987, 29.11.1988.

57 At the time of writing, 10,000 yen is approximately $US105.

58 *Kyōto shinbun*, 5.1.2008.

Chapter 4   The History of a Myth: The Sun-Goddess and the Rock-Cave

1 *NKBT* 1: 80–3; cf. Philippi 1969: 80–6.

2 Michael Witzel (2005: 1–69) compares myths on the theme of "releasing the sun from hiding" over a large area, stretching from Meso-America to Japan, India, Central Asia, and Europe. He boldly posits the existence of an ancient "Laurasian" prototype, going back tens of thousands of years.

3 Como 2009: ch. 7. This angle on Amaterasu was first pioneered by Orikuchi Shinobu.

4 *Nihon shoki*, entry Suinin 25/3; Aston 1972: I, 176. Tokoyo, which means "eternal world," refers to a divine land located across the sea. In this particular passage, there is a pun on *tokoyo*, a homonym meaning "eternal night": the roosters from the "eternal world" across the sea from Ise bring an end to the "eternal night" with their crowing. Michael Como has further thrown light on early connections between Tokoyo and, again, silkworm cults (Como 2008, ch. 2).

5 Aston 1972: I, 77, with minor changes.

6 On the same day Tenmu's "spirit-summoning rite" was performed, the Korean priest Pŏp-chang and a Japanese lay priest presented "an infusion of white *okera*," the medicinal herb *Atractylodes japonica* (Aston 1972: II, 373). David Bialock (2007: 76–84) sees this not just as a curative procedure but as a Daoist immortality rite. He argues that its aims of balancing Yin and Yang and pacifying the soul or spirit made for a perfect fit with the *chinkonsai*, which he (in contrast to Ooms) does connect to the rock-cave myth.

7 *Shōyūki*, entry 1031/8; quoted in Saitō 1996: 208.

8 In the ninth and tenth centuries, lecture series on *Nihon shoki* were held at the court roughly once every 30 years (812–14, 843, 878–81, 904–6, 936–43, 965). After 965, however, they were discontinued, and even court nobles no longer had any opportunity to see this text or hear about its contents. *Kojiki* was even more obscure.

9 This does not, of course, mean that there are no Chinese influences in *waka*; in content and subject matter, and even in phrasing, such influences are in fact obvious. The *Kokinshū* has two prefaces: one in pure Japanese and the other in Chinese; these prefaces do not say different things, but they say them in two different formats that were consciously kept apart by means of a rather extreme linguistic purism.

10 *Saibara* is a genre of court songs. This term will be explained further below.

11 The *Kokinshū* includes a very similar poem (no. 1081) in the section "kami songs" (*kamiasobi-no-uta*). Some editions carry a note explaining that "this is a *saibara* song in which the mode changes from minor to major" (cf. n. 25 below). In a slightly different form, the poem occurs also in collections of *saibara* pieces (see e.g. NKBT 3: 386).

12 *Shingon fuhō san'yōshō* (Notes on the transmission and essentials of Shingon; 1060).

13 Śākyamuni's erring cousin, who, among other things, plotted to kill him.

14 That is, meditative absorption and insight or understanding, the two main prerequisites for enlightenment.

15 *Nihon shoki* mentions that Ame-no-Uzume lit a bonfire when she performed her dance; *Kojiki* does not refer to this.

16 *ST* Tendai Shintō ge: 413.

17 Abe 2000: 75. The transmission document on which we draw is dated 1513.

18 Abe 2000: 76. The text places particular emphasis on the physicality of the heart/mind, as a red piece of "meat"; therefore I prefer the translation heart/mind rather than the more usual "mind." For another (and probably older) variant of this procedure, see Teeuwen 2000: 102–5.

19 *Shosha daiji* (Important matter of all shrines), Abe 2000: 78.

20 Famously, this song features in *The Tale of Genji* (early eleventh century), e.g., in the chapter *Wakana* 1, where we are witness to an amateur concert by nobles: "The singers were called to the top of the steps, where they sang in magnificent voice until the mode change came. The later the night, the sweeter the music, until by the time they reached Green Willow (*Aoyagi*), the very warbler on its perch might have wondered at such enchanting harmonies" (Tyler 2003: 591). In the original (*NKBT* 6: 245), the effect of the *Aoyagi* performance is further described as "extremely *omoshiroshi*."

21 Actually, the spirit possession of Ame-no-Uzume does not appear to have a clear function in the rock-cave myth; it remains unclear by which deity Ame-no-Uzume is possessed, and there is no oracle. It

appears to be there because it is a part of *kagura*, not because it fits the particular plot of this tale.

22 In fact, the word *kagura* is often said to derive from *kami-kura*, "kami seat," although other etymologies have also been proposed.

23 Another story in *Kojiki* and *Nihon shoki* tells how "Emperor Chūai" played the *koto*, causing the empress, Jingū Kōgō, to become possessed by a deity and pronounce an oracle. When this emperor, who is hardly a historical figure, refused to believe the deity's "words of instruction" and ceased playing, he was instantly killed by the deity (Philippi 1969: 257–8).

24 This is related in *Uji shūi monogatari* (Remaining tales of Uji; early thirteenth century), episode 74. The translation is taken from Mills 1970: 241. The emperor in question is Horikawa (r. 1086–1107). See Müller 1971: 108.

25 *Heihaku (gohei, mitegura)* are sticks with streams of cloth or paper attached to them, serving either as offerings or as symbols of a deity's presence.

26 Fujiwara-no-Munetada (1062–1141), *Chūyūki* (Records of the Minister of the Right, Munetada), entry Chōshō 3 (1134)/5/8.

27 Rimer and Yamazaki 1984: 31, with minor variations.

28 The work is *Shūgyoku tokka* (Gathering jewels and acquiring the flower; c. 1428?), written by Zeami as a brief overview of his views on Noh for his son-in-law and heir Zenchiku.

29 *SNKBT* 57: 127–32. This account is based on a performance of the Konparu Emaikai in Tokyo in November 2007.

30 On these matters, see Scheid and Teeuwen 2006.

31 On these two avenues of interpretation, see Nakai 2007: 11–39.

32 Ishizuka 2005 covers western Japan; on variants in eastern Japan, see Mitamura 2005: 53–64.

33 Shibuya Kuritsu Shōtō Bijutsukan 1999: 114 ff.

Chapter 5   The Daijōsai: A "Shinto" Rite of Imperial Accession

1 The third, the mirror or *shinkyō*, is permanently located in the Kashikodokoro, the palace shrine of the sun-goddess.

2 The postwar Constitution can be viewed online at http://www.ndl. go.jp/constitution/e/etc/c01.html#s10.

3 On Yasukuni, see Chapter 6 below.

4 *Jinja shinpō*, 11.7.2004.

5 *Jinja shinpō*, 29.10.1990.

6 *Asahi shinbun*, 20.10.1990; *Jinja shinpō*, 29.10.1990.

7 http://kokkai.ndl.go.jp/SENTAKU/syugiin/159/0107/15903110107
002a.html.

8 The American scholar Robert Ellwood is a notable exception. See
Ellwood 1973: 1–36.

9 *Yomiuri shinbun*, 15.4.1915.

10 *Yomiuri shinbun*, 20.7.1915.

11 *Yomiuri shinbun*, 14.11.1915.

12 Details about Shiga Prefecture's involvement in the enthronement
are drawn from the file *Gishiki* 3, *Tai ka* 21, which is kept in the
Shiga prefectural archives.

13 The Meiji Constitution can be viewed online at http://history.
hanover.edu/texts/1889con.html.

14 *Yomiuri shinbun*, 26.11.1915.

15 For an interestingly biased first-hand account of the Shōwa
enthronement rites, see Ponsonby-Fane 1959.

16 *Yomiuri shinbun*, 14.11.1928.

17 Philippi 1969 mistranslates *tatami yae* or "eight-layered" mats and
silks as "many layers"; the eight here is critical.

18 On the Dōkyō scandal, see Chapter 2.

19 On Kanetomo, see Chapter 2.

20 *Sōen wagen* is not easily rendered into English. *Wagen* means Japanese
words or speech; *sōen* refers to grass (*sō*) which bows (*en*) before the
wind. This is a metaphor for the virtue of the loyal subject being forever inferior to, and so prone before, the greater virtue of his lord.

21 There was, however, the case of Emperor Chūkyō (r. 1221) who is
known as *hantei* or half-emperor since he abdicated before he underwent either enthronement or *daijōsai*.

22 http://www.sangiin.go.jp/japanese/kenpou/keika_g/147_08g.htm.

23 http://kokkai.ndl.go.jp/SENTAKU/syugiin/159/0107/15903110107
002a.html.

24 http://www.sangiin.go.jp/japanese/kenpou/keika_g/159_08g.htm.

Chapter 6   Issues in Contemporary Shinto

1 The *niiname-sai* is a feast shared by emperor and sun-goddess. It is
the annual version of the *daijōsai* discussed in Chapter 5. On the
kinensai, see Chapter 2.

2 These rites celebrate respectively the founding of the imperial line, Jinmu's founding of Japan, the sun-goddess in Ise, and the birthdays of Emperor Meiji and the present emperor.

3 *Jinja shinpō*, 17.3.2008.

4 On the *Nakatomi ōharae*, see Chapter 2.

5 *Jinja shinpō*, 20.9.2008.

6 *Jinja shinpō*, 27.10.2008.

7 *Jinja shinpō*, 11.11.2008.

8 This translates literally as "Shinto political league" although the official English rendering avoids the "political" reference and opts for "the Shinto association of spiritual leadership" (SAS).

9 http://www.sinseiren.org.

10 *Asahi shinbun*, 16.5.2000.

11 *Jinja shinpō*, 16.6.2008.

12 On *ichi-no-miya* and *nijūnisha* shrines see Chapter 2. *Kanpei* and *kokuhei* are usually translated respectively as "great state-funded shrines" and "national shrines of senior rank." The former were regarded as distinctly more elevated in status than the latter.

13 *Jinja ni kansuru ishiki chōsa*, 2008.

14 The transfer ceremony is the headline article in *Jinja shinpō*, 29.9.2008.

15 *Jinja shinpō*, 17.3.2008.

16 *Jinja shinpō*, 3.12.2007.

17 *Jinja shinpō*, 16.6.2008.

18 *Shūkan shinchō*, 10.2.2004.

19 *Kokumin shinbun*, 8.10.2004.

20 See, for example, *Asahi shinbun*, 31.7.2004.

21 On Nikkō, see Chapter 2. On this incident see *Asahi shinbun*, 25.7.1985.

22 The website is http://www.keta.jp. The web page at the time of writing carries 42,879 messages of thanks from young women to the Keta kami for prayers answered.

23 For an overview of the Keta incident see *Asahi shinbun*, 17.9.2006. At the time of bringing this book to press, the *Yomiuri shinbun* is reporting that the Usa Hachiman Shrine is in dispute with NAS over the appointment of a successor to the recently deceased chief priest (*Yomiuri shinbun*, 8.3.2009). Usa Hachiman sought NAS approval for the daughter of the deceased to take over, but it was not forthcoming and NAS appointed an alternative. Usa Hachiman has responded by declaring its intention to pull out of NAS. How this will play out remains to be seen, but it should be noted that Usa Hachiman is the

head shrine of a national Hachiman network. It comprises some 7,800 shrines, more than any other category (Okada and Kase 2007).

24 *Asahi shinbun*, 6.10.2004. See also the extended reports of ongoing legal cases in *Asahi shinbun*, 30.5.2005, 21.10.2005, and 14.12.2007.

25 See the pages http://www.jinjahoncho.or.jp/en/view/ and especially http://www.jinjahoncho.or.jp/en/publications/nature/index.html. It should be added that a Japanese translation of the English text is provided, but this can only be accessed through the English-language website.

26 For a summary of the issues here, see Breen 2004a.

27 *Jinja shinpō*, 28.7.2008.

28 *Jinja shinpō*, 4.8.2008.

29 *Jinja shinpō*, 25.8.2008.

30 *Jinja shinpō*, 25.8.2008. The same issue of *Jinja shinpō* reported that 8,500 square meters of cypress, or 10,000 cypress trees, will be needed for the rebuilding and that, for every tree destroyed, one would be planted.

31 s-bunka.com.wp/index.php?page_id=5.

32 *Jinja shinpō* carried its first ever editorial on brain death on 7.7.2008.

33 Sonoda, chief priest of Chichibu Shrine in Saitama Prefecture, has pioneered Shinto concern with the environment. See, for example, Sonoda 2000.

34 The *Shasō gakkai* sponsored a striking pavilion at the 2005 Aichi expo which can be viewed at: www2.odn.ne.jp/shasou/expo.htm.

35 Thus proclaims the Shinrikyō page on the *Kyōha Shintō rengōkai* website: www.kyoharen.net.

36 3,000 is the figure given in Okada and Kase 2007: 11–12, which suggests that the cult of Inari is the fourth most popular in Japan. Only shrines venerating Hachiman, the Ise kami, and Tenjin, the spirit of Sugawara-no-Michizane, are more numerous. The Inari website suggests that the real number of Inari Shrines across Japan is closer to 30,000 (http://inari.jp).

37 http://inari.jp/c_sairei/index.html.

38 Smyers 1999 is a very interesting multidisciplinary study of the Inari cults.

39 For a fascinating discussion of Yasukuni in comparative context, see Selden 2008. Selden reaches a different conclusion to that offered here.

40 On this ruling, see Chapter 5.

41 For an apologist's spirited defence of the PM's right to visit Yasukuni, see Nitta 2008.

42 See Asō's fascinating speech of August 2006, entitled *Yasukuni ni iyasaka are* (Long live Yasukuni) at: http://www.aso-taro.jp/lecture/talk/060808.html.

43 See for example Nitta 2008: 130–3.

44 www.shinto.org/isri/jpn/forum/forum19/taidan2/htm.

45 *Kyōto shinbun*, 29.8.2008.

46 For details of the association and a full list of shrines and temples signed up, see Shinbutsu Reijōkai 2008.

References

Newspapers Cited

Asahi shinbun
Asahi shinbun (Kyōto furoku)
Chūgai denpō
Jinja shinpō
Kokumin shinbun
Kyōto shinbun
Ōsaka Asahi (Shigaban)
Sankei shinbun
Shūkan shinchō
Yomiuri shinbun

Online Sources

All sites were last accessed July 2, 2009.

www.ndl.go.jp/constitution/e/etc/c01.html#s10
www.sangiin.go.jp/japanese/kenpou/keika_g/147_08g.htm
kokkai.ndl.go.jp/SENTAKU/syugiin/159/0107/15903110107002a.html
www.sangiin.go.jp/japanese/kenpou/keika_g/159_08g.htm
www.sinseiren.org
www.keta.jp
www.jinjahoncho.or.jp/en/view/
ww.jinjahoncho.or.jp/en/pXublications/nature/index.html
www2.odn.ne.jp/shasou/expo.htm

www.kyoharen.net
inari.jp
inari.jp/c_sairei/index.html
www.aso-taro.jp/lecture/talk/060808.html
www.shinto.org/isri/jpn/forum/forum19/taidan2/htm

Other Sources

Abé, Ryuichi. 1999. *The weaving of mantra: Kūkai and the constitution of esoteric Buddhist discourse.* Columbia University Press.

Abe Yasurō. 2000. *Ninnaji shiryō shintō-hen, shintō kanjō injin.* Nagoya Daigaku Hikaku Jinbungaku Kenkyūshitsu.

Adolphson, Mikael. 1997. Enryakuji – An old power in a new era. In Jeffrey Mass, ed., *The origins of Japan's medieval world.* Stanford University Press.

Adolphson, Mikael. 2000. *The gates of power.* University of Hawai'i Press.

Akisato Ritō. 1944. *Ise sangū meisho zue,* ed. Ashida Koreto. Tōyōdō.

Ambrose, Barbara. 2008. *Emplacing a pilgrimage: The Ōyama cult and regional religion in early modern Japan.* Harvard University, Asia Center.

Arakawa Kusuo. 1989. Kōki Mitogaku ni okeru daijōsai no kenkyū. In Kōgakkan Daigaku Shintō Kenkyūjo, ed., *Daijōsai no kenkyū,* vol. 2. Kōgakkan Daigaku Shuppanbu.

Arichi, Meri. 2006. *Sannō miya mandara*: The iconography of Pure Land on this earth. *Japanese Journal of Religious Studies,* 33(2).

Ashizu Uzuhiko. 1986. *Shimaguni no tami no kokoro.* Shimazu Shobō.

Aston, W. G. 1972. *Nihongi: Chronicles of Japan from the earliest times to A. D. 697.* Tuttle.

Bentley, John R. 2006. *The authenticity of Sendai kuji hongi.* Brill.

Bialock, David T. 2007. *Eccentric spaces, hidden histories: Narrative, ritual and royal authority from* The Chronicles of Japan *to* The Tale of the Heike. Stanford University Press.

Blacker, Carmen. 1990. The *shinza* or God-seat in the *daijōsai*: Throne, bed, or incubation couch? *Japanese Journal of Religious Studies,* 17.

Bock, Felicia. 1970. *Engi-shiki: Procedures of the Engi era,* vol. 1. Sophia University Press.

Bock, Felicia. 1972. *Engi-shiki: Procedures of the Engi era,* vol. 2. Sophia University Press.

Bocking, Brian. 2001. *The Oracles of the Three Shrines: Windows on Japanese Religion.* Routledge.

Bouchy, Anne. 2003. Et le culte, sera-t-il shintô ou bouddhique? *Cipango*, 11.

Bowring, Richard. 2005. *The religious traditions of Japan, 500–1600*. Cambridge University Press.

Breen, John. 1990. Shintoists in Restoration Japan: Towards a reassessment. *Modern Asian Studies*, 24(3).

Breen, John. 2000. Ideologues, bureaucrats and priests: On Buddhism and Shintō in early Meiji Japan. In Breen and Teeuwen, eds., 2000.

Breen, John. 2004a. Death issues in 21st century Japan. *Mortality*, 9(1).

Breen, John. 2004b. The dead and the living in the land of peace: A sociology of Yasukuni. *Mortality*, 9(1).

Breen, John. 2007a. Meiji tennō o yomu. *Ratio*, 3.

Breen, John. 2007b. Inside Tokugawa religion: Stars, planets and the calendar-as-method. *Culture and cosmos*, 10(1–2).

Breen, John. 2007c. Kingendai Shintōshi no jidai kubun. In Shintō Kokusai Gakkai ed., *Shintōshi kenkyū no saikō*. Kokusai Bunka Kōbō.

Breen, John, ed. 2008a. *Yasukuni, the war dead and the struggle for Japan's past*. Columbia University Press.

Breen, John. 2008b. Introduction: A Yasukuni genealogy. In Breen, ed., 2008a.

Breen, John. 2008c. Yasukuni and the loss of historical memory. In Breen, ed., 2008a.

Breen, John and Teeuwen, Mark, eds. 2000. *Shintō in history: Ways of the kami*. University of Hawai'i Press.

Como, Michael. 2008. *Shōtoku: Ethnicity, ritual, and violence in the Japanese Buddhist tradition*. Oxford University Press.

Como, Michael. 2009. *Weaving and binding: Female shamans and immigrant gods in Nara Japan*. University of Hawai'i Press.

Davis, Winston. 1992. *Japanese religion and society: Paradigms of structure and change*. State University of New York Press.

DeCaroli, Robert. 2004. *Haunting the Buddha*. Oxford University Press.

Ellwood, Robert. 1973. *The feast of kingship: Accession ceremonies in ancient Japan*. Sophia University Press.

Endō Jun. 1998. The Shinto funeral movement in early modern and modern Japan. *Transactions of the Institute for Japanese Culture and Classics*, 82.

Endō Jun. 2004. Shintō kara mita kinsei to kindai: Shakaiteki bunmyaku ni okeru kotoba no imi o megutte. In *Iwanami kōza shūkyō, 3: Shūkyōshi no kanōsei*, Iwanami Shoten.

Endō Jun. 2008. *Hirata kokugaku to kinsei shakai*. Perikansha.

Faure, Bernard. 1998. *The red thread: Buddhist approaches to sexuality*. Princeton University Press.

Fridell, Wilbur M. 1973. *Japanese shrine mergers 1906–12: Shinto moves to the grassroots*. Sophia University.

Fukuyama Toshio. 1985. *Jinja kenchiku no kenkyū*. Chūō Kōron Bijutsu Shuppan.

Geinōshi Kenkyūkai, ed. 1982. *Nihon geinōshi*, vol. 2. Hōsei Daigaku.

Gishiki 3, *Tai ka* 21. MS (Historical Archives, Prefectural Office, Shiga Prefecture).

Grapard, Allan. 1984. Japan's ignored Cultural Revolution: The separation of Shinto and Buddhist divinities in Meiji ("shimbutsu bunri") and a case study: Tōnomine. *History of Religions*, 23(3).

Grapard, Allan. 1988. Institution, ritual, and ideology: The twenty-two shrine-temple multiplexes of Heian Japan. *History of Religions*, 27.

Grapard, Allan. 1992a. *The protocol of the gods: A study of the Kasuga cult in Japanese history*. University of California Press.

Grapard, Allan. 1992b. The Shinto of Yoshida Kanetomo. *Monumenta Nipponica*, 47(1).

Grapard. Allan. 2002. Shrines registered in ancient Japanese law: Shinto or not? *Japanese Journal of Religious Studies*, 29(3–4).

Hagiwara Tatsuo. 1962. *Chūsei saishi soshiki no kenkyū*. Yoshikawa Kōbunkan.

Hardacre, Helen, 1986. *Kurozumikyō and the new religions of Japan*. Princeton University Press.

Hardacre, Helen. 1989. *Shinto and the state, 1868–1988*. Princeton University Press.

Hardacre, Helen. 2002. *Religion and society in 19th century Japan*. Centre for Japanese Studies, University of Michigan Ann Arbor.

Harootunian, Harry D. 1998. Figuring the folk: History, poetics, and representation. In Vlastos, ed., 1998.

Hashimoto Kōsaku. 2005. *Buzen no kuni kagura kō*. Fukuoka: Kaichōsha.

Hashimoto Masanobu. 1997. Kanbun Gonen "Jinja jōmoku" no kinō. *Shintō shūkyō*, 168(9).

Hashimoto Mitsuru. 1998. *Chihō*: Yanagita Kunio's "Japan". In Vlastos, ed., 1998.

Hatakama Kazuhiro. 2007. Shingakusha. In Yokota Fuyuhiko, ed., *Chishiki to gakumon o ninau hitobito*. Yoshikawa Kōbunkan.

Hie Jinja, comp. *Issha kindai hennen ryakuki*. Undated MS (Hiyoshi Taisha).

Hie koshiki saiki. 1943. MS (Hiyoshi Taisha).

Hie sairei tenkō byōbu. 1850s.

Hie Sannō rishōki. In *ST* Hie.

Hie sairei kozu. 1822.

Hocart, A. M. 1927. *Kingship*. Oxford University Press.

Hoshino Teruoki. 1991. *Tairei Hongi*. Appendix to Miyachi Masato, 1991.

Imaizumi Yoshiko. 2007. Contested space: A genealogy of Meiji shrine. London University, unpublished PhD thesis.

Inoue Hiroshi. 2006. *Nihon no jinja to Shintō*. Kōsō Shobō.

Inoue Nobutaka. 2002. The formation of sect Shinto in modernizing Japan. *Japanese Journal of Religious Studies*, 29(3–4).

Inoue Nobutaka et al. 2003. *Shinto: A short history* (translated and adapted by Mark Teeuwen and John Breen). Routledge Curzon.

Inoue Suguru. 2000. Shiryō honkoku: Nishikawa Yoshisuke shokan (1), *Rittō rekishika minzoku hakubutsukan kiyō*, 6.

Inoue Takami. 2003. The interaction between Buddhist and Shinto traditions at Suwa Shrine. In Teeuwen and Rambelli, eds., 2003.

Ishizuka Takatoshi. 2005. *Sato-kagura no seiritsu ni kansuru kenkyū*. Iwata Shoin.

Isomae Jun'ichi. 2000a. Tanaka Yoshitō and the beginnings of *Shintōgaku*. In Breen and Teeuwen, eds., 2000.

Isomae Jun'ichi. 2000b. Reappropriating the Japanese myths: Motoori Norinaga and the creation myths of the *Kojiki* and *Nihon shoki. Japanese Journal of Religious Studies*, 27(1–2).

Isomae Jun'ichi and Ogura Shigeji. 2005. *Kinsei chōtei to Suika Shintō*. Perikansha.

Iwai Tadakuma and Okada Seishi, eds. 1989. *Tennō daigawari gishiki no rekishiteki tenkai*. Kashiwa Shobō.

Iwata Masaru. 1994. Kaguragoto ni okeru takusen-gata to akurei kyōsei-gata. In Yamaori Tetsuo and Miyamoto Kesao, eds., *Saigi to jujutsu*. Yoshikawa Kōbunkan.

Jōi on inori no ki. MS (Eizan bunko).

Jōkyō yonen Sannō sengū ki. 1687. MS (Hiyoshi Taisha).

Juge Shigekuni. *Hie sha negi kuden shō*. In *ST* Hie.

Juge Shigekuni. *Saijin oyobi kanjō nenki*. MS (Historical Archives, Prefectural Office, Stiga Prefecture).

Kageyama Haruki. 2001. *Shintaizan: Nihon no genshi shinkō o saguru*. Gakuseisha.

Kakushin. 1688. *Hie Sannō sairei shinki*. In *ST* Hie.

Kamikawa Michio. 1989. Chūsei no sokui girei to bukkyō. In Iwai and Okada, eds., 1989.

Kamikawa Michio. 1990. Accession rituals and Buddhism in Medieval Japan. *Japanese Journal of Religious Studies*, 17(2–3).

Kanpei Taisha Hie Jinja shamusho, ed. 1942. *Kanpei Taisha Hie Jinja dainenpyō*. Kanpei Taisha Hie Jinja shamusho.

Katagiri Yōichi. 1971–87. *Chūsei kokinshū chūshakusho kaidai*, 6 vols. Akao Shōbundō.

Katō Genchi. 1931. *Honpō seishi no kenkyū*. Meiji Seitoku Kinen Gakkai.

Klein, Susan B. 2002. *Allegories of desire: Esoteric literary commentaries of medieval Japan*. Harvard University Press.

Kobayashi Zuiho. 2008. Jinjakai ni okeru kōkeisha fusoku ni kansuru ishiki. *Shintō shūkyō*, 208(9).

Kōnoshi Takamitsu. 2000. Constructing imperial mythology: *Kojiki* and *Nihon shoki*. In Haruo Shirane and Tomi Suzuki, eds., *Inventing the classics*. Stanford University Press.

Kozawa Hiroshi. 1988. Minshū shūkyō no shinsō. In Tsukamoto Manabu, ed., *Nihon no shakaishi, 8: Seikatsu kankaku to shakai*. Iwanami Shoten.

Kuroda Ryūji. 1999. *Chūsei jisha shinkō no ba*. Shibunkaku.

Kuroda Toshio. 1981. Shinto in the history of Japanese religion. *Journal of Japanese Studies*, 7(1).

Kyōgaku Kenkyūjo Chōsashitsu, ed. 1997. *Jinja ni kansuru ishiki chōsa hōkokusho*. Jinja Honchō Kyōgaku Kenkyūjo.

Lincoln, Bruce. 1999. *Theorizing myth: Narrative, ideology, and scholarship*. University of Chicago Press.

Liscutin, Nicola. 2000. Mapping the sacred body: Shinto versus popular beliefs at Mt. Iwaki in Tsugaru. In Breen and Teeuwen, eds., 2000.

Maeda Natsushige. 1868. Hie Sannō ben. In *ST* Tendai Shintō ge.

Maeda Tsutomu. 2006. *Heigaku to shushigaku, rangaku, kokugaku*. Heibonsha.

Mase Kumiko. 1985. Bakuhansei kokka ni okeru jinja ronsō to chōbaku kankei: Yoshida Shirakawa o chūshin ni. *Nihonshi kenkyū*, 277.

Matsumae Takeshi. 1974. *Kodai denshō to kyūtei saishi*. Hanawa Shobō.

Mayumi Tsunetada. 1989. *Daijōsai no sekai*. Gakuseisha.

Mills, D. E. 1970. *A collection of tales from Uji*. Cambridge University Press.

Mitamura Yoshiko. 2005. *Sato-kagura handobukku: Fukushima, Kantō, Kōshin'etsu*. Ōfū.

Miyachi Masato, comp. 1988. Shūkyō kankei hōrei ichiran. In Miyachi Masato and Yasumaru Yoshio, eds., *Kindai Nihon shisō taikei, 5: Shūkyō to kokka*. Iwanami Shoten.

Miyachi Masato. 1991. Tennōsei ideorogii ni okeru daijōsai no kinō: Jōkyōdo no saikō yori konnichi made. *Rekishi Hyōron*, 492.

Miyake Kazuo. 1984. *Kiki shinwa no seiritsu*. Yoshikawa Kōbunkan.

Miyata Noboru. 1972. *Kinsei no hayarigami*. Hyōronsha.

Mizubayashi Takeshi. 2001. *Kiki shinwa to ōken no matsuri*. Iwanami Shoten.

Mizubayashi Takeshi. 2002. Kodai shinwa no ideorogii kōsei. In Amino Yoshihiko et al., eds., *Tennō to ōken o kangaeru*, 4: *Shūkyō to ken'i*. Iwanami Shoten.

Mizubayashi Takeshi. 2005. Kojiki to Nihon shoki. In Hara Takeshi and Yoshida Yutaka, eds., *Tennō kōshitsu jiten*. Iwanami Shoten.

Mizuno Masayoshi, ed. 1992. *Kodai o kangaeru: Ōmi*. Yoshikawa Kōbunkan.

Moerman, D. Max. 2006. *Localizing paradise: Kumano pilgrimage and the religious landscape of premodern Japan*. Harvard University Press.

Momochi Akira. 1995. Daijōsai kanren soshō hanketsu o megutte. *Meiji Seitoku Kinen Gakkai Kiyō*, 16.

Motoori Norinaga. 1991. Naobi no mitama; trans. Sey Nishimura, In the way of the gods: Motoori Norinaga's Naobi no Mitama. *Monumenta Nipponica*, 46(1).

Müller, Gerhild. 1971. *Kagura: Die Lieder der kagura-Zeremonie am Naishidokoro*. Harrassowitz.

Muraoka Tsunetsugu. 1920. Hirata Atsutane shingaku ni okeru Yasokyō no eikyō. *Geibun*, 11(3).

Myōhōinshi Kenkyūkai, ed. 1976. *Gyōjo shinnō nikki*. Yoshikawa Kōbunkan.

Nakai, Kate W. 1988. *Shogunal politics: Arai Hakuseki and the premises of Tokugawa rule*. Harvard East Asian Monograph. Harvard University Press.

Nakai, Kate W. 2007. The Age of the Gods in medieval and early modern historiography. In James C. Baxter and Joshua A. Vogel, eds., *Writing histories in Japan*. Kyoto: International Research Center for Japanese Studies.

Nakamura Ken. 1988. *Chūsei chiiki-shi no kenkyū*. Takashina Shoten.

Naumann, Nelly. 2000. The state cult of the Nara and early Heian periods. In Breen and Teeuwen, eds., 2000.

Nelson, John. 1996. *A year in the life of a Shinto shrine*. University of Washington Press.

Nelson, John. 2000. *Enduring identities: The guise of Shinto in contemporary Japan*. University of Hawai'i Press.

Nishida Nagao. 1978. *Nihon Shintōshi kenkyū*, vol. 7. Kōdansha.

Nishimiya Hideki. 2004. *Ritsuryō kokka to jingi saishi seido no kenkyū*. Hanawa Shobō.

Nishimiya Kazutami. 1979. *Shinten Nihon koten shūsei, Kojiki.* Shinchōsha.

Nishioka Kazuhiko. 2004. *Kinsei Izumo taisha no kisoteki kenkyū.* Hara Shobō.

Nitta Hitoshi. 2000. Shinto as a "non-religion": The origins and development of an idea. In Breen and Teeuwen, eds., 2000.

Nitta Hitoshi. 2008. And why shouldn't the prime minister worship at Yasukuni? In Breen, ed., 2008.

Okada Seishi. 1970. *Kodai ōken no saishi to shinwa.* Hanawa Shobō.

Okada Seishi. 1987. Hie Jinja to Tenji-chō Ōtsumiya. In *Nihon shoki kenkyū* vol. 16. Hanawa Shobō.

Okada Seishi. 1989. Taiō shūnin girei no genkei to sono tenkai. In Iwai and Okada, eds., 1989.

Okada Shōji. 1990. *Ōname no matsuri.* Gakuseisha.

Okada Shōji and Kase Naoya, eds. 2007. *Jinja no shinkō hanpu: Sono rekishiteki keii o kangaeru tame ni.* 21-Seiki COE Puroguramu, Kokugakuin Daigaku.

Okada Yoneo. 1987. Jingū to Jinja honchō. In Jingū shichō, ed., *Jingū Meiji hyakunenshi (jō).* Jingū Bunko.

Oketsume Osamu. 1981. Jisha ryō no hensen. In *Shinshū Ōtsu shishi,* 3: *Kinsei zenki,* Ōtsu shiyakusho.

Ōno Izuru. 2002. Omikuji. In Hayashi Makoto and Koike Jun'ichi, eds., *Onmyōdō no kōgi.* Sagano Shoin.

Ono Sokyō. 1962. *Shinto: The kami way.* Tuttle.

Ontaireki. In *Zenkoku Shinshokukai Kaihō,* vol. 205 (1915).

Ooms, Herman. 1985. *Tokugawa ideology: Early constructs, 1570–1680.* Princeton University Press.

Ooms, Herman. 2008. *Imperial politics and symbolics in imperial Japan: The Tenmu dynasty.* University of Hawai'i Press.

Orikuchi Shinobu zenshū. Chūō Kōronsha. 1975.

Philippi, Donald L. 1969. *Kojiki.* University of Tokyo Press.

Plutschow, Herbert. 1996. *Matsuri: The festivals of Japan.* Japan Library.

Ponsonby-Fane, Richard A. B. 1959. *The Imperial House of Japan,* Ponsonby-Fane Memorial Society.

Reader, Ian. 1994. *Religion in contemporary Japan.* Macmillan.

Reader, Ian and Tanabe, George J. Jr. 1998. *Practically religious: Worldly benefits and the common religion of Japan.* University of Hawai'i Press.

Rimer, J. Thomas and Yamazaki Masakazu. 1984. *On the art of nō drama: The major treatises of Zeami.* Princeton University Press.

Sagai Tatsuru. 1992. *Hiyoshi Taisha to Sannō Gongen.* Jinbun Shoin.

Saigō Nobutsuna. 1973. *Kojiki kenkyū.* Miraisha.

Saitō Hideki. 1996. *Amaterasu no fukami e*. Shin'yōsha.

Saitō Hideki. 2002. Mi-kagura no Amaterasu. In Inseiki Bunka Kenkyūkai, ed., *Inseiki bunka ronshū* 2: *Gensetsu to tekisutogaku*. Shinwasha.

Sakamoto Koremaru. 2000. The structure of state Shinto: Its creation, development and demise. In Breen and Teeuwen, eds., 2000.

Sakurai Tokutarō. 1988. *Kō shūdan no kenkyū. Sakurai Tokutarō chosakushū* 1. Yoshikawa Kōbunkan.

Samukawa Tatsukiyo. 1733. *Ōmi yochi shiryaku*.

Sanekata Yōko. 2000. Hie Sannō sairei zu byōbu o yomu: Umikita Yūsetsu no sōi to senryaku. *Izumiya Hakubutsukan kiyō*, 16.

Sasaki Kiyoshi. 1998. Amenominakanushi no kami in late Tokugawa period Kokugaku. In Inoue Nobutaka, ed., *Contemporary Papers on Japanese Religion*, 4: *Kami*. Institute for Japanese Culture and Classics, Kokugakuin University.

Satō Masato. 1984. Chūsei Hie sha no fugeki ni tsuite. *Kokugakuin zasshi*, 85(8).

Satō Masato. 1989. *Hie sha negi kuden shō* no seiritsu. *Ōkurayama Ronshū*, 25.

Satō Masato. 1993. Kinsei shake no Yoshida Shintō juyō: Hie shashi no jirei o megutte. *Ōkurayama Ronshū*, 33.

Satow, Ernest. 1871. FO 46/143 no. 140. Adams to Granville, 30 December 1871. National Archives, Kew.

Scheid, Bernhard. 2000. Reading the *Yuiitsu Shintō myōbō yōshū*: A modern exegesis of an esoteric Shinto text. In Breen and Teeuwen, eds., 2000.

Scheid, Bernhard. 2001. *Der Eine und Einzige Weg der Götter: Yoshida Kanetomo und die Erfindung des Shinto*. Verlag der Österreichischen Akademie der Wissenschaften.

Scheid, Bernhard and Teeuwen, Mark, eds. 2006. *The culture of secrecy in Japanese religion*. Routledge.

Sekimori, Gaynor. 2005. The separation of kami and buddha worship in Haguro Shugendō, 1869–1875. *Japanese Journal of Religious Studies*, 32(2).

Selden, Mark. 2008. Japan, the United States and Yasukuni nationalism: War, historical memory and the future of the Asia Pacific. *Japan Focus*, 1215.

Shibuya Jigai, ed. 2000. *Kōtei zōho Tendai zasu ki*. Daiichi Shobō.

Shibuya Kuritsu Shōtō Bijutsukan, ed. 1999. *Ukiyoeshi-tachi no shinbutsu*. Shibuya Kuritsu Shōtō Bijutsukan.

Shinbutsu Reijōkai, ed. 2008. *Kami to hotoke no michi o aruku*. Shūeisha.

Shōgenji Kitoku. *Hie jinja korei saishiki*. MS (Historical Archives, Prefectural Office, Shiga Prefecture).

Shōgenji Kiyo. *Ōyamakui shinden*. 1836. MS (Eizan bunko).

Shōgenji Yukimaru. 1577. *Hiesha Shintō himitsu ki*. In *ST* Hie.

Shōgenji Yukimaru. 1588. *Hiesha shin'yaku nenjū gyōji*. In *ST* Hie.

Smyers, Karen. 1999. *The fox and the jewel: Shared and private meanings in contemporary Inari worship*. University of Hawai'i Press.

Sonoda Minoru. 2000. Shinto in the natural environment. In Breen and Teeuwen, eds., 2000.

Stone, Jacqueline. 1999. *Original enlightenment and the transformation of medieval Japanese Buddhism*. University of Hawai'i Press.

Sugahara Shinkai. 1992. *Sannō Shintō no kenkyū*. Shunjūsha.

Suzuki Hajime. 2003. *Konkō Daijin*. Konkōkyōtosha.

Takano Toshihiko. 2003. Edo jidai no jinja seido. In Takano, ed., *Genroku no shakai to bunka*. Yoshikawa Kōbunkan.

Takashima Kōji. 1978. Edo jidai no sanmon kuninshū: Kageyamake kyūzō monjo o chūshin ni. *Kokushigaku Kenkyū*, 4.

Takeda Hideaki. 1996. *Ishinki Tennō saishi no kenkyū*. Taimeidō.

Tamura Enchō. 1996. *Ise Jingū no seiritsu*. Yoshikawa Kōbunkan.

Teeuwen, Mark. 1996. *Watarai Shintō: An intellectual history of the Outer Shrine of Ise*. CNWS Publications.

Teeuwen, Mark. 2000. The kami in esoteric Buddhist thought and practice. In Breen and Teeuwen, eds., 2000.

Teeuwen, Mark. 2002. From *jindō* to Shinto: A concept takes shape. *Japanese Journal of Religious Studies*, 29(3–4).

Teeuwen, Mark. 2006. Knowing vs. owning a secret: Secrecy in medieval Japan, as seen through the *sokui kanjō* enthronement unction. In Scheid and Teeuwen, eds., 2006.

Teeuwen, Mark. 2007a. Comparative perspectives on the emergence of *jindō* and Shinto. *Bulletin of SOAS*, 70(2).

Teeuwen, Mark. 2007b. *Sendai kuji hongi*: Authentic myths or forged history? *Monumenta Nipponica*, 62(1).

Teeuwen, Mark, and Rambelli, Fabio, eds. 2003. *Buddhas and kami in Japan: Honji suijaku as a combinatory paradigm*. RoutledgeCurzon.

Ten Grotenhuis, Elizabeth. 1999. *Japanese mandalas*. University of Hawai'i Press.

Thal, Sarah. 2005. *Rearranging the landscape of the gods*. University of Chicago Press.

Thornhill, Arthur H. III. 1993. *Six circles, one dewdrop: The religio-aesthetic world of Konparu Zenchiku*. Princeton University Press.

Tokoro Isao. 1993. Shiryō shōkai: Taishō Shōwa no *Tairei yōshi*. *Kyōto Sangyō Daigaku Sekai Mondai Kenkyūjo Kiyō*, 30.

Tokutomi Sohō. 1926. *Kinsei Nihon kokuminshi: Hōreki Meiwa hen*. Min'yūsha.

Toyoda Takeshi. 1982. Chūsei no shōnin to kōtsū. In *Toyoda Takeshi chosakushū*, 3. Yoshikawa Kōbunkan.

Tyler, Royall. 2003. *The tale of Genji*. Penguin Books.

Uwai Hisayoshi. 1988. *Nihon kodai no shinzoku to saishi*. Jinbun Shoin.

Vlastos, Stephen, ed. 1998. *Mirror of modernity: Invented traditions of modern Japan*. University of California Press.

Wada Mitsuo. 2006. Sakamoto ni okeru Sannō mandara no shosō. *Tendai shū 1200nen kinen, Tendai shū o mamoru kamigami: Sannō mandara no shosō*. Ōtsushi Rekishi Hakubutsukan.

Wakabayashi, Bob Tadashi. 1986. *Anti-foreignism and Western learning in early modern Japan: The New Theses of 1825*. Harvard East Asian Monograph. Harvard University Press.

Walthall, Anne. 1998. *The weak body of a useless woman: Matsuo Taseko and the Meiji Restoration*. University of Chicago Press.

Wang Zhixin. 2008. China, Japan and the spell of Yasukuni. In Breen, ed., 2008a.

Witzel, Michael. 2005. Vala and Iwato: The myth of the hidden sun in India, Japan, and beyond. *Electronic Journal of Vedic Studies*, 12(1).

Yamamoto Junya. 2002. Shiryō honkoku: Nishikawa Yoshisuke shokan (2). *Rittō Rekishi Minzoku Hakubutsukan kiyō*, 8.

Yamamura Akiyoshi. 2009. Ima Jinja Shintō ga abunai, *Shokun*, 41(3).

Yanagita Kunio. 1969. *Nihon no matsuri*. In *Teihon Yanagita Kunio shū*, vol. 10. Chikuma Shobō.

Yasumaru Yoshio and Miyachi Masato, eds. 1988. *Nihon kindai shisō taikei 5: Shūkyō to kokka*. Iwanami Shoten.

Yoshida Yuriko. 1995. Kunin to "ken'i". In Kurushima Hiroshi et al., eds., *Kinsei no shakai shūdan*. Yamakawa Shuppansha.

Index